D0592364

The Singer's Repertoire

Singer's Repertoire

Part IV
Baritone and Bass

Second Edition

by

Berton Coffin

The Scarecrow Press, Inc.
Lanham, Md., & London

To

George Hoffman

friend and artist

Foreword

"The Singer's Repertoire" in its second edition has been divided into four parts. Part I includes songs for Coloratura Soprano, Lyric Soprano and Dramatic Soprano. Part II includes songs for Mezzo Soprano and Contralto. Part III includes songs for Lyric Tenor and Dramatic Tenor and Part IV includes songs for Baritone and Bass. This has been thought to be a service to the individual singer who is primarily interested only in that material which is suitable for his particular voice.

Several of the song lists have been augmented and duets, trios, songs of limited range and chamber operas for two, three or four voices have been added. Intentionally no lists have been made of "easy" songs since this has been felt to be a misnomer. That which is easy for one is not necessarily easy for another. Young singers may have short ranges but they frequently have very fine tastes, possibly some language background and even fairly good musicianship due to previous instrumental study. Hence, instead of a list of "easy" songs, the compiler has listed a broad spectrum of songs with limited range.

"The Singer's Repertoire" is an effort to aid all singers and teachers of singing in their repertoire problems. The singer at no stage in his career is free from this problem. In the beginning he has to select the suitable songs for his vocal powers and development. As he becomes a successful amateur singer he secures various engagements which are always presenting new song needs. Should he become a professional singer the needs will be multiplied many times with a changing repertoire required season after season. Should he become a teacher of singing or a vocal coach he will have hundreds of potential singers, each one with different needs. Therefore, no matter with what phase of vocal work one is concerned, the repertoire problem is always present and one's storehouse is always changing, always being added to.

"The Singer's Repertoire" has profited in its growth and development by the advice, counsel and criticism of many experienced singers and many noted teachers of singing.

From these discussions, four repertoire aids appear to be paramount:

1. Aids for program building (for this problem the guide lists recital songs in the various languages; songs for opening and closing recitals; and songs by classification).

2. Aids for training repertoire (this problem has been approached by indexing technical characteristics of songs).

3. Aids for specific or seasonal occasions (see Christmas, Easter, Wedding and Patriotic lists).

4. Aids in sacred repertoire (hundreds of songs have been studied and those appropriate are listed).

The above aids are based on contemporarily performed songs and arias as programmed in countless recitals, in recordings and in the' media of radio and television. This mass of material has been interpolated into appropriate listings. The compiler has not assumed the position of musical analyst except for the sacred listing and in augmenting the smaller lists. Questions have not been asked as to why certain songs are sung or not sung; if the song has been found in the above mentioned sources, it is listed, otherwise it is not included in this volume. This book is based on the preselection of songs sung by noteworthy or accepted singers, and is not a compendium of all vocal repertoire which would surely approximate 100, 000 song titles. It is merely a distribution of some 8, 000 songs into 818 lists for the nine voice classifications rather than an annotated bibliography of songs. For each voice classification there are 71 - 92 lists whereby the characteristics of various songs are shown. It is well known to all teachers that a matching of song traits to the strengths and limitations of any singing personality will assure the individual's best success. This is a very difficult thing to do and it is hoped the problem will be made easier by the multiple listings of this work.

Due to the large number of programs examined, all voices should be represented in proportion to their natural distribution. The largest segments will be the lyric soprano and baritone, because there are more of those voices; the smallest segments will be the coloratura soprano, dramatic tenor and bass since these voices occur less frequently. The compiler has made no attempt to classify voices in this study but has merely listed the songs according to the voice classification stated on the programs.

A work of this kind can never be complete in contemporary song (although publication in this field is lamentably limited) since new songs are appearing and others are falling into disuse. However, the classic, romantic and impressionistic repertoire is now relatively stable. These songs comprise the living repertoire of today.

Boulder, Colorado

Table of Contents

Repertoire for the Bass Voice

Directions for Use

All songs are listed alphabetically by composer with the song listings alphabetized under each composer. The lists are to be read in the following manner: first, the composer's name is given, then the title, then the opera, operetta, cantata, oratorio, if it is an aria. In cases where a solo instrument accompanies the voice and piano that instrument has been indicated.

Next are shown the keys HML. The last letter of the key is important: should it be L – the low range is shown; if the last is M, the medium range is shown; and if it is H – the high. BF-EF indicates a range of B flat to E flat (CS-FS would indicate C sharp to F sharp). The three letters at the extreme right of page are a code for the publisher (code at front of book, i.e. GSC indicates G. Schirmer; SC indicates Schott). Where a dagger (†) appears the song is published by more than one firm.

The Miscellaneous listings are total lists including songs other than those found in the American, British, French, German and Italian listings. However, if there is a void in any of these lists (American, British, French, German, Italian), those songs will be included in the Miscellaneous list. Latin songs always appear in the Miscellaneous lists as do the Portuguese, Hungarian, Hebrew, etc.

This book does not include popular music as such but does have a separate listing of the lighter numbers which are frequently needed. These songs are found under the heading – Songs of Popular Appeal.

The Handel Songs are found in the British, German and Italian lists; Wagner in the German and French; and Mozart in the Italian, German and French. American compositions are found in the American lists regardless of whether French, German or Italian texts are used. Likewise English composers are in the English lists.

The classical Italian arias are listed under song rather than opera because the works are no longer staged and they are thought of as song literature.

Publisher Code

† - Published by more than one company

A

ABC - ABC Music Corp.
AHC - Asherberg, Hopwood and Crew
AMI - Amici
AMM - American Music
AMP - Associated Music Publishers
ARR - Arrow Music Press
ASB - Ashbrook
ASC - Arthur P. Schmidt
ASH - Ashdown
AUG - Augener
AXE - Axelrod

B

BAF - Bayley and Ferguson
BAR - Barenreiter
BER - Berlin
BES - Bessel
BIR - Birchard
BLO - C.A. Blodgett
BMI - Broadcast Music, Inc.
BOH - Boosey and Hawkes
BOO - Boosey
BON - Bongiovani
BOS - Boston
BOT - Bote and Bock
BRA - Brandus and Cie
BRE - Bregeman
BRH - Breitkof and Haertel
BRM - Barton and Mead
BRO - Broude
BVC - Bregman, Vocco and Conn

C

CAR - Cardilli
CFI - Carl Fischer
CHA - Chappel
CHE - Chester
CHM - Champagne
CHO - Choudens
CMC - Composers Music Corp.
CMP - Composers Press
CNN - Conn
CRA - Cramer
CRF - Crawford
CRZ - Cranz
CSC - Cos Cob
CST - Costallet
CUR - Curwen

D

DBH - Desylvia, Brown and Henderson
DES - DeSantis
DIT - Ditson
DRE - Dreiklang
DUR - Durand

E

ECS - E.C. Schirmer
ELK - Elkin
ELV - Elkan-Vogel
ENO - Enoch
ESC - Eschig

F

FAM - Famous
FEI - Feist
FLA - Flammer
FOE - Foetisch
FOX- Fox
FRA - Frank
FRL - Forlivesi
FRS - Forster
FST - Forsyth
FTZ - FitzSimmons

G

GAL - Galaxy
GAM - Gamble Hinged(GAH)
GER - Gershwin
GLO - Glocken Verlag
GOL - Goldsea
GOT - Goodwin and Tabb
GRA - H.W. Gray
GSC - G. Schirmer

H

HAC - Hachette
HAM - Hamelle
HAN - Hansen
HAR - Harms
HEU - Heugel
HHE - Hinds, Haydn and
        Eldredge
HNR - Heinrichofen
HNZ - Hunzinger
HOM - Homeyer
HRM - Harmonia (HMP)
HSC - Hans Schneider

I

INT - International

J

JCH - John Church
JFI - J. Fischer
JOB - Jobert
JUR - Jurgenson

JWI - J. Williams

K

KAL - Kalmus
KIS - Kistner
KSS - Kustner and Siegel

L

LAC - Lacour
LED - Leduc
LEE - Leeds
LEM - Lemoine

M

MAR - Marks
MAT - Mathot
MCG - MacGimsey
MCR - McLaughlin, Reilly
MER - Mercury
MET - Methuen
MLR - Miller
MLS - Mills
MOR - Morris, E. H.
MOV - Movietone
MUP - Music Press

N

NAG - Nagel Verlag
NEM - New Music
NOR - Norsky Verlag
NOV - Novello

O

OCT - Octava Music Co.
OXF - Oxford

P

PAR - Paragon
PEE - Peer
PET - Peters
PON - William Pont
PRE - Presser
PRM - Paramount

xviii

PRO - Prowse
PTR - Paterson

R

RBR - Riker, Brown and
      Wellington
REM - Remick
RIC - Ricordi
ROB - Robbins
ROG - Winthrop Rogers
ROM - Roma
ROU - Rouart, Lerolle
ROW - Row

S

SAL - Salabert
SC - Schott
SCH - Schlesinger
SEN - Senart
SHA - Shapiro
SHU - Schuberth
SIM - Simroch
SIR - Sirene
SON - Sonzogno
SOU - Southern Music Co.
SPA - Spada
STB - Stainer Bell
SUM - Summy

T

TEM - Templeton
TRA - Transcontinental

U

UME - Union Musical
      Española
UNI - Universal

V

VIC - Victoria
VLP - Valley Press

W

WEI - Weinberger
WHB - Whitney Blake
WHI - White Smith
WIL - Williamson
WIT - Witmark
WLL - Willis
WOO - Wood
WOR - Words and Music
WTR - Weintraub

Z

ZER - Zerboni

Part IV

Baritone

American Recital Songs

Baritone

Bacon	Brady			BOO
-----	Casey Jones			
Barber	Bessie Bobtail	M	C-F	GSC
-----	Dover Beach	M	BF-F	GSC
	String quartet			
-----	Here in this spot with you			
-----	I hear an army	LH	D-AF	GSC
-----	I ride the great black horses			
-----	Rain has fallen	HM	D-E	GSC
-----	Sure on this shining night	MH	D-G	GSC
-----	The daisies	M	C-F	GSC
-----	The Queen's face on the summery coin	L	C-E	GSC
-----	With rue my heart is laden	HL	CS-D	GSC
Barnett	Music, when soft voices die	M	C-E	GSC
Bartholomew	When we are parted	M	CS-E	GAL
Beach	Ah, love but a day			ASC
-----	The year's at the spring	MH	AF-AF	ASC
Bloch	Psalm 22	M	B-F	GSC
Bone and Fenton	Captain Kidd	MH	B-G	CFI
-----	Everything that I can spy	M	E-GF	CFI
-----	Green fields	MH	E-A	PRE
-----	Tryst	MH	FS-G	CFI
Bowles	Cabin	ML	CS-CS	GSC
-----	David	M	E-D	AMP

(Bowles)	Heavenly grass	ML	B-E	GSC
-----	I went to see my love			
-----	Lonesome man	M	DF-EF	GSC
-----	Once a lady was here	ML	C-EF	GSC
Boyd	Cape Horn gospel	L	BF-D	GAL
Braine	Dawn awakes	HML	A-D	ASC
Branscombe	At the postern gate	MH	DF-AF	ASC
-----	By St. Lawrence waters	HL		ASC
Burnham	Sing me a song of a lad that is gone	HL		GSC
Buzzi-Peccia	London bridge	ML	BF-DF	CFI
Cadman	Service	HML	BF-D	FLA
Campbell-Tipton	If I were king	HML	C-EF	GSC
-----	The crying of water	LH	FS-GS	GSC
Carpenter	Berceuse de guerre	M	C-G	GSC
-----	Don't ceare	M	C-D	GSC
-----	Go, lovely rose	M	DF-EF	GSC
-----	Looking glass river	M	B-D	GSC
-----	May the maiden			DIT
-----	On the day when death will knock at thy door	M	C-F	GSC
-----	Serenade	LH	CS-A	GSC
-----	Slumber song	ML	BF-F	GSC
-----	The cock shall crow	M	B-E	GSC
-----	The green river	M	B-E	GSC
-----	Young man chieftan	L	B-E	GSC
Carter	Dust of snow	M	D-E	AMP
Castelnuovo-Tedesco	Apemantus grace			CHE
-----	O mistress mine			CHE
-----	Springtime	M		CHE
-----	The horn			CHE
Chadwick	Allah	LH	CS-GS	ASC
-----	Drake's drum			
-----	O let night speak of me	HM	C-F	ASC
-----	The admirals			
-----	The danza	HM		ASC
Chanler	I rise when you enter	M	CS-G	GSC
Charles	Clouds	HML	C-EF	GSC
-----	My lady walks in loveliness	HM	C-EF	GSC
-----	Song of exaltation	M		GSC
-----	Sweet song of long ago	HML	A-D	GSC
-----	When I have sung my songs	HM	BF-EF	GSC
Clifton	If music be the food of love, play on			
Coombs	Her rose	ML	D-C	GSC

Copland	Long time ago			
Cowell	The donkey	M	D-F	MER
Crist	Into a ship dreaming	LMH	EF-GS	CFI
Davis	The jolly fat friar			
Dello Joio	Mill doors	M	D-E	CFI
-----	The assassination			CFI
-----	There is a lady sweet and kind	M	C-F	CFI
Diamond	David weeps for Absolom	M	D-A	MUP
Dobson	Cargoes	ML	C-EF	GSC
Dougherty	Blow ye winds	L	C-D	GSC
-----	Declaration of independence	L	C-C	GSC
-----	Hush'd be the camps today	M	BF-G	GSC
-----	Loveliest of trees	HM	C-E	BOH
-----	The bird and the beast			
Duke	Capri			
-----	Central Park at dusk	M		BOO
-----	Here in this spot with you	M	B-F	GSC
-----	I ride the great black horses	M	C-G	GSC
-----	Loveliest of trees	L	C-D	GSC
-----	Luke Havergal	M	BF-F	CFI
-----	Miniver Cheevy	L	G-F	CFI
-----	On a March day	M	B-GF	BOH
-----	Reveille			
-----	Richard Cory	L	A-EF	CFI
-----	White in the moon the long road lies	M		VLP
Edmunds	Billy boy	ML	BF-EF	ROW
-----	Fare you well	MH	F-AF	ROW
Elwell	Music I heard	M		AMP
-----	The road not taken	M	B-FS	GSC
Engel	Sea shell	M	EF-EF	GSC
Foote	I'm wearing awa'	HL		ASC
-----	Tranquillity	HL	BF-E	ASC
Foster, S.C.	Ah, may the red rose live always			GSC
-----	De Glendy Burke			GSC
-----	Ellen Bayne			DIT
-----	Gentle Annie			
Galloway	Alone upon the housetops			
Ganz	A memory	HM	B-D	GSC
Gilbert	Pirate song	L	C-EF	GRA
Golde	O beauty, passing beauty	MH	CS-GS	GSC
-----	Who knows	HM	BF-F	GSC
Griffes	An old song resung	LM	EF-F	GSC
-----	By a lonely forest pathway	HML	A-EF	GSC
-----	Phantoms	M	BF-F	GSC

(Griffes)	Sorrow of Mydath	M		GSC
-----	Symphony in yellow	M	D-GF	GSC
Guion	Black oxen			
Hadley	My shadow			ASC
Hageman	Don Juan Gomez	M		GAL
-----	Miranda	HL		GAL
-----	Music I heard with you	MH	E-A	GAL
-----	The donkey			BOO
-----	The rich man	M		GAL
Hammond	The pipes of Gordon's men	HL	D-F	GSC
Harris	Agatha Morley	M	C-D	CFI
Helm	She is not fair			
Hindemith	The whistling thief	M	E-F	AMP
Homer	Sing me a song of a lad that is gone	HL	C-EF	GSC
Hopkinson	Come fair Rosina			
-----	My days have been so wondrous free	LH	EF-G	†
-----	My generous heart disdains			
-----	O'er the hills	LH	C-G	†
Horsman	In the yellow dusk	MH	FS-A	GSC
-----	The bird of the wilderness	LMH	DF-BF	GSC
Howard	Love in thy youth			
Howe	When I died in Berners Street	H	C-G	GSC
Huhn	Courage	HML	BF-EF	GSC
Ives	Charlie Rutlage	M		ARR
-----	General William Booth enters into Heaven			
-----	The greatest man	M		ARR
-----	The white gulls			
James	The victory riders			
Kagen	Never more will the wind			
-----	Upstream	H	CS-F	WTR
Kernochan	Out of the rolling ocean			
-----	Smuggler's song			GAL
-----	We two together	H	EF-AF	GAL
Kingsford	Courage	M	C-F	GSC
Kleinsinger	The courtship of old Joe Clark			
Klemm	Animal man			CFI
Kramer	For a dream's sake	HL		JFI
-----	Minnelied	M	C-E	JFI
-----	Pleading	LH	D-GF	JFI
-----	Swans	HL		RIC
Kubik	I bought a bright sword			
-----	Shoe song			
La Forge	Hills	HL		RIC

26

(La Forge)	To a messenger	HLM	CF-G	GSC
-----	Voodoo spirits			CFI
Lang	Irish love song	HML	A-E	ASC
Levitzki	Do you remember?	HML	BF-EF	GSC
Loeffler	To Helen	M	DF-F	GSC
Mac Dowell	The sea	HL	D-D	BRH
-----	Thy beaming eyes	ML	BF-EF	ASC
Mac Gimsey	O Lord you made a Moses	M		CFI
-----	Thunderin' wonderin'	L	C-D	CFI
Malotte	One, two, three	M	C-F	GSC
-----	Upstream	M	C-F	GSC
Mana Zucca	I shall know			CNG
-----	Rachem	HML		CHA
-----	Thy will be done			CNG
Manning	In the Luxembourg gardens	HML	BF-D	GSC
Mason	A prophet	M	BF-GF	GSC
-----	A sea dirge			WIT
Mc Feeters	Exultation	HL	C-E	GSC
Metcalf	At nightfall	HML	C-DF	ASC
Miller	Boats of mine	HML	BF-EF	FLA
Mitchell	I must go down to the sea	M	BF-F	GAH
Moore	Adam was my grandfather			GAL
Naginski	Night song at Amalfi	M	D-EF	GSC
-----	Richard Cory	ML	A-E	GSC
Nordoff	Tell me, Thyrsis	H	E-G	AMP
Olmstead	The ladies of St. James's	L	BF-EF	GSC
-----	Thy sweet singing	HL	BF-EF	GSC
Paxson	Dusk at sea	HL	A-EF	GSC
-----	Laughing song	M	C-F	CFI
Porter, Q.	Music, when soft voices die	HM	D-C	MUP
-----	The desolate city			
Protheroe	The pilot			
Robertson	The Jolly Roger	HML	C-D	GSC
Rogers	War			DIT
-----	The last song	MLH	E-AF	GSC
-----	Time for making songs	HM	CS-F	DIT
-----	Wind song	LM	C-G	GSC
Rorem	From an unknown past			
Rose	Roadways			GAM
Russell	Fulfillment	LH	EF-GF	BOS
Sacco	Brother Will, brother John	M	C-F	GSC
-----	Drum of peace	M	D-F	CFI
-----	Johnny the one	HL	BF-D	GSC
-----	Mexican serenade	HL	D-EF	BOS

27

(Sacco)	Revelation	HL	DF-EF	BOS
-----	Spanish Johnny	HL	BF-F	GSC
-----	The ragpicker	MH	C-AF	GSC
Sachs	Grandma			FLA
-----	The three riders	M	C-F	GSC
Schindler	From a city window			
Schuman	Holiday song	M	C-F	GSC
Scott	Cherry ripe	L	B-E	ELK
Singer	This want of you	L	E-FS	BOH
Speaks	Shepherd, see thy horse's foaming mane			FLA
Spencer	For whom the bell tolls	MH	F-AF	BOS
Swanson	Joy	M	BF-EF	LEE
-----	The negro speaks of rivers	M		LEE
-----	The valley	L	BF-DF	LEE
Taylor	A song for lovers	MH	D-F	JFI
-----	Captain Stratton's fancy	L	CS-F	JFI
Thompson	Velvet shoes	M	C-E	ECS
Tureman	A winter sunset	L	BF-E	GSC
Tyson	Noon and night	LH	F-AF	GSC
-----	One little cloud	HL	BF-D	GSC
-----	Sea moods	LH	E-AF	GSC
Warner	Hurdy gurdy	M	D-F	CFI
Warren	By a fireside	HL	C-EF	GSC
-----	My parting gift			DIT
-----	Through my open window	HL	C-E	GSC
-----	We two	LH	E-A	GSC
-----	White horses of the sea	LH	F-G	GSC
Watts	Blue are her eyes	H	FS-FS	DIT
-----	Falmouth Town	M	B-FS	GSC
-----	Joy	HL	D-F	GSC
-----	Like music on the waters	H		GSC
-----	The poet sings	MH	EF-AF	DIT
Weaver	A book of verses	H	D-AF	GAL
-----	The Abbot of Derry	HL	B-EF	GSC
Wolfe	The hand-organ man	M	B-FS	GSC
Worth	The evening is hushed			

British Recital Songs

Baritone

Aiken	Sigh no more	HML		STB
Anon	False Phillis			
-----	Have you seen but a white lily grow?	H	E-F	GSC
Arne, T.	By the gaily circling glass	L		DIT

(Arne, T.)	Now Phoebus sinketh in the west			GSC
-----	Why so pale and wan?			GSC
Bainton	Ring out, wild bells	M	C-EF	OXF
Bantock	A feast of lanterns	HM	D-F	GAL
-----	Lament of Isis	L		AMP
-----	Silent strings	MH	F-G	BOO
-----	The celestial weaver			
-----	The golden nenuphar	HM	B-E	ELK
Bartlet	What thing is love			BOO
-----	Whither runneth my sweetheart			BOO
Bax	The enchanted fiddle			
Benjamin	Hedgerow			CUR
-----	The wasp			CUR
Berners	Dialogue between Tom Filuter and his man	M	D-F	CHE
-----	Theodore or the pirate king			CHE
Blow	The self banished	L	C-F	NOV
Boughton	Immanence	M	B-E	CUR
Bridge	All things that we clasp	HL		BOS
-----	Come to me in my dreams	HL	C-EF	BOH
-----	E'en as a lovely flower	HM	FS-E	BOH
-----	Isobel	HML		CHA
-----	Love went a-riding	HL		BOS
-----	O that it were so	LMH	D-G	CHA
Britten	The birds	M		BOO
Bury	There is a lady	HM	CS-E	CFI
Butterworth	Loveliest of trees			AUG
-----	When I was one and twenty			AUG
Campion	Follow thy fair sun			STB
-----	There is a garden in her face			DIT
-----	When to her lute Corinna sings			STB
Clarke	Shy one	HL	BF-G	BOH
Coleridge-Taylor	Eleanore	HML		NOV
-----	She rested by the broken brook	HL		DIT
Delius	Love's philosophy			†
-----	Twilight fancies	M	D-FS	CFI
Dowland	Awake, sweet love	M	E-F	STB
-----	Come again! sweet love	M	D-E	STB
-----	Come away			BOO
-----	Deare, if you change			BOO
-----	Fine knacks for ladies	M	E-F	STB
-----	Flow, my tears	M	D-E	STB
-----	I saw my lady weep	M	E-E	STB
-----	Say love, if ever thou didst find			STB

29

(Dowland)	Shall I sue?			STB
-----	Sorrow, sorrow stay	M	D-D	BOS
-----	The lowest trees have tops			STB
-----	What if I never speede?	M	D-D	BOS
-----	White as lilies was her face			STB
Dunhill	The cloths of heaven	LM	EF-G	STB
Elgar	My old tunes	M	D-EF	ELK
-----	To the children	M	C-E	ELK
Fisher	At Tankerton Inn	LM	B-G	BOO
-----	Spanish gold			BOO
Ford	Now I see thy look were feigned			BOO
-----	Since first I saw your face			DIT
-----	There is a lady sweet and kind	M	D-E	STB
Forsyth	The bell man			DIT
German	Charming Chloe	HML		NOV
-----	My song is of the sturdy north	ML		CHA
-----	Rolling down to Rio	ML	G-D	NOV
Gibbs	Five eyes	HL	D-D	BOS
-----	The market			CUR
Green	My lips shall speak the praise	M	E-F	OXF
Gurney	An epitaph			OXF
Hammond	Ballad of the bony fiddler			
Handel	On love's wings			
Harty	Homeward	L	C-E	NOV
Head	A vagabond song			BOO
-----	Money, O!			BOO
-----	Sweet chance that led my steps abroad	LM	C-F	BOH
-----	The ships of Arcady	ML	BF-EF	BOH
-----	When I think upon the maidens	LM	D-G	BOO
-----	Why have you stolen my delight?	LH		BOH
Hely-Hutchinson	Old mother Hubbard	HL	B-E	CFI
Henschel	The angels dear	M		PRE
Holst	Creation			GSC
-----	The heart worships	ML	BF-D	STB
-----	The Sergeant's song			ASH
-----	Weep ye no more	M		STB
Hook	Bright Phoebus	M	EF-F	GSC
Howells	Old skinflint	M	D-F	CUR
Hughes	Old mother Hubbard			CRA
Humphrey	I pass all my hours			DIT
Ireland	Great things			AUG
-----	I was not sorrowful	ML		BOO

30

(Ireland)	The soldier	HLM		BOO
-----	When lights go rolling round the sky			
Johnson	As I walked forth one summer day			DIT
Jones	Love is a bable			STB
-----	What if I speede?			BOO
Lawes	I am confirmed			BOO
Leveridge	The beggar's song	L	G-D	BOO
-----	The maiden's resolution			GSC
-----	When dull care			BOO
Longsteffe	When the Sergeant Major's on parade			CHA
Milford	So sweet love seemed	HL	D-D	GRA
Molloy	Punchinello	L	A-D	GSC
Morgan	Clorinda	HM	C-EF	ENO
Morley	It was a lover and his lass	HM		DIT
-----	Sweet nymph, come to thy lover	M	D-B	BOS
Munro	My lovely Celia			BIR
Novello	A page's road song			ENO
Parry	To Althea	M		NOV
-----	To Lucasta			
Peterkin	A curse on a closed gate (Voice and viola)	M	D-E	OXF
Pilkington	Rest, sweet nymphs			STB
Purcell, E.	Passing by	HM	D-D	DIT
Purcell, H.	Ah, how pleasant 'tis to love			AUG
-----	Arise, ye subterranean winds			
-----	Cease, o my sad soul			POT
-----	Evening hymn	M	C-F	OXF
-----	Hark! how all things with one sound rejoice			NOV
-----	Hence with your trifling deity			
-----	If music be the food of love	M	D-G	BOO
-----	I'll sail upon the dog star	HL	A-E	†
-----	Man is for woman made			
-----	Not all my torments			NOV
-----	Since from my dear			
-----	Sylvia, now your scorn give over			FSY
Quilter	Blow, blow thou winter wind	HL	C-E	BOO
-----	Drink to me only	LMH	GF-GF	BOH
-----	Go, lovely rose	LHM	F-GF	CHA
-----	Hey, ho the wind and the rain			BOO
-----	It was a lover and his lass	HL	CS-E	BOO

31

(Quilter)	I will go with my father a-plowing	MH	D-G	ELK
-----	Now sleeps the crimson petal	LMH	EF-GF	BOO
Rosseter	What then is love but mourning			STB
-----	When Laura smiles	LM	D-E	STB
Rowley	Cherry song			
-----	In Twinkledown valley			
-----	On Newlyn Hill			BOH
-----	The toll gate house			ROG
Russell	Poor man's garden	HML	A-D	BOO
Sanderson	Drumadune			BOH
-----	Quiet	ML	AF-EF	BOH
-----	The company Sergeant major			BOH
Shaw	Song of the Palanquin bearers	LH	E-F	CUR
Somervell	A kingdom by the sea	ML	DF-F	BOO
Stanford	Drake's drum			BOO
-----	The bold unbiddable child	ML	B-DF	STB
-----	The fairy lough	ML	A-EF	BOO
-----	The pilbroch			
Stephenson	Love is a sickness	HML	C-D	BOO
-----	Ships that pass in the night	HML	DF-DF	BOO
Taylor	The wind mill	M		OXF
Toye	The inn	L	C-E	CUR
Treharne	The fly			
Vaughan Williams	Boy Jonny	LH		BOH
-----	Bright is the ring of words	L		BOH
-----	Joy shipmate, joy			OXF
-----	Let beauty awake			
-----	Linden Lea	HML	C-D	BOS
-----	Orpheus with his lute			PRO
-----	See the chariot at hand			
-----	Silent noon			GSC
-----	The infinite shining heavens			BOH
-----	The roadside fire	HML	BF-EF	BOO
-----	The vagabond	ML	A-E	BOO
-----	The water mill	L	C-D	OXF
Walton	Sunset			
Warlock	As ever I saw	MH	DF-GF	ROG
-----	Captain Stratton's fancy			AUG
-----	Fair and true	M	EF-EF	CFI
-----	Good ale			AUG
-----	Jillian of Berry			OXF
-- ---	Milkmaids			
-----	My own country	M	C-E	CFI
-----	One more river	L	C-F	ROG
-----	Passing by	M	D-G	CFI
-----	Piggesnie	ML	B-E	AUG

(Warlock)	Pretty ring time	H	D-G	CFI
-----	Robin good-fellow			
-----	Sigh no more	M	EF-F	CFI
-----	Sleep			OXF
-----	The droll lover			
-----	The sweet o' the year			ELK
White	So we'll go no more a-roving			CHA
Wilson	Phillis has such charming graces	ML	CS-EF	BOO
-----	The sailor's life	M		BOO
-----	The pretty creature	L		BOO

French Recital Songs

Baritone

Aubert	La lettre			DUR
Auric	Le gloxinia			AMP
Benati	Air crois en mon coeur fidèle			ROU
Berton	Hymne d'amour	HM	B-DS	LRO
Beydts	Dans les ombres de mon âme			
Boieldieu	C'est la Princesse de Navane			DIT
Busser	Notre père qui êtes aux cieux			
Caplet	La ronde	M		DUR
-----	Le forêt			DUR
-----	Viens, une flûte invisible			DUR
Chabrier	Ballade des gros dindons	HL		†
-----	L'Île heureuse	M	B-F	†
-----	Villanelle des petits canards	HML	B-E	†
Chaminade	Ronde d'amour			
-----	Tu me dirais	LH	BF-AF	DIT
Charpentier	La ronde des compagnons			
Chausson	Apaisement	MH	EF-G	HAM
-----	Chanson de clown	M	D-EF	ROU
-----	Le charme	HM	BF-EF	HAM
-----	Le colibri	M	F-GF	BOS
-----	Le temps des lilas	MH	D-GS	†
-----	Les papillons	M	C-F	GSC
Debussy	Ballade des femmes de Paris			DUR
-----	Beau soir	LH	C-FS	†
-----	Chevaux de bois	H	C-G	†
-----	Colloque sentimental			DUR
-----	De soir	HL		†
-----	Green	H	C-AF	†
-----	Je tremble en voyant ton visage			DUR

(Debussy)	L'échelonnement des haies			HAM
-----	La grotte			DUR
-----	Le faune			DUR
-----	Le son du cor	HL		†
-----	Le temps a laissié son manteau			DUR
-----	Les ingénus			DUR
-----	Mandoline	HM	BF-F	†
-----	Noël des enfants qui n'ont plus de maisons			DUR
-----	Nuits d'étoiles	LH	E-A	MAR
-----	Romance	HM	C-E	†
Delibes	Sérénade à Ninon			
Dukas	Sonnet			DUR
Duparc	Chanson triste	MH	FS-AF	†
-----	Elégie	HM		ROU
-----	Extase	LMH	FS-A	†
-----	La vague et la cloche			ROU
-----	La vie antérieure	HL		†
-----	Lamento	ML	EF-EF	†
-----	Le manoir de Rosamunde	HL	B-F	BOS
-----	L'invitation au voyage	HM	E-F	†
-----	Pensée d'automne			
-----	Phidylé	MH	EF-AF	BOS
-----	Sérénade florentine	HL		INT
-----	Testament	HL		INT
Dupont	Les boeufs			SAL
Fauré	Adieu	MH	F-F	†
-----	Après un rêve	HM	C-F	†
-----	Arpège	MH	E-FS	HAM
-----	Au cimetière	LH	D-F	†
-----	Aurore	H	D-G	†
-----	Automne	MH	D-FS	GSC
-----	C'est l'extase	HL	C-FF	GSC
-----	Chanson de Shylock			HAM
-----	Chanson du pêcheur	H	E-A	HAM
-----	Chant d'automne	LH	G-G	HAM
-----	Clair de lune	MH	C-G	†
-----	Cygne sur l'eau			DUR
-----	Dans les ruines d'une abbaye	M	E-FS	†
-----	En prière	H	F-F	†
-----	En sourdine	HL	C-EF	†
-----	Green	HL	CS-GF	†
-----	L'absent	LH	C-G	HAM
-----	Le parfum impérissable	LH	GF-GF	
-----	Le secret	LH	F-G	MAR
-----	Le voyageur	H	F-G	MAR
-----	Les berceaux	LMH	BF-G	†
-----	Les roses d'Ispahan	HM	D-FS	†

(Fauré)	Lydia	MH	G-G	†
-----	Madrigal	MH	F-F	HAM
-----	Nell	LH	FS-AF	†
-----	Nocturne	H	F-A	MAR
-----	Notre amour	H	DS-B	†
-----	Prison	LH		†
-----	Rencontre	H	EF-AF	†
-----	Soir	LH	D-GS	†
-----	Spleen	H	E-FS	MAR
-----	Toujours	LH	F-AF	†
Ferrari	Le miroir	M	E-F	GSC
Février	L'intruse	M	B-DF	HEU
Fourdrain	Alger le soir	M		RIC
-----	Carnaval	M	C-F	RIC
-----	Promenade au mule			
Franck	Le mariage des roses	M	E-FS	BOS
-----	Lied	LH	FS-FS	†
-----	Nocturne	HL		†
Gevaert	Lamentation napolitaine			
Gounod	A la brise			
-----	Adore and be still	HL		GSC
-----	Au printemps	LMH	DF-AF	GSC
-----	Au rossignol	LMH	D-G	CHO
-----	Ce que je suis sans toi			SC
-----	Dernières volontés			
-----	Envoi de fleurs	MH	G-G	SC
-----	L'absent			
-----	Le soir	M	CS-FS	GSC
-----	Medjé (Chanson arabe)	MH	G-G	BOO
-----	O ma belle rebelle			
-----	Prière			
-----	Vénise	HL		INT
Hahn	D'une prison	L	BF-EF	HEU
-----	L'enamourée			HEU
-----	L'heure exquise	M	DF-F	†
-----	L'incrédule			HEU
-----	Les cygnes			HEU
-----	Offrande	M	D-D	†
-----	Paysage	MH	EF-G	HEU
-----	Phyllis			HEU
-----	Tous deux			BOS
-----	Trois jours de vendange	M		HEU
Holmès	Au pays	HM	C-F	CFI
-----	L'oiseau bleu			HEU
-----	La belle du roi			HEU
Honegger	Automne			
-----	Chanson (Ronsard)			SEN
	Flute and string quartet			
Hue	J'ai pleuré en rêve	HL	D-E	BOS

Indy	La chevauchée du cid	M		HAM
-----	Lied maritime	LH	B-G	†
-----	Madrigal			DIT
-----	Mirage			HAM
Koechlin	Le thé	HM	C-E	BOS
Lalo	Marine	LH	DS-FS	
Leguerney	L'adieu	M	B-FS	DUR
Lemaire	Chanson à manger	M	B-E	GSC
Lenormand	Quelle souffrance	HM	AF-F	HAM
Levade	Les vieilles de chez nous			
Martini	Plaisir d'amour	M	BF-EF	GSC
Massenet	Crépuscule	M	D-E	GSC
-----	Pensée d'automne	HML	B-E	GSC
Milhaud	Chant d'amour	M	C-GF	ESC
-----	Chant de Forgeron	M	C-FS	SC
-----	La tourterelle	M	B-G	DUR
Paladilhe	Lamento provinçal	M	CS-FS	HOM
-----	Les trois prières			
-----	Psyché	HM	BF-F	GSC
Pessard	L'adieu du matin	ML	BF-D	GSC
-----	Requiem du coeur			LED
Pierné	En barque	L	D-DF	GSC
Pillois	Mon feu			SEN
Poldowski	Colombine	H	D-GF	CHE
-----	Dansons la gigue	M	EF-G	MAR
Poulenc	A sa guitare	M	D-FS	DUR
-----	Chanson à boire	L	B-E	HEU
-----	Chanson d'Orkenise			AMP
-----	Couplets bachiques	L	C-FF	HEU
-----	Dans le jardin d'Anna			SAL
-----	Fleurs	M	DF-F	ROU
-----	Hôtel			AMP
-----	Invocation aux Parques			HEU
-----	L'anguille			ROU
-----	La belle jeunesse	L	D-F	HEU
-----	La grenouillère			DEI
-----	Le bal masque			SAL
-----	Le disparu			ROU
-----	Montparnasse	H	EF-G	ESC
-----	Priez pour paix	ML		ROU
-----	Reine des mouettes	M	FF-F	SAL
-----	Sanglots			AMP
-----	Sérénade			
-----	Voyage à Paris			AMP
Rameau	Le grillon			DUR
Ravel	Chanson à boire			DUR
-----	Chanson française			
-----	Chanson romanesque			DUR
-----	D'Anne qui me jecta	HM	CS-FS	GSC

(Ravel)	Dansant l'amique			
-----	Kaddisch	H	C-G	DUR
-----	La pintade			DUR
-----	Le martin-pêcheur			DUR
-----	Le paon	M	C-F	DUR
-----	Manteau de fleurs	H		INT
-----	Nicolette	L	B-FS	ELK
-----	Ronsard à son âme	L	CS-E	DUR
-----	Sainte	M	C-G	ELV
-----	Sur l'herbe	MH	C-G	DUR
-----	Tout gai!	MH	EF-F	
-----	Trois beaux oiseaux du paradis			DUR
Rhené-Baton	Nuit d'autrefois			DUR
Riquier	Chanson religieuse (Troubador song)			
Roussel	Coeur en péril			DUR
-----	Le jardin mouillé	M	C-FS	ROU
Saint-Saëns	Aimons-nous			DUR
-----	Danse macabre	L	BF-EF	AXE
-----	La cloche	LH	DF-AF	†
-----	Le lever de la lune			DUR
-----	Les pas d'armes du Roi Jean	HML	A-F	RIC
-----	Mai	H	G-FS	DUR
-----	Tournoiement			DUR
Satie	Daphénéo			ROU
-----	La statue da bronze			ROU
-----	Le chapelier			ROU
Severac	Chanson de la nuit durable			SAL
-----	Les hiboux			ROU
Szulc	Dansons la gigue	M		ROU
Tiersot	Les filles de la rochelle	H		GRA
Weckerlin	Bergère légère	M	D-E	BOS
Widor	Je ne veux pas autre chose	HL	C-EF	HAM

German Recital Songs

Baritone

Ahle	Bruenstiges Verlangen	M	E-E	GSC
Bach, J.S.	Bist due bei mir	HML	A-EF	†
-----	Gedenke doch, mein Geist, zurueck			PET
-----	Komm suesser Tod	MH	C-G	†
-----	Mein Jesu, was fuer Seelenweh			
-----	O Jesulein suess			
Beethoven	Adelaide	HML	BF-E	†
-----	An die Geliebte	M	E-E	†

37

(Beethoven)	An die Hoffnung	H	B-A	†
-----	Andenken			†
-----	Auf dem Huegel sitz' ich spaehend			†
-----	Aus Goethes Faust			
-----	Bitten			†
-----	Busslied			†
-----	Das Geheimnis			
-----	Delizia	M	C-F	GSC
-----	Der Kuss			†
-----	Der Wachtelschlag			†
-----	Die Ehre Gottes	HL	AF-EF	†
-----	Diese Wolken in den Hoehen			†
-----	Es kehret der Maien			
-----	Faithfu' Johnie			
-----	Ich liebe dich	HL	BF-DF	†
-----	In questa tomba	ML	A-CS	†
-----	Leichte Segler in den Hoehen			
-----	Nimm sie hin denn, diese Lieder			†
-----	Vom Tode	L	A-EF	GSC
-----	Wo die Berge so blau			†
-----	Wonne der Wehmut			†
Brahms	Am Sonntag Morgen	L	CS-FS	†
-----	An den Mond	HL	CS-EF	†
-----	An die Tauben	HL	CS-E	†
-----	Auf dem Kirchhofe	HL	BF-EF	†
-----	Auf dem See	HL	D-F	†
-----	Bei dir sind meine Gedanken	MH	E-FS	†
-----	Blinde Kuh			†
-----	Botschaft	HL	D-F	†
-----	Dein blaues Auge	MH	BF-G	†
-----	Denn es gehet dem Menschen	HL		†
-----	Der Schmied	HL	EF-EF	†
-----	Der Tod, das ist die kuehle Nacht	L	AF-F	†
-----	Der Ueberlaeufer			†
-----	Die Mainacht	HL	BF-FF	†
-----	Ein Sonett			†
-----	Feldeinsamkeit	HL	C-EF	†
-----	Geheimnis			†
-----	Heimkehr			†
-----	Ich wandte mich und sahe an	HL		†
-----	In Waldeseinsamkeit	H	ES-G	†
-----	Juchhe!			RIC
-----	Kein Haus, keine Heimat	HL	D-D	†
-----	Klage	LH	FS-FS	†

(Brahms)	Lerchengesang	LH	FS-GS	†
-----	Liebe kam aus fernen Landen	HL	C-E	†
-----	Meine Lieder	HL	D-DS	†
-----	Minnelied	MHL	C-EF	†
-----	Mit vierzig Jahren	HL	FS-D	†
-----	Muss es eine Trennung geben?	LH	FS-FS	†
-----	Nachtwandler			
-----	Nicht mehr zu dir zu gehen			†
-----	O kuehler Wald	MH	A-F	†
-----	O liebliche Wangen	MLH	E-G	†
-----	O wuesst' ich doch den Weg zurueck	H	E-FS	†
-----	Regenlied	HL	CS-F	†
-----	Ruhe, Suessliebchen	HL	BS-E	†
-----	Sapphische Ode	HML		†
-----	Schwermut			†
-----	Schwesterlein			†
-----	Sehnsucht	H	EF-AF	†
-----	Sind es Schmerzen	HL	BF-F	†
-----	Sonntag	H	D-G	†
-----	So willst du des Armen	HL	C-E	†
-----	Staendchen	HL	BF-E	†
-----	Steig' auf, geliebter Schatten	HL	BF-EF	CFI
-----	Tambourliédchen			†
-----	Treue Liebe	LMH	DS-E	†
-----	Unueberwindlich			†
-----	Vergebliches Staendchen	LMH		†
-----	Verrat	HL	FS-EF	†
-----	Verzagen	MH	CS-FS	†
-----	Von ewiger Liebe	LMH	B-AF	†
-----	Von waldbekraenzter Hoehe			†
-----	Wehe, so willst du mich wieder			†
-----	Wenn du nur zuweilen laechelst			†
-----	Wenn ich mit Menschen			†
-----	Wie bist du meine Koenigin	HL	C-E	†
-----	Wie froh und frisch	HL	B-E	†
-----	Wie Melodien zieht es	HL	A-E	†
-----	Willst du, dass ich geh'?	L	C-G	†
-----	Wir wandelten	LH	EF-GF	†
Bungert	Der Sandtraeger			
-----	Ich hab' ein kleines Lied erdacht			
Franz	For music	ML	C-D	†
-----	Im Herbst	HM	A-F	†
-----	Marie	HL	D-F	†
-----	Sonnenuntergang	HL	CS-FS	†

(Franz)	Sterne mit den gold'nen Fuesschen	HL	DS-E	DIT
-----	Stille Sicherheit	M	E-F	†
Gluck	Ode an den Tod			
Handel	Dank sei Dir, Herr	M	CS-E	†
Hassler	Tanzlied			SIM
Haydn	Liebes Maedchen, hoer' mir zu			HSC
-----	She never told her love	HL	B-D	DIT
-----	The sailor's song			
-----	The spirit's song	M	B-GF	†
-----	The wanderer			
Hildach	Wo du hingehst			
Humperdinck	Am Rhein			AMP
Jensen	Margreta	M	F-F	PET
Liszt	Am Rhein			
-----	Die drei Zigeuner	LM	B-G	GSC
-----	Die Lorelei	LH	BF-BF	†
-----	Es muss ein Wunderbares sein	M	C-EF	DUR
-----	Nimm einen Strahl der Sonne			DUR
-----	Wieder moecht' ich dir begegnen			DUR
Loewe	Archibald Douglas			†
-----	Der Noeck			SC
-----	Die Uhr	HML	AF-EF	†
-----	Edward	HL	F-E	†
-----	Erkennen			SC
-----	Erlkoenig	M	G-F	†
-----	Friedericus Rex			SC
-----	Heinrich der Vogler			SC
-----	Hochzeitlied			HSC
-----	Kleiner Haushalt			HSC
-----	Odins Meeresritt			SC
-----	Prinz Eugen			SC
-----	Suesses Begraebnis			SC
-----	Tom der Reimer			HSC
Mahler	Der Tamboursgesell	HL		INT
-----	Des Antonius von Padua Fischpredigt	HL	GF-F	†
-----	Die zwei blauen Augen	M	A-G	†
-----	Ging heut Morgen uebers Feld	M	A-FS	INT
-----	Ich bin der Welt abbanden gekommen	HL		INT
-----	Ich hab' ein gluehend Messer	M	BF-GF	WEI
-----	Urlicht	L	DF-E	†

(Mahler)	Wenn mein Schatz Hochzeit macht			WEI
Marx	An einen Herbstwald	M	CS-FS	UNI
-----	Der Rauch			UNI
-----	Der Ton	M	C-F	AMP
-----	Ein junger Dichter			AMP
Mendelssohn	An die Entfernte	M	F-F	
-----	Jagdlied	HL	BF-EF	DIT
-----	O wert thou in the cauld blast			
-----	On wings of song			†
-----	Schilflied	M	F-FS	
-----	Venetianisches Gondellied	LM	E-FS	AUG
-----	Volkslied	M	E-A	†
Mittler	Ueber den Bergen			
Mozart	Abendempfindung	M	E-F	
-----	Trennungslied			
-----	Verdankt sei es dem Glanz			DIT
-----	Warnung	HM	C-D	
Pfitzner	Abbitte			BOH
-----	Der Einsame			BOO
-----	Der Gaertner			
-----	Hast du von den Fischerkindern			
-----	In Danzig			
-----	Michaels Kirchplatz			
-----	Nachts			BOO
Reichardt	Rhapsodie			MOS
Schillings	Wie wundersam			AMP
Schoeck	Reiselied			
-----	Wanderlied der Prager Studenten			
Schoenberg	Dank			
-----	Der verlorene Haufen	L		UNI
Schubert	Abschied	HL	BF-F	†
-----	Alinde	HL	G-B	GSC
-----	Am Bach im Fruehling			PET
-----	Am Feierabend	HL	BF-F	†
-----	Am Flusse			PET
-----	Am Meer	HML	B-D	†
-----	Am See			PET
-----	An den Mond	HL	F-GF	†
-----	An die Leier	LM	BF-F	†
-----	An die Tueren	HL		†
-----	An Schwager Kronos	HL	G-E	†
-----	An Silvia			†
-----	Auf dem Flusse	HL	F-E	†
-----	Auf dem Wasser zu singen	MH	EF-GF	†
-----	Auf der Donau			PET
-----	Aufenthalt	HLM	A-F	†

41

(Schubert)	Ave Maria	LMH	F-F	†
-----	Das Fischermaedchen	L	A-EF	†
-----	Das Lied im Gruenen			PET
-----	Das Wandern	HLM	E-E	†
-----	Das Wirtshaus	HL	C-D	†
-----	Dass sie hier gewesen!			PET
-----	Dem Unendlichen	L	A-GF	†
-----	Der Atlas	HL	BF-F	†
-----	Der Blumenbrief	L	F-EF	†
-----	Der Doppelgaenger	HL	G-D	†
-----	Der entsuehnte Orest			PET
-----	Der Erlkoenig	HML	A-E	†
-----	Der Juengling an der Quelle	LH	E-A	†
-----	Der Juengling und der Tod	M	DF-FF	†
-----	Der Leiermann	ML	C-D	†
-----	Der Lindenbaum	HL	A-D	†
-----	Der Musensohn	LH	FS-G	†
-----	Der Neugierige	HL	CS-EF	†
-----	Der Pilgrim	LH	D-F	†
-----	Der Schiffer	LH	BF-A	†
-----	Der stuermische Morgen	HL		
-----	Der Wanderer	HML	FS-D	†
-----	Der Wanderer an den Mond	LM	D-F	PET
-----	Der Wegweiser	L	D-EF	†
-----	Der Zwerg	M	A-GF	PET
-----	Der zuernende Barde			PET
-----	Die Allmacht	HML	G-E	†
-----	Die Forelle	MLH	EF-GF	†
-----	Die junge Nonne	LH	C-GF	†
-----	Die Kraehe	HL	A-E	†
-----	Die liebe Farbe			
-----	Die Liebe hat gelogen	LM	G-F	†
-----	Die Nebensonnen	HL	F-D	†
-----	Die Post	HML	BF-EF	†
-----	Die Stadt	HL	A-E	†
-----	Die Sterne	LH		DIT
-----	Die Taubenpost	HL	D-EF	†
-----	Du liebst mich nicht	LH	E-FS	†
-----	Erstarrung	HL	D-F	†
-----	Erster Verlust	M	C-F	†
-----	Fahrt zum Hades	HL	G-DF	PET
-----	Fischerweise	L	C-D	†
-----	Florio			PET
-----	Fragment aus dem Aeschylus			PET
-----	Freude der Kinderjahre	LH	C-G	†
-----	Fruehlingsglaube	M	EF-F	†
-----	Fruehlingssehnsucht	HL	B-E	†

(Schubert)	Fruehlingstraum	HL	C-D	†
-----	Ganymed	LH	EF-G	†
-----	Gebet waehrend der Schlacht	M	CS-E	†
-----	Geheimes	HL	BF-EF	†
-----	Gruppe aus dem Tartarus	L	CS-EF	†
-----	Gute Nacht	LH	C-FS	†
-----	Heideroeslein			†
-----	Ihr Bild	HL	C-C	†
-----	Ihr Grab			PET
-----	Im Abendrot	HL	C-D	†
-----	Im Fruehling	LH	D-FS	†
-----	In der Ferne	HL		†
-----	Irrlicht			
-----	Kriegers Ahnung	HL	G-EF	†
-----	Lachen und Weinen	HL	C-EF	†
-----	Liebesbotschaft	H	E-G	GSC
-----	Liebeslauschen			PET
-----	Lied eines Schiffers an die Dioskuren	HL	A-C	†
-----	Litanei	HLM	C-EF	†
-----	Lob der Thraenen	LM	F-F	†
-----	Meeresstille	HL	B-D	†
-----	Mein!	HL		†
-----	Memnon	LM	AF-F	PET
-----	Mut	HL		†
-----	Nachtgesang			PET
-----	Nachtstueck	LH	D-G	†
-----	Nacht und Traeume	HL	C-DF	†
-----	Prometheus	HL		†
-----	Schwanengesang			†
-----	Sei mir gegruesst	LH	G-G	†
-----	Seligkeit			
-----	Staendchen			
-----	Totengraebers Heimweh	HL	G-EF	†
-----	Ueber Wildemann			PET
-----	Ungeduld	HML		†
-----	Vor meiner Wiege	HL	C-E	†
-----	Wanderers Nachtlied, 1	HL		†
-----	Wanderers Nachtlied, 2	LH	F-F	†
-----	Wehmuth	HL	B-D	†
-----	Wer nie sein Brot	HL	C-EF	†
-----	Wer sich der Einsamkeit ergibt	M	C-FS	†
-----	Widerschein			PET
-----	Wohin?	HL	B-E	†
Schuetz	Aus dem 119th Psalm			
-----	Eile mich, Gott, zu erretten			BAR
Schumann, C.	Er ist gekommen			

43

Schumann, R.	Alte Laute	HL	DF-DF	†
-----	An den Sonnenschein	HL	A-D	†
-----	Auftraege	HL	C-E	†
-----	Aus den Hebraeischen Gesaengen			
-----	Dein Angesicht	HL	B-EF	†
-----	Der Hidalgo	HL	BF-F	†
-----	Der Husar, trara			
-----	Der Knabe mit dem Wunderhorn			†
-----	Der Nussbaum	LMH	D-FS	†
-----	Der Sandmann	HL	AF-DF	†
-----	Der Soldat			
-----	Die beiden Grenadiere			
-----	Die Lotusblume	HLM	BF-F	†
-----	Du bist wie eine Blume	HM	F-EF	†
-----	Er ist's	HL	BF-EF	†
-----	Fruehlingsfahrt	HL	B-E	†
-----	Ich grolle nicht	HL	BF-D	†
-----	Ich hab' im Traum geweinet	HL	B-D	†
-----	Ich wandelte unter den Baeumen	HL	A-D	†
-----	Ihre Stimme	LH		CFI
-----	Im Rhein, im heiligen Strome	HM	D-F	
-----	Im Walde	HL	A-D	†
-----	In der Fremde	HL		†
-----	Jeden Morgen			
-----	Lieb, Liebchen	HL	B-E	†
-----	Melancholie			
-----	Mit Myrthen und Rosen	HL	A-D	†
-----	Mondnacht	M	E-FS	†
-----	Provenzalisches Lied	LH		†
-----	Requiem			†
-----	Romanze	HL	C-E	†
-----	Schoene Wiege meiner Leiden	HL	C-EF	†
-----	Staendchen			
-----	Stille Traenen	HL		†
-----	Talismane			
-----	Waldesgespraech	HL	A-FS	†
-----	Wanderlied	HL	A-E	†
-----	Wenn ich in deine Augen seh'	HL	EF-FF	†
-----	Wer machte dich so krank?			
-----	Widmung	HL	BF-F	†
Strauss	Ach wehe mir unglueckhaftem Manne			
-----	Allerseelen	HL	AS-E	†

44

(Strauss)	Befreit			HSC
-----	Caecilie	MH	E-B	†
-----	Die Nacht	HL		DIT
-----	Du meines Herzens Kroenelein	HL	CS-E	†
-----	Freundliche Vision	HL	C-F	†
-----	Fuer fuenfzehn Pfennige			†
-----	Geduld	LH	C-G	
-----	Heimkehr	HL	B-E	†
-----	Heimliche Aufforderung	HL	B-E	†
-----	Ich trage meine Minne	M		†
-----	Liebeshymnus			†
-----	Madrigal	LH	EF-GF	
-----	Mit deinen blauen Augen	LH	C-GS	†
-----	Morgen	HML	E-F	†
-----	Nachtgang			†
-----	Ruhe meine Seele			†
-----	Schlechtes Wetter			†
-----	Traum durch die Daemmerung	HML	BF-EF	†
-----	Waldseligkeit			†
-----	Wie sollten wir geheim sie halten	LH	D-A	
-----	Winterliebe			†
-----	Winterweihe			†
Trunk	In meiner Heimat			
-----	Mir traeumte von einem Koenigskind			
-----	Schnitterlied			
Weber	Reigen			PET
Weingartner	Die Post im Walde			
-----	Hochsommer			
-----	Liebesfeier			
Wolf	Abschied			†
-----	Ach, des Knaben Augen	HL		†
-----	Ach, im Maien	HL	C-E	†
-----	Alle gingen, Herz, zu Ruh	HL	C-EF	†
-----	Alles endet, was entstehet	HL	F-C	†
-----	Anakreons Grab	HL	D-D	†
-----	An die Geliebte			†
-----	Auch kleine Dinge	HM	D-E	†
-----	Auf dem gruenen Balkon	HL		†
-----	Auf ein altes Bild	HL	E-DS	†
-----	Auf einer Wanderung	HL		†
-----	Auftrag	HL		†
-----	Bedeckt mich mit Blumen	HL	B-D	†
-----	Begegnung	M	EF-GF	PET
-----	Benedeit die sel'ge Mutter	H	D-G	PET
-----	Biterolf	HL	D-F	DIT

(Wolf)	Cophtisches Lied, 2			†
-----	Dank des Paria			PET
-----	Das Koehlerweib ist trunken			PET
-----	Das Staendchen	HL		†
-----	Dass doch gemalt all deine Reize waeren			†
-----	Denk' es, o Seele	LH	EF-F	†
-----	Der Feuerreiter			†
-----	Der Freund	HM	BF-E	PET
-----	Der Gaertner	HL		†
-----	Der Genesene an die Hoffnung	H	BF-AF	PET
-----	Der Musikant	HL	CS-D	†
-----	Der Rattenfaenger	HL		†
-----	Der Schreckenberger			†
-----	Der Soldat, 1	LH	E-FS	†
-----	Der Soldat, 2	H	EF-AF	PET
-----	Der Tambour	HL		†
-----	Ein Staendchen euch zu bringen	HL		†
-----	Epiphanias	HL	B-D	†
-----	Er ist's	H	D-G	†
-----	Fuehlt meine Seele	L	A-D	†
-----	Fussreise	HL	D-E	†
-----	Ganymed	HL	CS-D	†
-----	Gesang Weylas	HL	DF-F	†
-----	Gesegnet sei, durch den die Welt	HL		†
-----	Hatt ich irgend wohl Bedenken			PET
-----	Heb' auf dein blondes Haupt	HL	G-DF	†
-----	Heimweh (Eichendorff Lieder)	M		†
-----	Heimweh (Moerike Lieder)			†
-----	Hoch beglueckt in deiner Liebe	HL	DF-F	†
-----	Im Fruehling	HL	BF-F	†
-----	In der Fruehe	HL	C-C	†
-----	Jaegerlied			PET
-----	Lebe wohl	HL	BF-F	†
-----	Lied eines Verliebten			†
-----	Morgenstimmung	LH	C-GS	†
-----	Morgentau	HL	D-D	†
-----	Nachtzauber	HL	B-E	†
-----	Neue Liebe	LH	D-AF	†
-----	Nimmersatte Liebe	LH	CF-AF	†
-----	Nun wandre, Maria	HL	EF-D	†
-----	Prometheus			PET
-----	Seemanns Abschiedslied	H	C-A	†

46

(Wolf)	Selbstgestaendnis			PET
-----	Trunken muessen wir alle sein	M	ES-FS	†
-----	Ueber Nacht	LH	D-G	†
-----	Um Mitternacht	HL	G-EF	†
-----	Und willst du deinen Liebsten sterben	HL		†
-----	Verborgenheit	HL	B-E	GSC
-----	Verschwiegene Liebe	LH	DF-FS	†
-----	Wenn du zu den Blumen gehst	HL	B-EF	†
-----	Wer sich der Einsamkeit	HL	B-F	†
-----	Wer tat deinen Fuesslein weh?			
-----	Wiegenlied			
-----	Wohl denk' ich oft	M	C-EF	†
-----	Zur Ruh', zur Ruh'	HL	A-GF	†
Wolff	Alle Dinge haben Sprache	M	BF-GF	†
-----	Der Steinklopfer	M	BS-F	HMP
-----	Du bist so jung			HMP
-----	Es ist alles wie ein wunderbarer Garten			HMP
-----	Es werde Licht			†
-----	Ewig			
-----	Faeden			
-----	Knabe und Veilchen	M	D-D	HMP
-----	Landschaft			
-----	Seidenschuh' ueber Leisten von Gold			
-----	Since you're near	M	BF-GF	†
-----	Sommernacht			
-----	Tag meines Lebens			
-----	Und alles gehoeret uns			HMP

Italian Recital Songs

Baritone

Bassani	Dormi, bella, dormi tu	L	EF-F	GSC
Bimboni	Sospiri miei	M	EF-EF	GAL
Bononcini	L'esperto nocchiero (Astarte)	HL	B-E	†
-----	Per la gloria	HL	C-EF	†
-----	Suol dar la vita all'or			CFI
Brogi	Un ricordo			
Caccini	Amarilli, mia bella	ML	C-D	†
Caldara	Alma del core			GSC
-----	Come raggio di sol	HL	D-F	†
-----	Mirti, faggi			PET

47

(Caldara)	Sebben crudele	HML	E-DS	†
-----	Selve amiche, ombrose piante	HM	E-E	†
Carissimi	A morire!	ML	C-D	
-----	Filli, non t'amo più	HL	B-D	†
-----	Vittoria, mio core!	HLM	B-E	†
Castelnuovo-Tedesco	La barba bianca			
Cavalli	Beato chi può (Serse)			HEU
-----	Donzelle fuggite	HL	C-EF	†
-----	Troppo soavi i gusti	HM	E-E	DIT
Cesti	Ah, quanto è vero (Il Pomo d'Oro)	HL	F-F	DIT
-----	Che angoscia, che affanno (Il Pomo d'Oro)	HL	C-DF	DIT
-----	E dove t'aggiri (Il Pomo d'Oro)	HM	D-EF	DIT
-----	Intorno all'idol mio (Orontea)	MH	D-F	†
Cimara	Fiocca la neve	H	G-G	GSC
-----	Stornellata marinara	HM		RIC
De Leva	Canta il mare			
Del Leuto	Dimmi, amor	M	C-F	GSC
De Luca	Non posso disperar	HL	C-E	GSC
Denza	Gallop my steed			GSC
Donaudy	O del mio amato ben	M	EF-F	RIC
-----	Quando ti rivedrò			RIC
-----	Spirate pur, spirate			RIC
-----	Vaghissima sembianza	H	E-A	RIC
Durante	Danza, danza fanciulla gentile	HM	BF-F	†
-----	Vergin, tutta amor	LM	C-EF	†
Falconieri	Bella fanciulla			
-----	Non più d'amore	HL	C-D	DIT
-----	Nudo arciero	HL	AF-AF	DIT
-----	O bellissimi capelli	HL	B-D	†
Fatuo	Mattinata	M		RIC
Frescobaldi	Se l'aura spira	HL	C-EF	DIT
Gaffi	Luci vezzose	HL	D-E	DIT
Gagliano	Dormi, amore	HL	CS-E	DIT
-----	Valli profonde (Il Dannato)			HEU
Gasparini	Caro laccio, dolce nodo	M	EF-EF	GSC
Giordani	Caro mio ben	HML	B-D	†
Gluck	Spiagge amate (Paride ed Elena)			†
Handel	Affani del pensier (Ottone)			†
-----	Alma mia (Floridante)	HM	CS-E	†
-----	Col raggio placido (Agrippina)			

(Handel)	Dammi pace (Tamerlano)			
-----	Furibondo spira (Partenope)			KIS
-----	No soffrir non può (Berenice)			MUP
-----	Non lo dirò (Tolomeo)			
-----	O rendetemi il mio bene (Amadigi)	L	CS-EF	CFI
-----	Ombra mai fu (Serse)	HM	BF-EF	†
-----	Sento la gioja			
-----	Si, tra i ceppi (Berenice)	L	B-D	†
-----	V'adoro pupille (Julius Caesar)			BOO
-----	Volate più dei venti (Muzio Scevola)			MUP
Legrenzi	Che fiero costume	HML	C-D	GSC
Lotti	Pur dicesti, o bocca bella	LMH	E-FS	GSC
Malipiero	Ballata	H		CHE
-----	Inno a Maria, Nostra Donna	H		CHE
Marcello	Non m'è grave morir per amore	L	C-E	GSC
Monteverdi	Lettera amorosa			
-----	Maledetto sia l'aspetto			PET
Mozart	Ridente la calma			BOS
Paisiello	Lode al ciel			
-----	Nel cor più non mi sento	HL	C-EF	†
Paradies	M'ha preso alla sua ragna	M	EF-F	GSC
Pasquini	Sussurrate interno a clori			
Pergolesi	Bella mia (Il Maestro di Musica)			GSC
-----	Nina	HL	CS-D	DIT
-----	Ogni pena più spietata	L	B-E	GSC
Peri	Invocazione di Orfeo (Euridice)	HL	E-CS	DIT
-----	Nel puro ardor (Euridice)	HL	EF-C	DIT
Piccini	O nuit, dresse du mystere (Le Faux Lord)			GSC
Pizzetti	Angeleca			
-----	Oscuro è il ciel	M		RIC
Quagliati	Apra il suo verde seno	HL	E-CS	DIT
Respighi	Bella porta di rubini			RIC
-----	E se un giorno tornasse	M		RIC
-----	Nebbie			†
-----	Notte			BON
-----	Pioggia			BON
Rontani	Or ch'io non segno più	HL	CS-E	DIT
-----	Se bel rio	ML	D-C	†
Rosa	Selve, voi che le speranze	MH	D-G	DIT

(Rosa)	Star vicino	HL	D-E	†
Rossellini	La chambre vide			
-----	Le cennamelle			
Rossini	La danza	MH	E-A	†
Sadero	Amuri, Amuri	M		CHE
Santoliquido	Canzone Araba			
-----	Nel giardino			FOR
-----	Riflessi			FOR
Sarti	Lungi dal caro bene	HL	G-D	GSC
	(Armide)			
Scarlatti, A.	Chi vuole innamorarsi	HL	D-EF	DIT
-----	Già il sole dal Gange	LH	EF-F	GSC
-----	La fortuna			BOS
-----	Le violette			
-----	O cessate di piagarmi	HL	DS-E	†
-----	Rugiadose odorose	HL	D-E	DIT
	(Il Pirro e Demetrio)			
-----	Sento nel core	M	E-F	†
-----	Son tutta duolo	M	D-EF	GSC
Scarlatti, D.	Consolati e spara amante	L	BF-E	GSC
Secchi	Love me or not			BOO
-----	Lungi dal caro	HL	A-FS	DIT
Sibella	La Girometta	HML	D-E	GSC
-----	Sotto il ciel	HM	C-F	GSC
Stradella	Col mio sangue comprenderei	HL	E-F	DIT
	(Il Floridoro)			
-----	Per pietà (Il Floridoro)	HM	D-F	DIT
-----	Pietà, Signore	HM	C-F	GSC
-----	Se nel ben			CFI
Torelli	Tu lo sai	HL	BF-F	†
Toselli	Serenade			HEU
Tosti	À vucchella	LH	F-G	RIC
-----	Addio	MH		RIC
-----	Aprile	LMH		RIC
-----	La serenata	HLM	D-EF	GSC
-----	Mattinata			RIC
-----	The last song	HL		RIC
-----	Voi dormite signora			
-----	Vorrei morir	HM		RIC
Verdi	Tre romanze			RIC
Vivaldi	Piango gemo			
-----	Un certo no so che	HL	BF-EF	†
Wolf-Ferrari	Sonnets from Dante's "La Vita Nuova"			

Russian Recital Songs

Baritone

Arensky	Autumn	H	CS-FS	GSC
-----	Let me dream			
-----	Revery	MH	DS-FS	DIT
Blumenfeld	The starving peasant			
Cui	Hunger song	LM	E-F	DIT
-----	The statue at Czarskoe-Selo	HM	DF-EF	†
Davidenko	The blacksmith			
Gliere	Now forgotten is my lyre			
Glinka	The midnight review			
Gretchaninoff	Freedom			
-----	Hushed the song of the nightingale	MH	E-G	DIT
-----	My native land	L	C-EF	GSC
-----	Night			
-----	Over the steppe	LM	C-G	GSC
-----	Quand la hache tombe			
-----	The captive			DIT
-----	To a cup bearer			
-----	Wounded birch	HL	B-EF	†
Koeneman	The blacksmith	L		CHE
-----	When the king went forth to war	ML	A-E	CHE
Malashkin	O could I but express in song	LH		CHE
Mednikoff	The hills of Gruzia	H	DS-A	LAC
Mussorgsky	After the battle			GSC
-----	Death and the peasant			GSC
-----	Death the commander			
-----	In my attic			GSC
-----	Le chef d'armes			
-----	My little room			
-----	Night			GSC
-----	On the Dnieper			GSC
-----	Savishna			BES
-----	Serenade			BES
-----	Sphinx			BRH
-----	The banks of the Don			GSC
-----	The classic			BRH
-----	The evening prayer	M	C-E	GSC
-----	The goat	HL	C-E	CFI
-----	The grave			BRH
-----	The seminarian			GSC
-----	The song of the flea	L	AS-G	GSC
-----	Tiny star where art thou	LH	DF-F	BOS

Rachmaninoff	A dream	H		BOO
-----	Fair maiden			
-----	Floods of spring	HL		DIT
-----	God took away from me			GSC
-----	How fair this spot	MH		GSC
-----	In the silence of night	LH	D-A	GSC
-----	Morning	ML	B-DS	GSC
-----	No prophet, I			BOO
-----	Oh, no, I pray do not depart	H		DIT
-----	O thou billowy harvest field	HL	CS-E	GSC
-----	The island	LH	DF-F	†
-----	The raising of Lazarus			BRH
Rimsky-Korsakov	In silent woods			GSC
-----	On the Georgian hills	HM		GSC
-----	The prophet			
Rubinstein	Extases			
-----	When I see those little feet	MH		GSC
Tchaikovsky	At the ball	MH		GSC
-----	Don Juan's serenade	HLM	B-E	GSC
-----	Evening	HM		GSC
-----	Night	H		GSC
-----	Pilgrim's song	HLM	B-E	GSC
-----	To the forest			BOO

Scandinavian Recital Songs

Baritone

Alnaes	Sidste reis			
-----	Til en ung mann			
Grieg	A dream			†
-----	A swan			†
-----	Autumnal gale	HL	A-F	CFI
-----	By the brook			GSC
-----	Eros	LM	C-F	†
-----	Good morning			†
-----	Hunter's song	L	DS-E	GSC
-----	I love thee	HML	E-F	†
-----	In the boat	LM	D-ES	†
-----	Når jeg vil dø	L	CS-EF	HAN
-----	Nu er aftenen lys og lang	L	C-E	HAN
-----	Ragna			†
-----	Saint John's Eve	L	DF-E	CFI
-----	Serenade til Welhaven			

(Greig)	Spillemand			
-----	Thanks for thy counsel			DIT
-----	The way of the world			DIT
-----	The wounded heart			PET
-----	Til en II	M	E-F	HAN
-----	Vaer hilset, I Damer	M	D-F	HAN
-----	Vandring i skoven	M	D-FS	HAN
-----	Ved Moders grav	M	C-F	HAN
Heise	Arnes sang			
-----	Kongesønnens romance			
Ikonen	Tuutilaulu			
Klipinen	Sprich Geliebte, o sprich			
-----	Summer night			
Lassen, E.	Ich hatte einst ein	HML	B-E	GSC
	Vaterland			
Melartin	O Herre			
Nielson	Den Danske sang			
-----	Havet omkring Danmark			
-----	Irmelin rose			HAN
Rangstroem	Klunkom, Welam Welamsson			
-----	Song to Karin			
-----	Vingar i natten			
Rostedt	Neula			
Sibelius	Black roses	M	A-ES	AMP
-----	Come away death			AMP
-----	Die stille Stadt			DIT
-----	Reeds, reeds rustle			
-----	The origin of fire			
-----	Under strandens granar			
Sinding	Light	M	BF-F	GSC
-----	Sylvelin	M	E-E	GSC
Sjoeberg	Visions	MH	F-AF	GAL
-----	The Seraglio's garden	HL		GSC
Soedermann	Kung Heimer och Aslog			

Spanish Recital Songs
Baritone

Alvarez	La partida	HL	DS-E	GSC
Calleia	Granadinas			DIT
Eakin	Ay gitanos			
Ginastera	Triste			RIC
Guastavino	Campanas			
-----	Déjame estavoz			
-----	La rose y la sauce			RIC
-----	Paisaje			RIC
-----	Se equivoca			
Lara	Granada			SOU
Lecuona	Dame de tus rosas			

(Lecuona)	Por eso te quiero			MAR
Mompou	Combat del somni			
Padilla	Princesita	M		BOS
Sandoval	Madrigal	HL	A-E	GSC
-----	Sin tu amor	H	E-G	GSC
Serrano	Marinela			

Miscellaneous Recital Songs

Baritone

Bach-Gounod	Ave Maria			
Bartok	Ujdalok			
Bizet	Agnus Dei	HLM	C-AF	
Chajes	Adarim			TRA
Dvořák	Clouds and darkness			
-----	God is my shepherd			AMP
-----	I will sing new songs of gladness	HL		
-----	Lord, Thou art my refuge and shield			AMP
-----	Songs my mother taught me	HM	E-E	
-----	Turn Thee to me			AMP
Franck	Panis angelicus	LM		
Gustaldon	Musica probita			
Kodaly	Kit kene elvenni			
Kotilainen	Kun joulu on			
Monteverdi	Laudate Dominum			
Ravel	Mayerke mein suhn			RAV
Saint-Saëns	Ave Maria	HM		DIT
-----	Ave Verum			DUR
Schubert	Ave Maria			
Schuetz	Fili mi Absalom			
	4 Trombones and harpsichord			
Villa-Lobos	A Viola			
-----	Cantilena no. 3			
-----	Remeiro de San Francisco			
-----	Xango			AMP

British Songs and Arias For Opening Recitals

Baritone

Dowland	I saw my lady weep	M	E-E	STB
Green	My lips shall speak the praise	M	E-F	OXF

Handel	Have mercy, Lord (Te Deum)	HM		†
-----	Hear me, ye winds and and waves (Scipione)	ML	G-EF	BOO
-----	Let me wander not unseen (L'Allegro)	M	D-G	†
-----	Silent worship (Tolomeo)	LM	D-E	CUR
-----	Tears such as tender fathers shed (Deborah)	L		†
-----	Wher'er you walk (Semele)	HML	C-D	†
Purcell	Ah, how pleasant 'tis to love			AUG
-----	Evening hymn	M	C-F	OXF
-----	If music be the food of love	M	D-G	BOO
-----	Music for a while (Oedipus)	LH		SC
-----	Not all my torments			NOV

German Songs for Opening Recitals

Baritone

Bach, J.S.	Bist du bei mir	HML	A-EF	†
-----	O Jesulein suess			
Beethoven	Adelaide	HML	BF-E	†
-----	Andenken			†
-----	Ich liebe dich	HL	BF-DF	†
Brahms	Verzagen	MH	CS-FS	†
Bungert	Der Sandtraeger			
Gluck	Ode an den Tod			
Handel	Dank sei Dir, Herr	M	CS-E	†
Schubert	Das Wandern	HLM	E-E	†
-----	Ganymed	LH	EF-G	†
-----	Liebesbotschaft	H	E-G	†
Schuetz	Eile mich, Gott, zu erretten			BAR
Schumann	Mit Myrthen und Rosen	HL	A-D	†
Wolf	Ueber Nacht	LH	D-G	†

Italian Songs and Arias For Opening Recitals

Baritc e

Caccini	Amarilli, mia bella	ML	C-D	†
Caldara	Sebben crudele	HML	E-DS	†
Carissimi	Vittoria, mio core	HLM	B-E	†
Cavalli	Beato chi può (Serse)			HEU
-----	Donzelle fuggite	HL	C-EF	†

Cesti	Ah, quanto è vero (Il Pomo d'Oro)	HL	F-F	DIT
-----	Che angoscia, che affanno (Il Pomo d'Oro)	HL	C-DF	DIT
-----	E dove t'aggiri (Il Pomo d'Oro)			DIT
Cimara	Stornellata marinara	HM		RIC
Donaudy	Quando ti rivedrò			RIC
Durante	Vergin, tutta amor	LM	C-EF	†
Falconieri	O bellissimi capelli	HL	B-D	†
Gluck	Spiagge amate (Paride ed Elena)			†
Handel	Affani del pensier (Ottone)			†
-----	Furibondo spira (Partenope)			KIS
-----	Lascia ch'io pianga (Rinaldo)	HM	EF-F	†
-----	O rendetemi il mio bene (Amadigi)	L	CS-EF	CFI
-----	Sei mia gioia (Pathenope)	HL	C-F	CFI
-----	Si, tra i ceppi (Berenice)	L	B-D	GSC
-----	V'adoro pupille (Julius Caesar)			BOO
Lotti	Pur dicesti, o bocca bella	LMH	E-FS	GSC
Monteverdi	Ahi, troppo è duro (Il Balletto delle Ingrate)	HL	C-EF	DIT
Mozart	Ridente la calma			BOS
Paisiello	Nel cor più non mi sento	HL	C-EF	†
Pergolesi	Salve Regina			
Peri	Invocazione di Orfeo (Euridice)	HL	E-CS	DIT
Piccini	O nuit, dresse du mystere (Le Faux Lord)			GSC
Rosa	Star vicino	HL	D-E	†
Sarti	Lungi dal caro bene (Armide)	HL	G-D	GSC
Scarlatti, A.	Già il sole dal Gange	LH	EF-F	GSC
-----	Sento nel core	M	E-F	†
Stradella	Per pietà (Il Floridoro)	HM	D-F	DIT
-----	Pietà, Signore	HM	C-F	GSC
-----	Se nel ben			CFI
Vivaldi	Piango gemo			
-----	Un certo no so che	HL	BF-EF	†

American Songs For Closing Recitals

Baritone

Bacon	Casey Jones			
Barber	Bessie Bobtail	M	C-F	GSC
-----	I hear an army	LH	D-AF	GSC
-----	Sure on this shining night	MH	D-G	GSC
Branscombe	At the postern gate	MH	DF-AF	ASC
Carpenter	Serenade	LH	CS-A	GSC
Castelnuovo-Tedesco	Springtime	M		CHE
Chanler	I rise when you enter	M	CS-G	GSC
Charles	When I have sung my songs	HM	BF-EF	GSC
Copland	Old American songs			
Curran	Life	HM	BF-F	GSC
Dougherty	Everyone sang			
Duke	I ride the great black horses	M	C-G	GSC
-----	On a March day	M	B-GF	BOH
Foster	My journey's end	HLM	DF-G	GSC
Golde	Who knows	HM	BF-F	GSC
Hageman	Don Juan Gomez	M		GAL
-----	Miranda	HL		GAL
Horsman	The bird of the wilderness	LMH	DF-BF	GSC
Kernochan	We two together	H	EF-AF	GAL
Kingsford	Courage	M	C-F	GSC
Kleinsinger	The courtship of old Joe Clark			
La Forge	Hills	HL		RIC
-----	Song of the open	MH	EF-AF	DIT
-----	To a messenger	HLM	CF-G	GSC
Mac Gimsey	Jeri Jericho	M	C-G	CFI
-----	Land uv degradashun	M	BF-F	CFI
-----	O Lord you made a Moses	M		CFI
-----	Thunderin' wonderin'	L	C-D	CFI
Malotte	Blow me eyes	MH	C-G	GSC
-----	Mister Jim	M	D-F	GSC
-----	Song of the open road			ABC
-----	Upstream	M	C-F	GSC
Mana Zucca	Rachem	HML		CHA
Nordoff	Tell me, Thyrsis	H	E-G	AMP
Paxson	Laughing song	M	C-F	CFI
Rogers	The last song	MLH	E-AF	GSC
-----	Time for making songs	HM	CS-F	DIT
Sacco	Drum of peace	M	D-F	CFI
-----	Johnny the one	HL	BF-D	GSC

57

Sachs	The three riders	M	C-F	GSC
Schindler	From a city window			
Schuman	Holiday song	M	C-F	GSC
Singer	This want of you	L	E-FS	BOH
Swanson	Joy	M	BF-EF	LEE
Taylor	Captain Stratton's fancy	L	CS-F	JFI
Tyson	Sea moods	LH	E-AF	GSC
Warren	My parting gift			DIT
-----	We two	LH	E-A	GSC
-----	White horses of the sea	LH	F-G	GSC
Watts	Joy	HL	D-F	GSC
Weaver	The Abbot of Derry	HL	B-EF	GSC
Wolfe	Bone come a-knittin'			FLA
-----	Who's gonna mourn for me	LMH	D-A	ROB

(See also Negro Spirituals and Folk Songs.)

Miscellaneous Songs For
Closing Recitals

Baritone

Brahms	Juchhe!			†
-----	Wenn du nur zuweilen laechelst			†
-----	Wie froh und frisch	HL	B-E	†
-----	Willst du, dass ich geh'?	L	C-G	†
Bridge	Love went a-riding	HL		BOS
Britten	Oliver Cromwell			BOH
Cimara	Canto di primavera		D-G	FRL
Cowen	Border ballad	LM	D-E	BOO
Debussy	Chevaux de bois	H	C-G	†
De Lamarter	Break, new born year			WIT
Delius	Love's philosophy			†
Durante	Danza, danza fanciulla gentile	HM	BF-F	†
Eakin	Ay gitanos			
Falla	Jota	LH		AMP
-----	Polo	HL		AMP
German	My song is of the sturdy north	ML		CHA
Gretchaninoff	My native land	L	C-EF	GSC
Grieg	By the brook			GSC
-----	Good morning			†
-----	Hunter's song	L	DS-E	GSC
-----	Vaer hilset, I Damer	M	D-F	HAN
Head	A vagabond song			BOO

(Head)	When I think upon the maidens	LM	D-G	BOO
Hely-Hutchinson	Old mother Hubbard	HL	B-E	CFI
Hughes	Old mother Hubbard			CRA
Ireland	Great things			AUG
-----	When lights go rolling round the sky			
Keel	Trade winds	HL	BF-EF	BOH
Marx	Der Ton	M	C-F	AMP
Quilter	Blow, blow thou winter wind	HL	C-E	BOO
-----	Over the mountains			BOS
Rachmaninoff	Floods of spring	HL		DIT
-----	Oh, no, I pray do not depart	H		DIT
Rangstroem	Song to Karin			
Respighi	Pioggia			BON
Schubert	Die Forelle	MLH	EF-GF	†
-----	Ueber Wildemann			PET
Schumann	Er ist's	HL	BF-EF	†
Sinding	Light	M	BF-F	GSC
Strauss	Ich liebe dich			†
Vaughan Williams	The roadside fire	HML	BF-EF	BOO
Warlock	Yarmouth Fair	HL	B-E	CFI
Wolf	Er ist's	H	D-G	
-----	Morgenstimmung	LH	C-GS	†

American Atmospheric Songs

Baritone

Barber	Rain has fallen	HM	D-E	GSC
Bone and Fenton	Green fields	MH	E-A	PRE
-----	Tryst	MH	FS-G	CFI
Burleigh	Sometimes I feel like a motherless child	HML		RIC
Carpenter	Go, lovely rose	M	DF-EF	GSC
-----	Looking glass river	M	B-D	GSC
-----	Slumber song	ML	BF-F	GSC
-----	The green river	M	B-E	GSC
Carter	Dust of snow	M	D-E	AMP
Charles	Clouds	HML	C-EF	GSC
-----	My lady walks in loveliness	HM	C-EF	GSC

(Charles)	When I have sung my songs	HM	BF-EF	GSC
Crist	Into a ship dreaming	LMH	EF-GS	CFI
Curran	Nocturne Violin	HML	B-DS	GSC
Dougherty	Loveliest of trees	HM	C-E	BOH
Duke	Central Park at dusk	M		BOO
-----	Loveliest of trees	L	C-D	GSC
Ganz	A memory	HM	B-D	GSC
Griffes	Symphony in yellow	M	D-GF	GSC
Kramer	Minnelied	M	C-E	JFI
-----	Pleading	LH	D-GF	JFI
-----	Swans	HL		RIC
Loeffler	To Helen	M	DF-F	GSC
Mac Dowell	The sea	HL	D-D	BRH
Mac Gimsey	Sweet little Jesus boy	ML	D-D	CFI
Naginski	Night song at Amalfi	M	D-EF	GSC
Niles	I wonder as I wander	HL	BF-D	GSC
-----	Jesus, Jesus rest your head	HL	A-D	GSC
-----	The gambler's lament	HL	B-E	GSC
Robinson	Water boy	M	B-E	BOS
Sacco	The ragpicker	MH	C-AF	GSC
Tureman	A winter sunset	L	BF-E	GSC
Tyson	Noon and night	LH	F-AF	GSC
Watts	Blue are her eyes	H	FS-FS	DIT

British Atmospheric Songs

Baritone

Anon	Have you seen but a white lily grow?	H	E-F	GSC
Bridge	E'en as a lovely flower	HM	FS-E	BOH
Del Riego	O dry those tears	LMH	E-GS	CHA
Dunhill	The cloths of heaven	LM	EF-G	STB
Forsyth	The bell man			DIT
Handel	O sleep why dost thou leave me (Semele)	H	DS-GS	†
Harty	My lagan love	ML	BF-EF	BOO
Holst	The heart worships	ML	BF-D	STB
Hughes	A Ballynure ballad	L	BF-D	BOH
Quilter	Now sleeps the crimson petal	LMH	EF-GF	BOO
Sanderson	Quiet	ML	AF-EF	BOH
Somervell	A kingdom by the sea	ML	DF-F	BOO
Stanford	The fairy lough	ML	A-EF	BOO

Vaughan				
Williams	Bright is the ring of words L			BOH
-----	Silent noon			GSC
-----	The infinite shining heavens			BOH
Warlock	Sleep			OXF

French Atmospheric Songs and Arias

Baritone

Chausson	Apaisement	MH	EF-G	HAM
-----	Les papillons	M	C-F	GSC
Debussy	Nuits d'etoiles	LH	E-A	MAR
Delibes	Lakmé, ton doux regards (Lakmé)			HEU
Duparc	La vie antérieure	HL		†
Fauré	En sourdine	HL	C-EF	†
Ferrari	Le miroir	M	E-F	GSC
Février	L'ihtruse	M	B-DF	HEU
Gluck	Un ruisselet bien clair (La Rencontre Imprévue)			LEM
Gounod	Sérénade	LMH	D-A	GSC
Hahn	D'une prison	L	BF-EF	HEU
-----	L'heure exquise	M	DF-F	†
-----	Paysage	MH	EF-G	HEU
Holmès	Au pays	HM	C-F	CFI
Leguerney	L'adieu	M	B-FS	DUR
Massenet	Chanson de la Touraine (Panurge)	M	EF-EF	HEU
Paladilhe	Psyché	HM	BF-F	GSC
Poulenc	Fleurs	M	DF-F	ROU
Ravel	Sainte	M	C-G	ELV
-----	Sur l'herbe	MH	C-G	DUR
Roussel	Le jardin mouillé	M	C-FS	ROU

German Atmospheric Songs and Arias

Baritone

Brahms	Nachtwandler			
-----	Steig' auf, geliebter Schatten	HL	BF-EF	†
Franz	Sterne mit den gold'nen Fuesschen	HL	DS-E	†
Haydn	She never told her love	HL	B-D	DIT
Schubert	Gute Nacht	LH	C-FS	†
-----	Nacht und Traeume	HL	C-DF	†

61

Schumann	Dein Angesicht	HL	B-EF	†
-----	Der Nussbaum	LMH	D-FS	†
-----	Ich hab' im Traum geweinet	HL	B-D	†
-----	Im Walde	HL	A-D	†
Strauss	Die Nacht	HL		†
-----	Traum durch die Daemmerung	HML	BF-EF	†
Wolf	Verborgenheit	HL	B-E	†

Miscellaneous Atmospheric Songs

Baritone

Cui	The statue at Czarskoe-Selo	HM	DF-EF	†
Grieg	A dream			†
-----	A swan			†
-----	In the boat	LM	D-ES	†
-----	Når jeg vil dø	L	CS-EF	HAN
-----	Ragna			†
-----	Til En II	M	E-F	HAN
Mussorgsky	My little room			
-----	Tiny star where art thou	LH	DF-F	BOS
Rachmaninoff	Morning	ML	B-DS	GSC
Sibelius	Reeds, reeds rustle			
Sinding	Sylvelin	M	E-E	GSC

American Dramatic Songs

Baritone

Barber	Bessie Bobtail	M	C-F	GSC
-----	I hear an army	LH	D-AF	GSC
Beach	Ah, love but a day			ASC
-----	The year's at the spring	MH	AF-AF	ASC
Bloch	Psalm 22	M	B-F	GSC
Campbell-Tipton	The crying of water	LH	FS-GS	GSC
Carpenter	Berceuse de guerre	M	C-G	GSC
-----	On the day when death will knock at thy door	M	C-F	GSC
-----	Slumber song	ML	BF-F	GSC
-----	The green river	M	B-E	GSC
Chadwick	O let night speak of me	HM	C-F	ASC
Curran	Life	HM	BF-F	GSC
Damrosch	Danny Deever	L	A-F	PRE
Diamond	David weeps for Absolom	M	D-A	MUP

Duke	Capri			
-----	Here in this spot with you	M	B-F	GSC
-----	I ride the great black horses	M	C-G	GSC
-----	On a March day	M	B-GF	BOH
Foster	My journey's end	HLM	DF-G	GSC
Geehl	For you alone			SHU
Gilbert	Pirate song	L	C-EF	GRA
Griffes	An old song resung	LM	EF-F	GSC
-----	Phantoms	M	BF-F	GSC
-----	Sorrow of Mydath	M		GSC
Hageman	Don Juan Gomez	M		GAL
-----	Music I heard with you	MH	E-A	GAL
Horsman	The bird of the wilderness	LMH	DF-BF	GSC
Huhn	Invictus	ML	BF-DF	ASC
Ives	Charlie Rutlage	M		ARR
Johnson	Roll, Jerd'n roll	M	EF-F	GSC
Kernochan	We two together	H	EF-AF	GAL
La Forge	Song of the open	MH	EF-AF	DIT
Loeffler	To Helen	M	DF-F	GSC
Mac Dowell	The sea	HL	D-D	BRH
Mac Gimsey	Land uv degradashun	M	BF-F	CFI
Malotte	Song of the open road			ABC
Manz-Zucca	I love life	LM	F-F	PRE
Moore	Adam was my grandfather			GAL
Nordoff	Tell me, Thyrsis	H	E-G	AMP
Rogers	The last song	MLH	E-AF	GSC
-----	Time for making songs	HM	CS-F	DIT
Singer	This want of you	L	E-FS	BOH
Speaks	Morning	HML	BF-D	GSC
-----	Shepherd, see thy horse's foaming mane			FLA
Taylor	Captain Stratton's fancy	L	CS-F	JFI
Tyson	Sea moods	LH	E-AF	GSC
Warren	We two	LH	E-A	GSC
-----	White horses of the sea	LH	F-G	GSC
Wolfe	De glory road	L	A-F	GSC
-----	Gwine to Hebb'n	LM	B-E	GSC
-----	Who's gonna mourn for me	LMH	D-A	ROB

British Dramatic Songs and Arias

Baritone

Arne, T.	Preach not me your musty rules (Comus)	HML		ROW

Bainton	Ring out, wild bells	M	C-EF	OXF
Bridge	O that it were so	LMH	D-G	CHA
Cowen	Border ballad	LM	D-E	BOO
Delius	Twilight fancies	M	D-FS	CFI
Del Riego	Homing	HML	BF-E	CHA
Dix	The trumpeter	HML	A-C	BOH
Dowland	Fine knacks for ladies	M	E-F	STB
German	My song is of the sturdy north	ML		CHA
-----	Rolling down to Rio	ML	G-D	NOV
Grainger	Shallow brown	M	F-F	GSC
Handel	But who may abide (The Messiah)	L	G-E	†
-----	Why do the nations (The Messiah)	L	B-E	†
Holst	The Sergeant's song			ASH
Ireland	Great things			AUG
Leveridge	When dull care			BOO
Purcell	I'll sail upon the dog star	HL	A-E	†
Quilter	Blow, blow thou winter wind	HL	C-E	BOO
Ronald	Prelude	HML	B-D	ENO
Sanderson	Shipmates of mine	LL	G-D	BOO
Sullivan	The lost chord	HL	C-F	GSC
Templeton	Wi' a hundred pipers	L	BF-EF	GSC
Vaughan Williams	Joy, shipmate joy			OXF
-----	The vagabond	ML	A-E	BOO

French Dramatic Songs and Arias

Baritone

Bizet	Chanson du toreador (Carmen)	HL	BF-F	†
-----	L'orage s'est calmé (Les Pêcheurs des Perles)			CHO
-----	Quand la flamme de l'amour (Le Jolie Fille de Perth)			CHO
Caplet	Le forêt			DUR
Charpentier	Les pauvre gens peuvent-ils être heureux (Louise)			HEU
Debussy	Chevaux de bois	H	C-G	†
-----	Colloque sentimental			DUR
-----	Noël des enfants qui n'ont plus de maisons			DUR
Duparc	La vague et la cloche			ROU
-----	La vie antérieure	HL		†
-----	Le manoir de Rosamunde	HL	B-F	BOS

64

(Duparc)	Phidylé	MH	EF-AF	BOS
-----	Testament	HL		INT
Fauré	Automne	MH	D-FS	GSC
-----	Poème d'un jour			HAM
-----	Prison	LH		†
-----	Toujours	LH	F-AF	†
Février	L'intruse	M	B-DF	HEU
Hahn	D'une prison	L	BF-EF	HEU
-----	Offrande	M	D-D	†
Holmès	Au pays	HM	C-F	CFI
Hue	J'ai pleuré en rêve	HL	D-E	BOS
Indy	Lied maritime	LH	B-G	ROU
-----	Mirage			HAM
Lalo	Marine	LH	DS-FS	
Lenormand	Quelle souffrance	HM	AF-F	HAM
Massenet	Promesse de mon avenir (Le Roi de Lahore)	L	DF-GF	GSC
-----	Salomé, Salomé (Hérodiade)			GSC
-----	Vision fugitive (Hérodiade)	LM	C-GF	GSC
Meyerbeer	Adamastor, roi des vagues profondes (L'Africaine)	L	D-E	GSC
-----	Fille des rois (L'Africaine)			BRO
-----	Nonnes qui reposez (Robert le Diable)			GSC
Offenbach	Scintille diamant (Tales of Hoffman)	M		GSC
Paladilhe	Lamento provincal	M	CS-FS	HOM
Pessard	Requiem du coeur			LED
Poldowski	Dansons la gigue	M	EF-G	MAR
Saint-Saëns	Danse macabre	L	BF-EF	AXE
-----	Les pas d'armes du Roi Jean	HML	A-F	RIC
Thomas	Chanson bachique (O vin dissipe) (Hamlet)			GSC
-----	Comme une pâle fleur (Hamlet)			HEU

German Dramatic Songs and Arias

Baritone

Beethoven	In questa tomba	ML	A-CS	†
Brahms	Am Sonntag Morgen	L	CS-FS	†
-----	Nicht mehr zu dir zu gehen			†
-----	Treue Liebe	LMH	DS-E	†
-----	Verrat	HL	FS-EF	†
-----	Von ewiger Liebe	LMH	B-AF	†
Franz	Im Herbst	HM	A-F	†
Liszt	Die drei Zigeuner	LM	B-G	GSC

(Liszt)	Die Lorelei	LH	BF-BF	†
Loewe	Archibald Douglas			†
-----	Edward	HL	F-E	†
-----	Erkennen			SC
-----	Odins Meeresritt			SC
Mahler	Der Tamboursgesell	HL		INT
-----	Ich hab' ein gluehend Messer	M	BF-GF	WEI
-----	Lieder eines fahrenden Gesellen	M		INT
Marx	An einen Herbstwald	M	CS-FS	UNI
-----	Hat dich die Liebe beruehrt	MH	EF-BF	AMP
Mendelssohn	Is not His word like a fire (Elijah)	M	B-F	†
-----	It is enough (Elijah)	L	A-E	†
-----	Schilflied	M	F-FS	
Schubert	Am Feierabend	HL	BF-F	GSC
-----	Am Meer	HML	B-D	†
-----	An Schwager Kronos	HL	G-E	†
-----	Auf dem Flusse	HL	F-E	†
-----	Aufenthalt	HLM	A-F	†
-----	Dem Unendlichen	L	A-GF	†
-----	Der Atlas	HL	BF-F	†
-----	Der Doppelgaenger	HL	G-D	†
-----	Der Erlkoenig	HML	A-E	†
-----	Der Lindenbaum	HL	A-D	†
-----	Der Schiffer	LH	BF-A	†
-----	Die Allmacht	HML	G-E	†
-----	Die junge Nonne	LH	C-GF	†
-----	Die Kraehe	HL	A-E	†
-----	Die Liebe hat gelogen	LM	G-F	†
-----	Die Stadt	HL	A-E	†
-----	Du liebst mich nicht	LH	E-FS	†
-----	Erstarrung	HL	D-F	†
-----	Fahrt zum Hades	HL	G-DF	PET
-----	Fragment aus dem Aeschylus			PET
-----	Fruehlingstraum	HL	C-D	†
-----	Ganymed	LH	EF-G	†
-----	Gebet waehrend der Schlacht	M	CS-E	†
-----	Gruppe aus dem Tartarus	L	CS-EF	†
-----	In der Ferne	HL		†
-----	Kriegers Ahnung	HL	G-EF	†
-----	Mut	HL		GSC
-----	Prometheus	HL		†
-----	Totengraebers Heimweh	HL	G-EF	†
Schumann	Der arme Peter	HL	B-G	†

(Schumann)	Der Husar, Trara!			
-----	Der Soldat			
-----	Fruehlingsfahrt	HL	B-E	†
-----	Ich grolle nicht	HL	BF-D	†
-----	Mit Myrthen und Rosen	HL	A-D	†
-----	Schoene Wiege meiner Leiden	HL	C-EF	†
-----	Talismane			
-----	Waldesgespraech	HL	A-FS	†
Strauss	Caecilie	MH	E-B	†
-----	Madrigal	LH	EF-GF	
-----	Ruhe meine Seele			†
Wagner	Die Frist ist um (Der Fliegende Hollaender)			†
-----	Leb' wohl, du kuehnes, herrliches Kind (Die Walkuere)	L	B-E	†
Weber	Wo berg' ich mich (Euryanthe)			†
Wolf	Alle gingen, Herz, zu Ruh	HL	C-EF	†
-----	Das Koehlerweib ist trunken			PET
-----	Denk' es, o Seele	LH	EF-F	†
-----	Der Feuerreiter			†
-----	Der Freund	HM	BF-E	PET
-----	Der Rattenfaenger	HL		INT
-----	Epiphanias	HL	B-D	†
-----	Lebe wohl	HL	BF-F	†
-----	Nachtzauber	HL	B-E	†
-----	Prometheus			PET
-----	Seemanns Abschiedslied	H	C-A	†
-----	Ueber Nacht	LH	D-G	†
-----	Zur Ruh', zur Ruh'	HL	A-GF	†

Italian Dramatic Songs and Arias

Baritone

Cimara	Canto di primavera		D-G	FRL
Donizetti	Vien, Leonora a piedi tuoi (La Favorita)			BRO
Durante	Vergin, tutta amor	LM	C-EF	†
Giordano	Nemico della patria (Andrea Chenier)	L	B-FS	SON
Leoncavallo	Zaza, piccola zingara (Zaza)			SON
Mascagni	Il cavallo scalpita (Cavalleria Rusticana)			GSC
Piccini	O nuit, dresse du mystere (Le Faux Lord)			GSC
Ponchielli	O monumento (La Gioconda)			RIC

Puccini	Se la giurata fede (Tosca)	M	DF-F	RIC
Respighi	Nebbie			†
Verdi	Cortigiani, vil razza (Rigoletto)			GSC
-----	Credo (Otello)	M	AS-FS	JCH
-----	Eri tu (Un Ballo in Maschera)	M	A-G	†
-----	Ford's monologue (E sogno) (Falstaff)			RIC
-----	Il mio sangue (Luisa Miller)			RIC
-----	In braccio alle dovizie (I Vespri Siciliani)			RIC
-----	O de' verd'anni miei (Ernani)			RIC
-----	O vecchio cor, che batti (I Due Foscari)			RIC
-----	Per me giunto (Don Carlos)			RIC
-----	Urna fatale (La Forza del Destino)			RIC

Miscellaneous Dramatic Songs

Baritone

Alvarez	La partida	HL	DS-E	GSC
Cui	Hunger song	LM	E-F	DIT
Dvořák	Hear my prayer, O Lord			AMP
Gliere	Now forgotten is my lyre			
Gretchaninoff	Over the steppe	LM	C-G	GSC
-----	The captive			DIT
-----	Wounded birch	HL	B-EF	†
Grieg	A dream			†
-----	A swan			†
-----	Autumnal gale	HL	A-F	CFI
-----	Eros	LM	C-F	†
-----	In the boat	LM	D-ES	†
-----	Vaer hilset, I Damer	M	D-F	HAN
Koeneman	When the king went forth to war	ML	A-E	CHE
Korbay	Had a horse, a finer no one ever saw			SC
Malashkin	O could I but express in song	LH		CHE
Mussorgsky	After the battle			GSC
-----	On the Dnieper			GSC
-----	Siege of Kazan (Boris Godunoff)	L	F-E	GSC

(Mussorgsky)	The song of the flea	L	AS-G	GSC
Rachmaninoff	Christ is risen	LM	D-F	GAL
-----	Floods of spring	HL		DIT
-----	God took away from me			GSC
-----	Oh, no, I pray, do not depart	H		DIT
-----	O thou billowy harvest field	HL	CS-E	GSC
-----	To the children	MH	F-G	DIT
Rimsky- Korsakov	On the Georgian hills	HM		GSC
Sibelius	Black roses	M	A-ES	AMP
Sinding	Light	M	BF-F	GSC
Tchaikovsky	None but the lonely heart	HLM	C-F	DIT
-----	Pilgrim's song	HLM	B-E	GSC

American Humorous Songs
Baritone

Bone and Fenton	Captain Kidd	MH	B-G	CFI
Brockway	The swapping song			GSC
Carpenter	Don't ceare	M	C-D	GSC
Chanler	I rise when you enter	M	CS-G	GSC
Dougherty	Declaration of independence	L	C-C	GSC
Guion	What shall we do with a drunken sailor	HML	C-D	GSC
Hadley	My shadow			ASC
Hindemith	The whistling thief	M	E-F	AMP
Mac Gimsey	Egg-a-bread			MCG
-----	Jonah and the whale	M	BF-EF	CFI
Malotte	Blow me eyes	MH	C-G	GSC
-----	Mister Jim	M	D-F	GSC
Mana-Zucca	The big brown bear	HML	C-F	GSC
Mason	A grain of salt	L	A-D	GSC
-----	I ain't afeared of the Admiral	L	A-E	GSC
-----	Nautical lays of a landsman	L	A-E	GSC
-----	The constant cannibal maiden	L	C-FS	GSC
Moore	Adam was my grandfather			GAL
Niles	The gambler's lament	HL	B-E	GSC
Paxson	Laughing song	M	C-F	CFI
Porter	Brush up your Shakespeare (Kiss me Kate)			HAR
Powell	The deaf woman's courtship	M		JFI
Rodgers	Soliloquy (Carousel)			CHA

69

Romberg	The fireman's bride (Up in Central Park)	M	D-EF	WIL
Sacco	Brother Will, brother John	M	C-F	GSC
-----	Mexican serenade	HL	D-EF	BOS
Schuman	Holiday song	M	C-F	GSC
Scott	The drunken sailor			
Taylor	Captain Stratton's fancy	L	CS-F	JFI
Weaver	The Abbot of Derry	HL	B-EF	GSC
Wolfe	Sailormen	HM	D-FS	GSC
-----	Short'nin' bread	LHM	D-D	FLA

British Humorous Songs

Baritone

Arden and Wille	Cockles and mussels	HM	E-E	ROW
Arne, T.	Why so pale and wan?			GSC
Berners	Dialogue between Tom Filuter and his man	M	D-F	CHE
-----	Theodore or the pirate king			CHE
Britten	Oliver Cromwell			BOH
Charles, W.	The green eyed dragon	M	BF-E	BOH
Clarke	Shy one	HL	BF-G	BOH
Coates	Stone cracker John	L		BOO
Gibbs	Five eyes	HL	D-D	BOS
-----	The market			CUR
Head	When I think upon the maidens	LM	D-G	BOO
Hely-Hutchinson	Old mother Hubbard	HL	B-E	CFI
Hughes	A Ballynure ballad	L	BF-D	BOH
-----	Kitty, my love, will you marry me?	M	C-F	BOH
-----	Old mother Hubbard			CRA
-----	The stuttering lovers	MH	E-FS	CHA
Johnston	Because I were shy	L	B-E	CRA
Jones	Love is a bable			STB
Lawes	I am confirmed			BOO
Leveridge	The maiden's resolution			GSC
Liddle	The garden where the praties grow	LMH	E-FS	STB
Lohr	The little Irish girl	HLM	C-E	CHA
Old English	Young Richard			PRE
Sanderson	Captain Mac	ML	G-E	BOO
-----	Laughing cavalier	LM	BF-F	BOO
Stanford	The little admiral	L	C-G	STB

70

Sullivan	The Lord Chancellor's insomnia (Iolanthe)			
Torrence	Smilin' Kitty O'Day	ML	CS-D	BOO
Warlock	The droll lover			

French Humorous Songs and Arias

Baritone

Bizet	Quand la flamme de l'amour (Le Jolie Fille de Perth)			CHO
Chabrier	Ballade des gros dindons	HL		†
-----	Villanelle des petits canards	HML	B-E	†
Debussy	Ballade des femmes de Paris			DUR
Grétry	Nièces, neuveux (Les Deux Avares)			JOB
Lemaire	Chanson à manger	M	B-E	GSC
Messager	Long ago in Alcala	M		CHA
Poulenc	Chanson à boire	L	B-E	HEU
-----	La belle jeunesse	L	D-F	HEU
-----	Le bestiaire String quartet, flute, clarinet and bassoon	M		AMP
Ravel	Sur l'herbe	MH	C-G	DUR
Satie	La statue de bronze			ROU
-----	Le chapelier			ROU

German Humorous Songs and Arias

Baritone

Beethoven	Aus Goethes Faust			
-----	Der Kuss			†
Brahms	Vergebliches Staendchen	LHM	E-FS	†
Mahler	Des Antonius von Padua Fischpredigt	HL	GF-F	†
Mendelssohn	Ich bin ein vielgerister Mann (Heimkehr aus der Fremde)	ML		DIT
Mozart	Der Vogelfaenger bin ich ja (Die Zauberfloete)	L	D-E	†
-----	Warnung	HM	C-D	
Reichardt	Rhapsodie			MOS
Schubert	Heidenroeslein			
Strauss, J.	Open road, open sky (The Gypsy Baron)			GSC
Strauss, R.	Fuer fuenfzehn Pfennige			†

Wolf	Abschied			†
-----	Der Musikant	HL	CS-D	†
-----	Der Soldat, 1	LH	E-FS	†
-----	Der Tambour	HL		†
-----	Epiphanias	HL	B-D	†
-----	Nimmersatte Liebe	LH	CF-AF	†

Italian Humorous Songs and Arias

Baritone

Mozart	Ho capito, Signor (Don Giovanni)			
-----	Aprite un po' quegli occhi (Le Nozze di Figaro)			
-----	Der Vogelfaenger bin ich ja (Zauberfloete)			†
-----	Madamina! Il catalogo e questo (Don Giovanni)			†
-----	Non più andrai (Le Nozze di Figaro)	L	C-E	†
Pergolesi	Son imbrogliato io gia (La Serva Padrona)	L		RIC
Rontani	Or ch'io non segno più	HL	CS-E	DIT
Rossini	Largo al factotum (Il Barbieri di Siviglia)			†
Scarlatti, A.	Chi vuole innamorarsi	HL	D-EF	DIT
Wolf- Ferrari	Aprila, o bella (Jewels of the Madonna)	HL	D-FS	GSC

Miscellaneous Humorous Songs

Baritone

Grieg	The way of the world			DIT
Mussorgsky	Song of the parrot (Boris Godunoff)			DIT
-----	The evening prayer	M	C-E	GSC
-----	The seminarian			GSC
-----	The song of the flea	L	AS-G	GSC

American Folk Songs (Arr.)

Baritone

Bacon	Adam and Eve	M	B-D	CFI
-----	The Erie canal	L	D-C	CFI
Bartholomew	Pretty Saro	M	D-D	GSC
-----	Little Mawhee			GSC
Brockway	Barbara Allen			GRA
-----	Frog went-a-courting			GRA
-----	Sourwood mountain			GRA
-----	The barnyard song			GRA
-----	The swapping song			GSC
Burleigh	The dove and the lily	HL		RIC
Copland	I bought me a cat			
-----	Old American songs			
Davis	He's gone away	M	C-E	GAL
Dougherty	Across the western ocean	M	D-D	GSC
-----	Five sea chanties	L	A-EF	GSC
-----	Mobile bay	M	BF-EF	GSC
-----	Rio Grande	M	EF-EF	GSC
-----	Shenandoah	L	A-D	GSC
Guion	All day on the prarie	M	EF-F	GSC
-----	Home on the range	HLM	C-F	GSC
-----	What shall we do with a drunken sailor	HML	C-D	GSC
Hughes	The warranty deed			GSC
Niles	Black is the color of my true love's hair			
-----	Down in the valley			GSC
-----	Gambler, don't lose your place	HM	C-F	GSC
-----	Gambler's song of the Big Sandy River	HM	CS-FS	GSC
-----	I wonder as I wander	HL	BF-D	GSC
-----	Jesus, Jesus rest your head	HL	A-D	GSC
-----	The black oak tree			CFI
-----	The gambler's lament	HL	B-E	GSC
-----	The rovin' gambler	HL	BF-EF	GSC
Paxson	Bid your love			
-----	Blow ye winds			
-----	Sally Brown			
-----	Shenandoah			
Powell	At the foot of Yonders mountain	M		JFI
-----	Five Virginian folk songs			JFI
-----	The deaf woman's courtship	M		JFI

(Powell)	The rich old woman	M		JFI
Robinson	Water boy	M	B-E	BOS
Scott	Blow the man down			
-----	The drunken sailor			
-----	Wailie, wailie	M	D-E	JCH
Shaw	Black is the color of my true love's hair	M	C-F	DIT
Siegmeister	Bury me not on the lone prairie			
-----	Poor way faring stranger			
Wellesley	Sing me a chanty	HLM	B-E	FOX

British Folk Songs (Arr.)

Baritone

Arden and Wille	Cockles and mussels	HM	E-E	ROW
Britten	Oliver Cromwell			BOH
-----	The ash grove			BOH
Broadwood	Some rival has stolen my true love	LM	D-E	BOO
Clayton	O men from the fields	M	C-F	BOS
Corder	The Bailiff's daughter of Islington			JWM
Gatty	Bendemeer's stream	LMH		BOO
Grainger	Shallow Brown	M	F-F	GSC
Harty	My lagan love	ML	BF-EF	BOO
-----	The game played in Erin-Go-Bragh			CFI
Hatton	The minstrel boy			BOO
Hopekirk	Annie Laurie			DIT
-----	Loch Lomond			DIT
-----	Ye banks and braes	LM	D-C	DIT
Hughes	A Ballynure ballad	L	BF-D	BOH
-----	Down by the Sally gardens			BOO
-----	Has sorrow thy young days shaded			BOO
-----	Kitty, my love, will you marry me?	M	C-F	BOH
-----	Oft in the stilly night			
-----	The lark in clear air	ML	BF-D	BOO
-----	The stuttering lovers	MH	E-FS	CHA
Johnston	Because I were shy	L	B-E	CRA
Kennedy-Fraser	An Eriskay love lilt			BOO
-----	The bens of Jura			BOO
-----	The farmer's pride			CHA

74

(Kennedy-Fraser)	The road to the isles			BOO
Lawson	Turn ye to me	M	B-E	GSC
Liddle	The garden where the praties grow	LMH	E-FS	STB
Mc Gill	Lord Randall			BOO
Moss	The floral dance	HML	A-D	CHA
Old English	Young Richard			PRE
Page	The foggy dew			DIT
-----	The harp that once through Tara's halls			DIT
Peel	In summertime on Bredon	ML	BF-EF	CHA
-----	The bonnie Earl o' Moray			
Peterkin	I wish and I wish	M	B-E	OXF
Quilter	Over the mountains			BOS
Reid	Turn ye to me			BOO
Scott	Lord Randal	L	E-F	GAL
Shaw	The land of heart's desire	M	C-E	CUR
Somervell	David of the white rock			
Stanford	Trottin' to the fair	M		BOO
Tarrnsch	Early one morning			
Taylor	May day carol			JFI
Templeton	Wi' a hundred pipers	L	BF-EF	GSC
Vaughn Williams	And all in the morning	L	D-E	GAL
-----	Rolling in the dew			OXF
Warlock	Yarmouth Fair	HL	B-E	CFI
Welsh	All through the night			
Wilson	Come let's be merry			BOO
-----	Mary of Allendale	HML	BF-EF	BOO

Miscellaneous Folk Songs (Arr.)

Baritone

Brahms	In stiller Nacht			†
-----	Mein Maedel hat einen Rosenmund	M	F-F	†
Dvořák	Gypsy songs	LH	D-A	AMP
Falla	Asturiana	HL		AMP
-----	El pano moruno	HL		AMP
-----	Jota	LH		AMP
-----	Nana	HL		AMP
-----	Polo	HL		AMP
-----	Seguidilla murciana	HL		AMP
Ferrari	Valparaiso			
Korbay	Had a horse, a finer no one ever saw			SC

75

Milhaud	Two bretonne folk songs			ESC
Obradors	Con amores a mi madre			RIC
Ravel	Chanson espagnole	LH	D-BF	DUR
-----	Chanson italienne			DUR
-----	Là-bas, vers l'église	MH	GS-E	DUR
-----	Quel galant!	M	D-F	DUR
Serradell	La golondrina	H	C-A	GSC
Tiersot	J'ai vu la beauté ma mie			
-----	L'amours de moi	M	EF-F	HEU
Weckerlin	Aminte	M	C-D	†
-----	Chantons les amours de Jean	H	D-G	GSC
-----	Lison dormait	M	D-D	CFI
-----	Menuet d'Exaudet	H	D-G	GSC
-----	O ma tendre musette	LM	A-E	GSC
-----	Trop aimable Sylvia	M	D-E	GSC
-----	Venez, agréable printemps	M	C-F	

Negro Spirituals

Baritone

Boatner	Oh, what a beautiful city!	HL	D-E	GSC
-----	On mah journey	LH	EF-EF	RIC
-----	Trampin' (Tryin' to make heaven my home)	L	D-F	ELK
Brown	Dere's no hidin' place down dere			CFI
-----	Every time I feel de spirit			AMP
-----	Sometimes I feel like a motherless child	L		AMP
Burleigh	Balm in Gilead	HL		RIC
-----	De gospel train	HL		RIC
-----	Deep river	HML		RIC
-----	Go down, Moses	HL		RIC
-----	Hard trials	M		RIC
-----	He's just de same today	HL		RIC
-----	I stood on de ribber ob Jerdon	HL		RIC
-----	Joshua fit de battle ob Jericho	LH	DS-E	RIC
-----	My Lord, what a mornin'			
-----	Nobody knows de trouble I've seen	HL		RIC
-----	Oh, didn't it rain	LH		RIC
-----	Oh, Peter, go ring-a-dem bells			RIC

(Burleigh)	Sometimes I feel like a motherless child	HML		RIC
-----	Were you there?	HML		RIC
Dett	Sit down servant			GSC
Johnson	At the feet of Jesus	L		
-----	City called Heaven			ROB
-----	Dere's no hidin' place down dere			
-----	Fix me, Jesus	L	BF-DF	GSC
-----	Hold on			ROB
-----	Honor, honor	HM	C-E	CFI
-----	John Henry			CFI
-----	Oh, glory			
-----	Ride on, King Jesus			CFI
-----	Roll Jerd'n roll	M	EF-F	GSC
-----	Take my mother home	M	BF-EF	CFI
-----	Witness	HM	D-F	CFI
Kerby-Forrest	He's got the whole world in His hands	M	G-E	MLS
Lawrence	Let us break bread together	HML	BF-EF	MCR
Mac Gimsey	Daniel in the lion's den	M		CFI
-----	Land uv degradashun	M	BF-F	CFI
-----	Shadrack	HM	C-EF	CFI
-----	Sweet little Jesus boy	ML	D-D	CFI
Payne	Crucifixion	L	C-C	GSC
Price	My soul's been anchored in the Lord			GAM
Ryder	Let us break bread together	LH	D-G	JFI
Saunders	The Lord's prayer	L	BF-C	BOH
Singer	Go down Moses	M	E-E	CFI

American Songs Employing Agility

Baritone

Barber	I hear an army	LH	D-AF	GSC
Diack	Little Jack Horner			CFI
Dichmont	Ma little banjo	ML	E-CS	GSC
Hageman	Miranda	HL		GAL
Hopkinson	O'er the hills	LH	C-G	†
Manning	Shoes	M	EF-F	GSC
Nordoff	There shall be more joy	M		AMP
Schuman	Holiday song	M	C-F	GSC
Speaks	In May time	HL	D-E	JCH

British Songs and Arias Employing Agility

Baritone

Aiken	Sigh no more	HML		STB
Arne, T.	Now Phoebus sinketh in the west			GSC
-----	Preach not me your musty rules (Comus)	HML		ROW
German	Charming Chloe	HML		NOV
-----	Rolling down to Rio	ML	G-D	NOV
Green	My lips shall speak the praise	M	E-F	OXF
Handel	Arm, arm ye brave (Judas Maccabaeus)	L	B-E	†
-----	O ruddier than the cherry (Acis and Galatea)	L	G-F	DIT
-----	O sleep why dost thou leave me (Semele)	H	DS-GS	†
-----	Revenge, Timotheus cries (Alexander's Feast)	L	G-D	†
-----	See the raging flames arise (Joshua)			†
-----	The trumpet shall sound (The Messiah) Trumpet	L		†
-----	Thy glorious deeds (Samson)	M	C-F	†
-----	Why do the nations? (The Messiah)	L	B-E	†
Hely- Hutchinson	Old mother Hubbard	HL	B-E	CFI
Hook	Bright Phoebus	M	EF-F	GSC
Hughes	Old mother Hubbard			CRA
Morgan	Clorinda	HM	C-EF	ENO
Morley	It was a lover and his lass	HM		DIT
-----	Sweet nymph, come to thy lover	M	D-B	BOS
Purcell	Hark! how all things with one sound rejoice			NOV
-----	I attempt from love's sickness to fly (The Indian Queen)	MH	CS-E	†
-----	I'll sail upon the dog star	HL	A-E	†
Wilson	Come let's be merry			BOO
-----	Phillis has such charming graces	ML	CS-EF	BOO

French Songs and Arias Employing Agility

Baritone

Berlioz	Sérénade de Mephisto			DIT
	(La Damnation de Faust)			
Chausson	Le colibri	M		BOS
-----	Les papillons	M	C-F	GSC
Gounod	Au rossignol	LMH	D-G	CHO
-----	Sérénade	LMH	D-A	GSC
Grétry	O Richard, O mon roi			
	(Richard Coeur-De-Lion)			
Lemaire	Chanson a manger	M	B-E	GSC
Meyerbeer	Adamastor, roi des vagues	L	D-E	GSC
	profondes (L'Africaine)			
Ravel	Chanson à boire			DUR
-----	Kaddisch	H	C-G	DUR
Spontini	Dans le sein d'un Ami			
	(La Vestale)			

German Songs and Arias Employing Agility

Baritone

Bach, J.S.	Doch weichet, ihr tollen			NOV
	vergeblichen (Cantata 8)			
	Flute			
-----	Wie will ich lustig lachen			OXF
	(Cantata 205)			
Brahms	Botschaft	HL	D-F	†
-----	O liebliche Wangen	MLH	E-G	†
Haydn	Rolling in foaming billows	L	C-F	†
	(The Creation)			
-----	With joy th' impatient	L	B-E	†
	husbandman (The Seasons)			
Mahler	Des Antonius von Padua	HL	GF-F	†
	Fischpredigt			
-----	Ich bin der Welt abbanden		HL	INT
	gekommen			
Mendelssohn	Is not His word like a fire	M	B-F	†
	(Elijah)			
Mozart	Der Vogelfaenger bin ich ja	L	D-E	†
	(Die Zauberfloete)			
Schubert	Am See			PET
-----	Auf dem Wasser zu singen	MH	EF-GF	†
-----	Das Wandern	HLM	E-E	†
-----	Irrlicht			
-----	Liebesbotschaft	H	E-G	†

(Schubert)	Mein!	HL		†
-----	Ungeduld	HML		†
Schumann	Auftraege	HL	C-E	†
-----	Mondnacht	M	E-FS	GSC
-----	Waldesgespraech	HL	A-FS	†
Strauss	Fuer fuenfzehn Pfennige			†

Italian Songs and Arias Employing Agility

Baritone

Bononcini	L'esperto nocchiero (Astarte)	HL	B-E	†
-----	Per la gloria	HL	C-EF	†
Caldara	Alma del core			GSC
-----	Selve amiche, ombrose piante	HM	E-E	†
Carissimi	Filli, non t'amo più	HL	B-D	†
-----	Vittoria, mio core	HLM	B-E	†
Cimara	Canto di primavera		D-G	FRL
Donaudy	Spirate pur, spirate			RIC
Donizetti	Cruda funesta smania (Lucia di Lammermoor)			BRO
Durante	Danza, danza fanciulla gentile	HM	BF-F	†
Handel	Affani del pensier (Ottone)			†
-----	Furibondo spira (Partenope)			KIS
-----	Sei mia gioia (Parthenope)	HL	C-F	CFI
-----	Si, tra i ceppi (Berenice)	L	B-D	†
-----	Volate più dei venti (Muzio Scevola)			MUP
Lotti	Pur dicesti, o bocca bella	LMH	E-FS	GSC
Mozart	Aprite un po quegl' occhi (Le Nozze di Figaro)			†
-----	Mentre ti lascio	L		BOO
Pergolesi	Ogni pena più spietata	L	B-E	GSC
Rossini	La danza	MH	E-A	†
-----	Largo al factotum (Il Barbiere di Siviglia)	L	D-G	†
Scarlatti, A.	Già il sole dal Gange	LH	EF-F	GSC
-----	La fortuna			BOS
-----	Rugiadose odorose (Il Pirro e Demetrio)	HL	D-E	DIT
Scarlatti, D.	Consolati e spara amante	L	BF-E	GSC
Verdi	Il mio sangue (Luisa Miller)			RIC

80

Vivaldi	Un certo no so che	HL	BF-EF	†

Miscellaneous Songs
Employing Agility

Baritone

Alvarez	La partida	HL	DS-E	GSC
Falla	Nana murciana	HL		AMP
-----	Polo	HL		AMP
-----	Seguidilla	HL		AMP
Grieg	Good morning			†
Mussorgsky	Oriental chant (Josua Navine Cantata)	ML	BF-E	GSC
-----	Tiny star, where art thou	LH	DF-F	BOS

American Songs Employing
Crescendo and Diminuendo

Baritone

Barber	Rain has fallen	HM	D-E	GSC
--↓---	The daisies	M	C-F	GSC
Beach	Ah, love but a day			ASC
Campbell-Tipton	The crying of water	LH	FS-GS	GSC
Carpenter	Go, lovely rose	M	DF-EF	GSC
-----	Looking glass river	M	B-D	GSC
Charles	Clouds	HML	C-EF	GSC
Duke	Loveliest of trees	L	C-D	GSC
Engel	Sea shell	M	EF-EF	GSC
Hopkinson	My days have been so wondrous free	LH	EF-G	†
La Forge	Hills	HL		RIC
Loeffler	To Helen	M	DF-F	GSC
Niles	I wonder as I wander	HL	BF-D	GSC
-----	Jesus, Jesus rest your head	HL	A-D	GSC
Rogers	At parting	LH	CS-FS	GSC
Thompson	Velvet shoes	M	C-E	ECS

British Songs and Arias Employing
Crescendo and Diminuendo

Baritone

Benjamin	The wasp			CUR
Bridge	E'en as a lovely flower	HM	FS-E	BOH
Clarke	Shy one	HL	BF-G	BOH
Handel	Let me wander not unseen (L'Allegro)	M	D-G	†
-----	O sleep why dost thou leave me (Semele)	H	DS-GS	†
Head	The ships of Arcady	ML	BF-EF	BOH
Leveridge	The maiden's resolution			GSC
Morley	Sweet nymph, come to thy lover	M	D-B	BOS
Purcell	I attempt from love's sickness to fly (The Indian Queen)	MH	CS-E	†
-----	Sylvia, now your scorn give over			FSY
Quilter	Now sleeps the crimson petal	LMH	EF-GF	BOO
Shaw	Song of the Palanquin bearers	LH	E-F	CUR
Vaughan Williams	The infinite shining heavens			BOH

French Songs and Arias Employing
Crescendo and Diminuendo

Baritone

Berlioz	Le repos de la Ste. Famille (L'Enfance du Christ)	MH		CST
Debussy	Green	H	C-AF	†
-----	Les ingénus			DUR
Duparc	Chanson triste	MH	FS-AF	†
-----	L'invitation au voyage	HM	E-F	†
-----	Phidylé	MH	EF-AF	BOS
-----	Sérénade	HL		INT
Fauré	Adieu	MH	F-F	†
-----	Arpège	MH	E-FS	HAM
-----	Clair de lune	MH	C-G	†
-----	En prière	H	F-F	†
-----	Green	HL	CS-GF	†
-----	Le secret	LH	F-G	†
-----	Les roses d'Ispahan	HM	D-FS	†

82

(Fauré)	Lydia	MH	G-G	†
-----	Nell	LH	FS-AF	†
-----	Spleen	H	E-FS	MAR
Gounod	Envoi de fleurs	MH	G-G	SC
-----	Medjé (Chanson arabe)	MH	G-G	BOO
Martini	Plaisir d'amour	M	BF-EF	GSC
Mehul	Femme sensible (Ariodant)			
Paladilhe	Psyché	HM	BF-F	GSC
Rameau	A l'amour rendez les armes (Hippolyte et Aricie)			CHO
-----	Dans ces doux asiles (Castor et Pollux)			LEM
-----	Le grillon			DUR
Satie	Daphénéo			ROU

German Songs Employing
Crescendo and Diminuendo

Baritone

Beethoven	Andenken			†
Brahms	Auf dem See	HL	D-F	†
-----	Geheimnis			†
-----	Sonntag	H	D-G	†
-----	Wie Melodien zieht es	HL	A-E	†
Franz	Sterne mit den gold'nen Fuesschen	HL	DS-E	†
-----	Stille Sicherheit	M	E-F	†
Haydn	Liebes Maedchen, hoer' mir zu			HSC
Mendelssohn	Venetianisches Gondellied	LM	E-FS	AUG
Schubert	Abschied	HL	BF-F	†
-----	Am See			PET
-----	An den Mond	HL	F-GF	†
-----	Auf dem Wasser zu singen	MH	EF-GF	†
-----	Das Lied im Gruenen			PET
-----	Der Musensohn	LH	FS-G	†
-----	Der Wanderer	HML	FS-D	†
-----	Der Wanderer an den Mond	LM	D-F	PET
-----	Die Taubenpost	HL	D-EF	†
-----	Fruehlingstraum	HL	C-D	†
-----	Geheimes	HL	BF-EF	†
-----	Hark! hark! the lark	LMH	F-G	†
-----	Im Fruehling	LH	D-FS	GSC
-----	Lachen und Weinen	HL	C-EF	†
-----	Liebesbotschaft	H	E-G	†
-----	Nacht und Traeume	HL	C-DF	†

83

Schumann	Der Nussbaum	LMH	D-FS	†
-----	Der Sandmann	HL	AF-DF	†
-----	Provenzalisches Lied	LH		†
-----	Romanze	HL	C-E	†
-----	Staendchen			
Strauss	Die Nacht	HL		†
Wolf	Auch kleine Dinge	HM	D-E	†
-----	Der Gaertner	HL		†
-----	Morgentau	HL	D-D	†
-----	Nun wandre, Maria	HL	EF-D	†
-----	Und willst du deinen Liebsten sterben	HL		†
-----	Verschwiegene Liebe	LH	DF-FS	†
-----	Wenn du zu den Blumen gehst	HL	B-EF	†
Wolff	Faeden			
-----	Knabe und Veilchen	M	D-D	HMP

Italian Songs and Arias Employing Crescendo and Diminuendo

Baritone

Bononcini	Per la gloria	HL	C-EF	†
Caldara	Alma del core			GSC
-----	Sebben crudele	HML	E-DS	†
-----	Selve amiche, ombrose piante	HM	E-E	†
Cesti	Intorno all'idol mio (Orontea)	MH	D-F	†
De Luca	Non posso disperar	HL	C-E	GSC
Falconieri	O bellissimi capelli	HL	B-D	†
Frescobaldi	Se l'aura spira	HL	C-EF	DIT
Handel	Affani del pensier (Ottone)			†
-----	Ombra mai fu (Serse)	HM	BF-EF	†
Marcello	Non m'é grave morir per amore	L	C-E	GSC
Monteverdi	Lasciatemi morire (Arianna)	ML	D-D	†
Respighi	Bella porta di rubini			RIC
Rontani	Se bel rio	ML	D-C	†
Rosa	Selve, voi che le speranze	MH	D-G	DIT
Scarlatti, A.	La fortuna			BOS
-----	Sento nel core	M	E-F	†
Secchi	Love me or not			BOO

Miscellaneous Songs Employing
Crescendo and Diminuendo

Baritone

Gretchaninoff	My native land	L	C-EF	GSC
Grieg	En fuglevise			
-----	In the boat	LM	D-ES	†
-----	Nu er aftenen lys og lang	L	C-E	HAN
-----	Springtide			
Mussorgsky	Oriental chant (Josua Navine Cantata)	ML	BF-E	GSC
-----	The banks of the Don			GSC
-----	The evening prayer	M	C-E	GSC
Rachmaninoff	The island	LH	DF-F	†

American Songs Employing
Piano Singing

Baritone

Barber	With rue my heart is laden	HL	CS-D	GSC
Burleigh	Jean	HML		PRE
Carpenter	May the maiden			DIT
-----	The green river	M	B-E	GSC
Charles	My lady walks in loveliness	HM	C-EF	GSC
-----	When I have sung my songs	HM	BF-EF	GSC
De Rose	I heard a forest praying	MH	EF-GF	CHA
Foote	Tranquillity	HL	BF-E	ASC
Ganz	A memory	HM	B-D	GSC
Griffes	Symphony in yellow	M	D-GF	GSC
Guion	Mam'selle Marie	M	D-E	GSC
Kramer	Minnelied	M	C-E	JFI
-----	Pleading	LH	D-GF	JFI
-----	Swans	HL		RIC
Mac Dowell	The sea	HL	D-D	BRH
Mac Gimsey	Sweet little Jesus boy	ML	D-D	CFI
Manning	In the Luxembourg gardens	HML	BF-D	GSC
-----	Shoes	M	EF-F	GSC
Naginski	Night song at Amalfi	M	D-EF	GSC
Taylor	A song for lovers	MH	D-F	JFI
Watts	Blue are her eyes	H	FS-FS	DIT

British Songs Employing
Piano Singing

Baritone

Anon	Have you seen but a white lily grow?	H	E-F	GSC
Arden and Wille	Cockles and mussels	HM	E-E	ROW
Coleridge-Taylor	She rested by the broken brook	HL		DIT
Delius	So white, so soft, is she	LH	B-FS	BOH
-----	Twilight fancies	M	D-FS	CFI
Del Riego	O dry those tears	LMH	E-GS	CHA
Dunhill	The cloths of heaven	LM	EF-G	STB
Forsyth	The bell man			DIT
Gurney	An epitaph			OXF
Handel	Silent worship (Tolomeo)	LM	D-E	CUR
Harty	My lagan love	ML	BF-EF	BOO
Ireland	I was not sorrowful	ML		BOO
Pilkington	Rest, sweet nymphs			STB
Sanderson	Quiet	ML	AF-EF	BOH
Shaw	The land of heart's desire	M	C-E	CUR
Vaughan Williams	Orpheus with his lute			PRO
-----	Silent noon			GSC

French Songs and Arias Employing
Piano Singing

Baritone

Aubert	La lettre			DUR
Berlioz	Voici des roses (La Damnation de Faust)			CST
Debussy	La grotte			DUR
-----	Nuits d'etoiles	LH	E-A	MAR
Delibes	Lakmé, ton doux regards (Lakmé)			HEU
Dukas	Sonnet			DUR
Duparc	Extase	LMH	FS-A	†
Fauré	Après un rêve	HM	C-F	†
-----	C'est l'extase	HL	C-FF	GSC
-----	Dans les ruines d'une abbaye	M	E-FS	†
-----	En sourdine	HL	C-EF	†
Ferrari	Le miroir	M	E-F	GSC

Février	L'intruse	M	B-DF	HEU
Franck	Le mariage des roses	M	E-FS	BOS
Gounod	Au rossignol	LMH	D-G	CHO
-----	Sérénade	LMH	D-A	GSC
Hahn	D'une prison	L	BF-EF	HEU
-----	L'heure exquise	M	DF-F	†
-----	Offrande	M	D-D	†
-----	Paysage	MH	EF-G	HEU
Lully	Bois épais (Amadis)	ML	C-EF	†
Massenet	Crépuscule	M	D-E	GSC
-----	Légende de la sauge (Jongleur de Notre-Dame)	M	CS-F	HEU
Pessard	L'adieu du matin	ML	BF-D	GSC
Poulenc	Invocation aux Parques			HEU
-----	Montparnasse	H	EF-G	ESC
Ravel	D'Anne qui me jecta	HM	CS-FS	GSC
-----	Sainte	M	C-G	ELV
-----	Sur l'herbe	MH	C-G	DUR
-----	Trois beaux oiseaux du paradis			DUR
Roussel	Le jardin mouillé	M	C-FS	ROU
Saint-Saëns	Mai	H	G-FS	DUR
Weckerlin	Aminte	M	C-D	†
-----	Bergère légère	M	D-E	BOS
-----	Menuet d'Exaudet	H	D-G	GSC
-----	O ma tendre musette	LM	A-E	GSC
-----	Trop aimable Sylvia	M	D-E	GSC
Widor	Je ne veux pas autre chose	HL	C-EF	HAM

German Songs and Arias Employing Piano Singing

Baritone

Beethoven	Ich liebe dich	HL	BF-DF	†
Brahms	In Waldeseinsamkeit	H	ES-G	†
-----	Lerchengesang	LH	FS-GS	†
-----	Nachtwandler			
-----	Sapphische Ode	HML		†
-----	Staendchen	HL	BF-E	†
-----	Steig' auf, geliebter Schatten	HL	BF-EF	†
Franz	Marie	HL	D-F	†
Hassler	Tanzlied			SIM
Mahler	Die zwei blauen Augen	M	A-G	†
-----	Ich bin der Welt abbanden gekommen	HL		INT

Marx	Der Rauch			UNI
Mendelssohn	It is enough (Elijah)	L	A-E	†
-----	Lord God of Abraham (Elijah)	L	B-E	†
Schubert	Ave Maria	LMH	F-F	†
-----	Du bist die Ruh	LMH	EF-AF	†
-----	Im Abendrot	HL	C-D	†
-----	Lob der Thraenen	LM	F-F	†
-----	Totengraebers Heimweh	HL	G-EF	†
Schumann	Mondnacht	M	E-FS	†
-----	Requiem			†
Strauss	Allerseelen	HL	AS-E	†
-----	Freundliche Vision	HL	C-F	BOO
-----	Heimkehr	HL	B-E	†
-----	Ich trage meine Minne	M		†
-----	Nachtgang			†
-----	Traum durch die Daemmerung	HML	BF-EF	†
Trunk	In meiner Heimat			
Wagner	O du, mein holder Abendstern (Tannhaeuser)	L	BF-E	†
Wolf	Ach, des Knaben Augen	HL		†
-----	An die Geliebte			†
-----	Auf ein altes Bild	HL	E-DS	†
-----	Jaegerlied			PET
-----	Nachtzauber	HL	B-E	†
-----	Schlafendes Jesuskind	HL	AS-F	†
-----	Verborgenheit	HL	B-E	†

Italian Songs and Arias Employing
Piano Singing

Baritone

Bononcini	Deh, più a me non v'ascondete	LH		†
Brogi	Venitian vision	M	D-F	RIC
Cimara	Fiocca la neve	H	G-G	GSC
Durante	Vergin tutto amor			†
Gagliano	Dormi, amore (La Flora)	HL	CS-E	DIT
Gluck	O del mio dolce ardor (Paride ed Elena)			GSC
Mozart	Deh vieni alla finestra (Don Giovanni)	L	D-E	†
Respighi	Notte			BON
Scarlatti, A.	Già mai			
Secchi	Lungi dal caro bene	HL	A-FS	DIT

88

Miscellaneous Songs Employing
Piano Singing

Baritone

Arensky	Revery	MH	DS-FS	DIT
Cui	The statue at Czarskoe-Selo	HM	DF-EF	†
Dvořák	God is my shepherd			AMP
-----	Goin' home			DIT
-----	Songs my mother taught me	HM	E-E	†
Gretchaninoff	Hushed the song of the nightingale	MH	E-G	DIT
Grieg	A dream			†
-----	A swan			†
-----	Ragna			†
-----	Til En II	M	E-F	HAN
Mednikoff	The hills of Gruzia	H	DS-A	LAC
Mussorgsky	My little room			
Rachmaninoff	In the silence of night	LH	D-A	GSC
Rimsky-Korsakov	In silent woods			GSC
Sibelius	Die stille Stadt			DIT
Sinding	Sylvelin	M	E-E	GSC
Tchaikovsky	Evening	HM		GSC

American Songs Employing
Rapid Enunciation

Baritone

Boatner	Oh, what a beautiful city!	HL	D-E	GSC
Brockway	The swapping song			GSC
Burleigh	Joshua fit de battle ob Jericho	LH	DS-E	RIC
Carpenter	Don't ceare	M	C-D	GSC
-----	The cock shall crow	M	B-E	GSC
Guion	What shall we do with a drunken sailor	HML	C-D	GSC
Hadley	My shadow			ASC
Hageman	Don Juan Gomez	M		GAL
Kernochan	Smuggler's song			GAL
Kountz	The sleigh	HL	D-FS	GSC
Leoni	Tally-ho!			GSC
Mac Gimsey	Egg-a-bread			MCG
Mana-Zucca	The big brown bear	HML	C-F	GSC
Naginski	Richard Cory	ML	A-E	GSC

Sacco	Brother Will, brother John	M	C-F	GSC
-----	Mexican serenade	HL	D-EF	BOS
Speaks	Shepherd see thy horse's foaming mane			FLA
Warner	Hurdy gurdy	M	D-F	CFI
Weaver	The Abbot of Derry	HL	B-EF	GSC
Wolfe	De glory road	L	A-F	GSC
-----	Short'nin' bread	LHM	D-D	FLA

British Songs Employing Rapid Enunciation

Baritone

Bantock	A feast of lanterns	HM	D-F	GAL
Bartlet	Whither runneth my sweetheart			BOO
Bax	The enchanted fiddle			
Berners	Dialogue between Tom Filuter and his man	M	D-F	CHE
Britten	Oliver Cromwell			BOH
Charles	The green eyed dragon	M	BF-E	BOH
Cowen	Border ballad	LM	D-E	BOO
Dowland	Shall I sue?			STB
Fisher	At Tankerton Inn	LM	B-G	BOO
Gibbs	Five eyes	HL	D-D	BOS
Head	When I think upon the maidens	LM	D-G	BOO
Hughes	Kitty, my love, will you marry me?	M	C-F	BOH
-----	The stuttering lovers	MH	E-FS	CHA
Lehmann	Myself when young	LL	A-E	GSC
Leveridge	The beggar's song	L	G-D	BOO
Liddle	The garden where the praties grow	LMH	E-FS	STB
Molloy	The Kerry dance	LH	C-G	GSC
Moss	The floral dance	HML	A-D	CHA
Old English	Young Richard			PRE
Sanderson	Susan is her name	LM	D-E	BOH
Shaw	Song of the Palanquin bearers	LH	E-F	CUR
Sullivan	Ho, Jolly Jenkin (Ivanhoe)	LM	C-F	CHA
Templeton	Wi' a hundred pipers	L	BF-EF	GSC
Vaughan Williams	The water mill	L	C-D	OXF
Warlock	Good ale			AUG

90

French Songs Employing
Rapid Enunciation

Baritone

Caplet	La ronde	M		DUR
Chabrier	Villanelle des petits canards	HML	B-E	†
Debussy	Ballade des femmes de Paris			DUR
-----	Chevaux de bois	H	C-G	†
-----	Green	H	C-AF	†
-----	Le temps a laissié son manteau			DUR
-----	Mandoline	HM	BF-F	†
Fauré	Dans les ruines d'une abbaye	M	E-FS	†
-----	Notre amour	H	DS-B	†
-----	Poème d'un jour			HAM
-----	Toujours	LH	F-AF	†
Fourdrain	Carnaval	M	C-F	RIC
Gounod	Ballade de la reine Mab (Roméo et Juliette)			JCH
Milhaud	La tourterelle	M	B-G	DUR
Pessard	L'adieu du matin	ML	BF-D	GSC
Poldowski	Dansons la gigue	M	EF-G	MAR
Poulenc	Couplets bachiques	L	C-FF	HEU
-----	La belle jeunesse	L	D-F	HEU
Ravel	Manteau de fleurs	H		INT
-----	Nicolette	L	B-FS	ELK
Saint-Saëns	Danse macabre	L	BF-EF	AXE
-----	Mai	H	G-FS	DUR
-----	Tournoiement			DUR
Weckerlin	Aminte	M	C-D	†
-----	Chantons les amours de Jean	H	D-G	GSC
-----	Trop aimable Sylvia	M	D-E	GSC

German Songs Employing
Rapid Enunciation

Baritone

Brahms	Blinde Kuh			†
-----	Juchhe!			†
-----	Staendchen	HL	BF-E	†
-----	Tambourliedchen			†
-----	Vergebliches Staendchen	LHM	E-FS	†

91

Jensen	Margreta	M	F-F	PET
Mendelssohn	An die Entfernte	M	F-F	
Mozart	Warnung	HM	C-D	
Schubert	Abschied	HL	BF-F	†
-----	Am Feierabend	HL	BF-F	†
-----	Das Lied im Gruenen			PET
-----	Der Musensohn	LH	FS-G	†
-----	Der Schiffer	LH	BF-A	†
-----	Der zuernende Barde			PET
-----	Die Forelle	MLH	EF-GF	†
-----	Die Post	HML	BF-EF	†
-----	Erstarrung	HL	D-F	†
-----	Fischerweise	L	C-D	†
-----	Fruehlingssehnsucht	HL	B-E	†
-----	Ueber Wildemann			PET
-----	Wohin?	HL	B-E	†
Wolf	Der Feuerreiter			†
-----	Ein Staendchen euch zu bringen	HL		†
-----	Jaegerlied			PET

Italian Songs and Arias Employing Rapid Enunciation

Baritone

Cavalli	Donzelle fuggite	HL	C-EF	†
De Luca	Non posso disperar	HL	C-E	GSC
Falconieri	Non più d'amore	HL	C-D	DIT
-----	Nudo arciero	HL	AF-AF	DIT
Legrenzi	Che fiero costume	HML	C-D	†
Malipiero	Ballata	H		CHE
Mascagni	Il cavallo scalpita (Cavalleria Rusticana)			GSC
Mozart	Finch' han dal vino (Don Giovanni)	L	D-EF	†
-----	Ho capito, Signor (Con Giovanni)			
-----	Non più andrai (Le Nozze di Figaro)	L	C-E	†
-----	Se vuol ballare (Le Nozze di Figaro)	L		†
Paradies	M' ha preso alla sua ragna	M	EF-F	GSC
Pergolesi	Son imbrogliato io già (La Serva Padrona)	L		RIC
Rontani	Or ch'io non segno più	HL	CS-E	DIT
Scarlatti, A.	Chi vuole innamorarsi	HL	D-EF	DIT
Tosti	À vucchella	LH	F-G	RIC

Miscellaneous Songs Employing
Rapid Enunciation

Baritone

Falla	Seguidilla murciana	HL		AMP
Grieg	In the boat	LM	D-ES	†
-----	Nu er aftenen lys og lang	L	C-E	HAN
-----	The way of the world			DIT
-----	With a water lily	HM	CS-EF	†
Mussorgsky	The evening prayer	M	C-E	GSC
-----	Siege of Kazan (Boris Godunoff)			GSC
-----	The seminarian			GSC

American Songs Employing
Sustained Singing

Baritone

Andrews	Sea fever	L	A-D	GSC
Barber	Sure on this shining night	MH	D-G	GSC
Burleigh	Deep river	HML		RIC
-----	Sometimes I feel like a motherless child	HML		RIC
-----	Were you there?	HML		RIC
Carpenter	Slumber song	ML	BF-F	GSC
Chadwick	Allah	LH	CS-GS	ASC
-----	O let night speak of me	HM	C-F	ASC
Coombs	Her rose	ML	D-C	GSC
Curran	Nocturne	HML	B-DS	GSC
Edwards	By the bend of the river	HML	C-E	GSC
-----	Into the night	HML	C-DF	GSC
Foote	I'm wearing awa'	HL		ASC
Foster, S.C.	Ah, may the red rose live always			GSC
-----	Gentle Annie			BOS
Golde	O beauty, passing beauty	MH	CS-GS	GSC
Griffes	By a lonely forest pathway	HML	A-EF	GSC
Guion	Home on the range	HLM	C-F	GSC
Hageman	Music I heard with you	MH	E-A	GAL
Horsman	In the yellow dusk	MH	FS-A	GSC
-----	The bird of the wilderness	LMH	DF-BF	GSC
Kernochan	We two together	H	EF-AF	GAL
Kramer	For a dream's sake	HL		JFI
Lang	Irish love song	HML	A-E	ASC
Levitzki	Do you remember?	HML	BF-EF	GSC
Mac Dowell	Thy beaming eyes	ML	BF-EF	ASC

93

Mana-Zucca	Nichavo	HLM	F-G	JCH
Metcalf	At nightfall	HML	C-DF	ASC
Nevin	The Rosary	HML	C-D	BOS
Porter, Q.	Music, when soft voices die	HM	D-C	MUP
Rasbach	Trees	LMH	CS-GS	GSC
Robinson	Water boy	M	B-E	BOS
Rogers	Wind song	LM	C-G	GSC
Scott	Think on me	HML	D-EF	GAL
Speaks	Sylvia	HML	AF-DF	GSC
Tyson	Noon and night	LH	F-AF	GSC
Watts	The poet sings	MH	EF-AF	DIT

British Songs and Arias Employing Sustained Singing

Baritone

Balfe	The heart bowed down (The Bohemian Girl)			†
Bantock	Silent strings	MH	F-G	BOO
Blow	The self banished	L	C-F	NOV
Bridge	All things that we clasp	HL		BOS
-----	Isobel	HML		CHA
-----	O that it were so	LMH	D-G	CHA
Bury	There is a lady	HM	CS-E	CFI
Butterworth	Loveliest of trees			AUG
Campion	Follow thy fair sun			STB
-----	There is a garden in her face			DIT
-----	When to her lute Corinna sings			STB
Clarke	The blind ploughman	HML	C-D	CHA
Del Riego	Homing	HML	BF-E	CHA
Dowland	Flow, my tears	M	D-E	STB
-----	I saw my lady weep	M	E-E	STB
-----	Sorrow, sorrow stay	M	D-D	BOS
Dunhill	To the Queen of Heaven	M	C-G	GSC
Elgar	I am the good shepherd (Light of Life)			NOV
Ford	Now I see thy looks were feigned			BOO
-----	Since first I saw your face			DIT
-----	There is a lady sweet and kind	M	D-E	STB
Glover	Rose of Tralee	LMH	E-G	MOV
Handel	But who may abide (The Messiah)	L	G-E	†
-----	Defend her! Heaven (Theodora)			STB
-----	Hear me, ye winds and waves (Scipione)	ML	G-EF	BOO

94

(Handel)	Loathsome urns disclose your treasure (Triumph of Time and Truth)			DIT
-----	Shall I in Mamre's fertile plain (Joshua)	L	G-EF	DIT
-----	Tears such as tender fathers shed (Deborah)	L		†
-----	The people that walked in darkness (The Messiah)			†
-----	Wher'er you walk (Semele)	HML	C-D	†
Holst	The heart worships	ML	BF-D	STB
Humphrey	I pass all my hours			DIT
Johnson	As I walked forth one summer day			DIT
Mc Gill	Duna	HML	BF-D	BOO
Milford	So sweet love seemed	HL	D-D	GRA
Purcell	Cease, o my sad soul			POT
-----	If music be the food of love	M	D-G	BOO
-----	Music for a while (Oedipus)	LH		SC
-----	Since from my dear			
Quilter	Drink to me only	LMH	GF-GF	BOH
-----	Go, lovely rose	LHM	F-GF	CHA
Ronald	Prelude	HML	B-D	ENO
Sanderson	Drumadune			BOH
Scott	Lord Randal	L	E-F	GAL
Stephenson	Love is a sickness	HML	C-D	BOO
Sullivan	The lost chord	HL	C-F	GSC
Vaughan Williams	Bright is the ring of words	L		BOH
-----	Linden Lea	HML	C-D	BOS
Warlock	Passing by	M	D-G	CFI
-----	Sleep			OXF
Welsh	All through the night			
Wood	I look into your garden	LMH	F-AF	CHA

French Songs and Arias Employing Sustained Singing

Baritone

Bizet	L'orage s'est calmé (Les Pecheurs des Perles)			CHO
Caplet	Le forêt			DUR
Chausson	Apaisement	MH	EF-G	HAM
-----	Chanson de clown	M	D-EF	ROU
-----	Le charme	HM	BF-EF	HAM

(Chausson)	Le colibri	M	F-GF	BOS
-----	Le temps des lilas	MH	D-GS	†
Debussy	Beau soir	LH	C-FS	†
-----	Colloque sentimental			DUR
-----	Faites silence! écoutez tous! (L'Enfant Prodigue)			DUR
-----	Je tremble en voyant ton visage			DUR
-----	Le son du cor	HL		†
-----	Romance	HM	C-E	†
Duparc	Elégie	HM		ROU
-----	La vie antérieure	HL		†
-----	Lamento	ML	EF-EF	†
Fauré	Au cimetière	LH	D-F	†
-----	Aurore	H	D-G	†
-----	Automne	MH	D-FS	GSC
-----	Le parfum impérissable	LH	GF-GF	
-----	Les berceaux	LMH	BF-G	†
-----	Nocturne	H	F-A	MAR
-----	Prison	LH		†
-----	Rencontre	H	EF-AF	MAR
-----	Soir	LH	D-GS	†
Franck	Nocturne	HL		†
Gounod	Avant de quitter ces lieux (Faust)	HM	DF-F	†
Grétry	O Richard, ô mon Roi (Richard Coeur-De-Lion)	L	BF-G	LEM
-----	Songe enchanteur (Anacréon)			LEM
Honegger	Chanson (Ronsard)			SEN
Hue	J'ai pleuré en rêve	HL	D-E	BOS
Indy	Lied maritime	LH	B-G	†
-----	Madrigal			DIT
Lalo	Marine	LH	DS-FS	
Leguerney	L'adieu	M	B-FS	DUR
Lenormand	Quelle souffrançe	HM	AF-F	HAM
Massenet	Elégie	LM	C-GF	GSC
-----	Promesse de mon avenir (Le Roi de Lahore)	L	DF-GF	GSC
-----	Salomé, Salomé (Hérodiade)			GSC
-----	Vision fugitive (Hérodiade)	LM	C-GF	GSC
Messager	La maison grise (Fortuno)			CHO
Monsigny	Adieu, chère Louise (Le déserteur)			JOB
Offenbach	Scintille diamant (Tales of Hoffman)	M		GSC
Paladilhe	Lamento provinçal	M	CS-FS	HOM
Poulenc	A sa guitare	M	D-FS	DUR
-----	Chanson à boire	L	B-E	HEU
-----	Fleurs	M	DF-F	ROU

Ravel	Chanson italienne			DUR
-----	Kaddisch	H	C-G	DUR
-----	Là-bas vers l'église	MH	GS-E	DUR
-----	Le martin-pêcheur			DUR
-----	Le paon	M	C-F	DUR
-----	Ronsard à son âme	L	CS-E	DUR
Saint-Saëns	Aimons-nous			DUR
-----	La cloche	LH	DF-AF	†
-----	Le lever de la lune			DUR
Severac	Les hiboux			ROU
Spontini	Dans le sein d'un ami			PET
	(La Vestale)			
Thomas	Comme une pâle fleur			HEU
﹀	(Hamlet)			
Tiersot	L'amours de moi	M	EF-F	HEU
Weckerlin	Venez, agréable printemps	M	C-F	

German Songs and Arias Employing
Sustained Singing

Baritone

Ahle	Bruenstiges Verlangen	M	E-E	GSC
Bach, J.S.	Bist du bei mir	HML	A-EF	†
-----	Consider, O my soul			†
	(St. John Passion)			
-----	Hier in meines Vaters Staette			AUG
	(Cantata 32) Violin			
Beethoven	Adelaide	HML	BF-E	†
-----	An die ferne Geliebte	HL	C-E	†
-----	Das Geheimnis			
-----	Delizia	M	C-F	GSC
-----	Die Ehre Gottes	HL	AF-EF	†
-----	Faithfu' Johnie			
-----	In questa tomba	ML	A-CS	†
-----	Vom Tode	L	A-EF	GSC
-----	Wonne der Wehmut			†
Brahms	An den Mond	HL	CS-EF	†
-----	Auf dem Kirchhofe	HL	BF-EF	†
-----	Dein blaues Auge	MH	BF-G	†
-----	Der Tod, das ist die	L	AF-F	†
	kuehle Nacht			
-----	Der Ueberlaeufer			†
-----	Die Mainacht	HL	BF-FF	†
-----	Feldeinsamkeit	HL	C-EF	†
-----	Minnelied	MHL	C-EF	†
-----	Mit vierzig Jahren	HL	FS-D	†

97

(Brahms)	Muss es eine Trennung geben?	LH	FS-FS	CFI
-----	O kuehler Wald	MH	A-F	†
-----	O wuesst' ich doch den Weg zurueck	H	E-FS	†
-----	Ruhe, Suessliebchen	HL	BS-E	†
-----	Schwermut			†
-----	Treue Liebe	LMH	DS-E	†
-----	Verzagen	MH	CS-FS	†
-----	Wenn du nur zuweilen laechelst			†
-----	Wie bist du meine Koenigin	HL	C-E	†
-----	Wir wandelten	LH	EF-GF	†
Franz	Dedication	HML	BF-C	†
-----	For music	ML	C-D	†
-----	Im Herbst	HM	A-F	†
Haydn	Now heav'n in fullest glory shone (The Creation)	L		†
-----	She never told her love	HL	B-D	DIT
Humperdinck	Am Rhein			AMP
Liszt	Es muss ein Wunderbares sein		C-EF	DUR
Loewe	Suesses Begraebnis			SC
Mahler	Wenn mein Schatz Hochzeit			WEI
Marx	Der Ton	M	C-F	AMP
-----	Hat dich die Liebe beruehrt	MH	EF-BF	AMP
Mendelssohn	O God, have mercy (Saint Paul)	L	B-D	GSC
-----	On wings of song			†
Mozart	Abendempfindung	M	E-F	
-----	Verdankt sei es dem Glanz			DIT
Schubert	Am Bach im Fruehling			PET
-----	Am Flusse			PET
-----	Am Meer	HML	B-D	†
-----	An die Leier	LM	BF-F	†
-----	An die Musik	HL	A-DS	†
-----	An die Tueren	HL		†
-----	Auf dem Flusse	HL	F-E	†
-----	Das Wirtshaus	HL	C-D	†
-----	Der Doppelgaenger	HL	G-D	†
-----	Der Leiermann	ML	C-D	†
-----	Der Lindenbaum	HL	A-D	†
-----	Der Neugierige	HL	CS-EF	†
-----	Der Wegweiser	L	D-EF	†
-----	Die Allmacht	HML	G-E	†
-----	Die Kraehe	HL	A-E	†
-----	Die Liebe hat gelogen	LM	G-F	†
-----	Die Nebensonnen	HL	F-D	†

(Schubert)	Die Stadt	HL	A-E	†
-----	Du liebst mich nicht	LH	E-FS	†
-----	Erster Verlust	M	C-F	†
-----	Fruehlingsglaube	M	EF-F	†
-----	Ganymed	LH	EF-G	†
-----	Gute Nacht	LH	C-FS	
-----	Ihr Bild	HL	C-C	†
-----	In der Ferne	HL		†
-----	Lied eines Schiffers an die Dioskuren	HL	A-C	†
-----	Litanei	HLM	C-EF	†
-----	Memnon	LM	AF-F	PET
-----	Nachtgesang			PET
-----	Sei mir gegruesst	LH	G-G	†
-----	Wanderers Nachtlied, 1	HL		†
-----	Wanderers Nachtlied, 2	LH	F-F	†
-----	Wehmuth	HL	B-D	†
-----	Wer nie sein Brot	HL	C-EF	†
-----	Wer sich der Einsamkeit ergibt	M	C-FS	†
Schuetz	Aus dem 119th Psalm			
Schumann	An den Sonnenschein	HL	A-D	†
-----	Aus den Hebraeischen Gesaengen			
-----	Dein Angesicht	HL	B-EF	†
-----	Die Lotusblume	HLM	BF-F	†
-----	Du bist wie eine Blume	HM	F-EF	†
-----	Ich grolle nicht	HL	BF-D	†
-----	Ich hab' im Traum geweinet	HL	B-D	†
-----	Ich wandelte unter den Baeumen	HL	A-D	†
-----	Ihre Stimme	LH		†
-----	Im Rhein, im heiligen Strome	HM	D-F	
-----	In der Fremde	HL		DIT
-----	Mit Myrthen und Rosen	HL	A-D	†
-----	Stille Traenen	HL		†
-----	Wenn ich in deine Augen seh'	HL	EF-FF	†
-----	Wer machte dich so krank?			
Strauss	Befreit			HSC
-----	Liebeshymnus			†
-----	Madrigal	LH	EF-GF	
-----	Mit deinen blauen Augen	LH	C-GS	†
-----	Morgen	HML	E-F	†
-----	Ruhe meine Seele			†
Wolf	Alle gingen, Herz, zu Ruh	HL	C-EF	†
-----	Alles endet, was entstehet	HL	F-C	†

(Wolf)	Anakreons Grab	HL	D-D	†
-----	Bedeckt mich mit Blumen	HL	B-D	†
-----	Biterolf	HL	D-F	†
-----	Das Staendchen	HL		†
-----	Denk' es, o Seele	LH	EF-F	INT
-----	Der Genesene an die Hoffnung	H	BF-AF	PET
-----	Fuehlt meine Seele	L	A-D	†
-----	Gebet	HL		†
-----	Gesang Weylas	HL	DF-F	†
-----	Gesegnet sei, durch den die Welt	HL		†
-----	Heb' auf dein blondes Haupt	HL	G-DF	†
-----	Heimweh (Eichendorff Lieder)	M		†
-----	Herr, was traegt der Boden	HL	B-DS	†
-----	Im Fruehling	HL	BF-F	†
-----	In der Fruehe	HL	C-C	†
-----	Lebe wohl	HL	BF-F	†
-----	Morgenstimmung	LH	C-GS	†
-----	Neue Liebe	LH	D-AF	†
-----	Um Mitternacht	HL	G-EF	†
-----	Wohl denk' ich oft	M	C-EF	†
-----	Zur Ruh', zur Ruh'	HL	A-GF	†
Wolff	Alle Dinge haben Sprache	M	BF-GF	†
-----	Du bist so jung			HMP
-----	Ewig			

Italian Songs and Arias Employing Sustained Singing

Baritone

Bimboni	Sospiri miei	M	EF-EF	GAL
Caccini	Amarilli, mia bella	ML	C-D	†
Caldara	Come raggio di sol	HL	D-F	†
Cavalli	Beato chi può (Serse)			HEU
-----	Troppo soavi i gusti	HM	E-E	DIT
Cesti	Che angoscia, che affanno (Il Pomo d'Oro)	HL	C-DF	DIT
-----	E dove t'aggiri (Il Pomo d'Oro)			DIT
Cimara	Stornellata marinara	HM		RIC
Del Leuto	Dimmi, amor	M	C-F	GSC
Diaz	O splendore infinito (Benvenuto)	L	A-F	GRU

Donaudy	O del mio amato ben	M	EF-F	RIC
-----	Quando ti rivedrò			RIC
-----	Vaghissima sembianza	H	E-A	RIC
Donizetti	Ambo nati in questa valle			RIC
	(Linda di Chamounix)			
-----	Bella siccome un angelo			BRO
	(Don Pasquale)			
Durante	Vergin, tutta amor	LM	C-EF	†
Giordano	Nemico della patria	L	B-FS	SON
	(Andrea Chenier)			
Gluck	Spiagge amate (Paride ed Elena)			CFI
Handel	Lascia ch'io pianga (Rinaldo)	HM	EF-F	†
-----	No soffrir non può (Berenice)			MUP
-----	O rendetemi il mio bene	L	CS-EF	CFI
	(Amadigi)			
-----	V'adoro pupille			BOO
	(Julius Caesar)			
Leoncavallo	Prologue (I Pagliacci)	M	BF-A	CFI
-----	Zaza, piccola zingara (Zaza)			SON
Mattei	Non è ver	HML		DIT
Monteverdi	Ahi, troppo è duro	HL	C-EF	DIT
	(Il Balletto delle Ingrate)			
Mozart	Ridente la calma			BOS
Paisiello	Nel cor più non mi sento	HL	C-EF	†
Pergolesi	Bella mia (Il Maestro			GSC
	di Musica)			
-----	Nina	HL	CS-D	DIT
Peri	Invocazione di Orfeo	HL	E-CS	DIT
	(Euridice)			
Piccini	O nuit, dresse du mystere			GSC
	(Le Faux Lord)			
Puccini	Se la giurata fede	M	DF-F	RIC
	(Tosca)			
Respighi	Nebbie			†
Rosa	Star vicino	HL	D-E	†
Santoliquido	Nel giardino			FOR
Scarlatti, A.	O cessate di piagarmi	HL	DS-E	GSC
-----	Son tutta duolo	M	D-EF	GSC
Stradella	Col mio sangue comprenderei	HL	E-F	DIT
	(Il Floridoro)			
-----	Per pietà (Il Floridoro)	HM	D-F	DIT
-----	Pietà, Signore	HM	C-F	GSC
-----	Se nel ben			CFI
Torelli	Tu lo sai	HL	BF-F	†
Tosti	Aprile	LMH		RIC

Miscellaneous Songs Employing
Sustained Singing

Baritone

Arensky	Autumn	H	CS-FS	GSC
Dvořák	Hear my prayer, O Lord			AMP
-----	Lord, thou art my refuge and shield			AMP
-----	Turn Thee to me			AMP
Gretchaninoff	Over the steppe	LM	C-G	GSC
-----	The captive			DIT
-----	Wounded birch	HL	B-EF	†
Grieg	I love thee	HML	E-F	†
Malashkin	O could I but express in song	LH		CHE
Mussorgsky	In my attic			GSC
-----	On the Dnieper			GSC
-----	Sphinx			BRH
-----	The grave			BRH
Rachmaninoff	Christ is risen	LM	D-F	GAL
-----	O thou billowy harvest field	HL	CS-E	GSC
-----	To the children	MH	F-G	DIT
Rimsky-Korsakov	On the Georgian hills	HM		GSC
Sibelius	Black roses	M	A-ES	AMP
Sjoegren	The Seraglio's garden	HL		GSC
Tchaikovsky	A legend	M	D-E	GSC
-----	None but the lonely heart	HLM	C-F	DIT
-----	Pilgrim's song	HLM	B-E	GSC

American Songs Employing
Spirited Singing

Baritone

Barber	I hear an army	LH	D-AF	GSC
Beach	The year's at the spring	MH	AF-AF	ASC
Boatner	Oh, what a beautiful city!	HL	D-E	GSC
Boyd	Cape Horn gospel	L	BF-D	GAL
Burleigh	Joshua fit de battle ob Jericho	LH	DS-E	RIC
Carpenter	Don't ceare	M	C-D	GSC
-----	Serenade	LH	CS-A	GSC
-----	The cock shall crow	M	B-E	GSC
Castelnuovo-Tedesco	O mistress mine			CHE

Chadwick	Drake's drum			
-----	The admirals			
Chanler	I rise when you enter	M	CS-G	GSC
Curran	Life	HM	BF-F	GSC
Damrosch	Danny Deever	L	A-F	PRE
Dobson	Cargoes	ML	C-EF	GSC
Duke	On a March day	M	B-GF	BOH
Elwell	The road not taken	M	B-FS	GSC
Griffes	An old song resung	LM	EF-F	GSC
Guion	All day on the prarie	M	EF-F	GSC
-----	What shall we do with a drunken sailor	HML	C-D	GSC
Hadley	My shadow			ASC
Hageman	Don Juan Gomez	M		GAL
-----	Miranda	HL		GAL
Hindemith	The whistling thief	M	E-F	AMP
Hopkinson	O'er the hills	LH	C-G	†
Johnson	Roll Jerd'n roll	M	EF-F	GSC
Kountz	The sleigh	HL	D-FS	GSC
La Forge	Song of the open	MH	EF-AF	DIT
Malotte	Mister Jim	M	D-F	GSC
Mana-Zucca	I love life	LM	F-F	PRE
Margetson	Tommy, lad	HML	A-D	BOH
Mason	A sea dirge			WIT
Moore	Adam was my grandfather			GAL
Niles	The rovin' gambler	HL	BF-EF	GSC
Rogers	The last song	MLH	E-AF	GSC
Sacco	Brother Will, brother John	M	C-F	GSC
-----	Mexican serenade	HL	D-EF	BOS
Schuman	Holiday song	M	C-F	GSC
Speaks	Morning	HML	BF-D	GSC
-----	On the road to Mandalay	HL	BF-F	PRE
-----	Shepherd, see thy horse's foaming mane			FLA
Taylor	Captain Stratton's fancy	L	CS-F	JFI
Warner	Hurdy gurdy	M	D-F	CFI
Warren	White horses of the sea	LH	F-G	GSC
Weaver	The Abbot of Derry	HL	B-EF	GSC
Wolfe	Short'nin' bread	LHM	D-D	FLA

British Songs and Arias Employing
Spirited Singing

Baritone

Arne, T.	By the gaily circling glass	L		DIT

(Arne, T.)	Now Phoebus sinketh in the west			GSC
-----	Preach not me your musty rules (Comus)	HML		ROW
-----	Why so pale and wan			GSC
Bantock	A feast of lanterns	HM	D-F	GAL
Bartlet	Whither runneth my sweetheart			BOO
Bax	The enchanted fiddle			
Benjamin	Hedgerow			CUR
Bridge	Love went a-riding	HL		BOS
Butterworth	When I was one and twenty			AUG
Charles, W.	The green eyed dragon	M	BF-E	BOH
Cowen	Border ballad	LM	D-E	BOO
Dowland	Awake, sweet love	M	E-F	STB
-----	Come again! sweet love	M	D-E	STB
-----	Say love, if ever thou didst find			STB
-----	Shall I sue?			STB
-----	What if I never speede?	M	D-D	BOS
German	Charming Chloe	HML		NOV
-----	My song is of the sturdy north	ML		CHA
-----	Rolling down to Rio	ML	G-D	NOV
Gibbs	Five eyes	HL	D-D	BOS
Handel	Arm, arm, ye brave (Judas Maccabaeus)	L	B-E	†
-----	O ruddier than the cherry (Acis and Galatea)	L	G-F	DIT
-----	Revenge, Timotheus cries (Alexander's Feast)	L	G-D	†
-----	See the raging flames arise (Joshua)			†
-----	Thy glorious deeds (Samson)	M	C-F	†
Head	Money, o!			BOO
-----	When I think upon the maidens	LM	D-G	BOO
Holst	The Sergeant's song			ASH
Hook	Bright Phoebus	M	EF-F	GSC
Hopekirk	Ye banks and braes	LM	D-C	DIT
Hughes	The stuttering lovers	MH	E-FS	CHA
Ireland	Great things			AUG
Johnston	Because I were shy	L	B-E	CRA
Jones	Love is a bable			STB
-----	What if I speede			BOO
Keel	Trade winds	HL	BF-EF	BOH
Lawes	I am confirmed			BOO
Leveridge	The beggar's song	L	G-D	BOO

(Leveridge)	When dull care			BOO
Liddle	The garden where the praties grow	LMH	E-FS	STB
Martin	Come to the fair	HML	D-D	BOO
Molloy	The Kerry Dance	LH	C-G	GSC
Morgan	Clorinda	HM	C-EF	ENO
Morley	It was a lover and his lass	HM		DIT
Moss	The floral dance	HML	A-D	CHA
Purcell	Hark! how all things with one sound rejoice			NOV
-----	I'll sail upon the dog star	HL	A-E	†
Quilter	Blow, blow thou winter wind	HL	C-E	BOO
-----	It was a lover and his lass	HL	CS-E	BOO
-----	I will go with my father a-plowing	MH	D-G	ELK
Rowley	The toll gate house			ROG
Sanderson	Captain Mac	ML	G-E	BOO
-----	Laughing cavalier	LM	BF-F	BOO
Sullivan	Ho, Jolly Jenkin (Ivanhoe)	LM	C-F	CHA
Toye	The inn	L	C-E	CUR
Vaughan Williams	Joy shipmate, joy			OXF
-----	The roadside fire	HML	BF-EF	BOO
-----	The vagabond	ML	A-E	BOO
Warlock	As ever I saw	MH	DF-GF	ROG
-----	Captain Stratton's fancy			AUG
-----	Good ale			AUG
-----	Pretty ring time	H	D-G	CFI

French Songs and Arias Employing Spirited Singing

Baritone

Berlioz	Chanson de la puce (La Damnation de Faust)			CST
-----	Sérénade de Mephisto (La Damnation de Faust)			DIT
Bizet	Chanson du toreador (Carmen)	HL	BF-F	†
-----	Quand la flamme de l'amour (Le Jolie Fille de Perth)			CHO
Caplet	La ronde	M		DUR
Chabrier	L'ile heureuse	M	B-F	†
-----	Villanelle des petits canards	HML	B-E	†
Chausson	Les papillons	M	C-F	GSC

105

Debussy	Ballade des femmes de Paris			DUR
-----	Chevaux de bois	H	C-G	†
-----	De soir	HL		†
-----	Le faune			DUR
-----	Le temps a laissié son manteau			DUR
-----	Mandoline	HM	BF-F	†
-----	Noël des enfants qui n'ont plus de maisons			DUR
Duparc	Le manoir de Rosamunde	HL	B-F	BOS
-----	Testament	HL		INT
Fauré	Noël	LH	EF-AF	GSC
-----	Notre amour	H	DS-B	†
-----	Poème d'un jour			HAM
-----	Toujours	LH	F-AF	MAR
Gluck	C'est en vain que l'enfer compte (Alceste)			†
-----	Un ruisselet bien clair (La Rencontre Imprévue)			LEM
Gounod	Au printemps	LMH	DF-AF	GSC
-----	Ballade de la reine Mab (Roméo et Juliette)			JCH
-----	Vénise	HL		INT
Grétry	Nièces neuveux (Les Deux Avares)			JOB
Koechlin	Le thé	HM	C-E	BOS
Lully	Il faut passer (Alceste)			LEM
Massenet	Chanson de la Touraine (Panurge)	M	EF-EF	HEU
Meyerbeer	Adamastor, roi des vagues profondes (L'Africaine)	L	D-E	GSC
-----	Fille des rois (L'Africaine)			BRO
Milhaud	Chant d'amour	M	C-GF	ESC
-----	La tourterelle	M	B-G	DUR
Poldowski	Colombine	H	D-GF	CHE
-----	Dansons la gigue	M	EF-G	MAR
Poulenc	La belle jeunesse	L	D-F	HEU
Ravel	Chanson à boire			DUR
-----	Chanson espagnole	LH	D-BF	DUR
-----	Manteau de fleurs	H		INT
-----	Nicolette	L	B-FS	ELK
-----	Quel galant!	M	D-F	DUR
Saint-Saëns	Danse macabre	L	BF-EF	AXE
-----	Les pas d'armes du roi Jean	HML	A-F	RIC
-----	Qui donc commande (Henry VIII)			GSC
-----	Tournoiement			DUR
Weckerlin	Chantons les amours de Jean	H	D-G	GSC

German Songs and Arias Employing
Spirited Singing

Baritone

Beethoven	An die Geliebte	M	E-E	†
-----	Aus Goethes Faust			
-----	Busslied			†
-----	Der Kuss			†
Brahms	Bei dir sind meine Gedanken	MH	E-FS	†
-----	Blinde Kuh			†
-----	Botschaft	HL	D-F	†
-----	Der Gang zur Liebsten	HL		†
-----	Der Schmied	HL	EF-EF	†
-----	Heimkehr			†
-----	Juchhe!			†
-----	Klage	LH	FS-FS	†
-----	Liebe kam aus fernen Landen	HL	C-E	†
-----	Meine Lieder	HL	D-DS	†
-----	O liebliche Wangen	MLH	E-G	†
-----	Sehnsucht	H	EF-AF	†
-----	Sind es Schmerzen	HL	BF-F	†
-----	Tambourliedchen			†
-----	Vergebliches Staendchen	LHM	E-FS	†
-----	Wie froh und frisch	HL	B-E	†
Franz	Sonnenuntergang	HL	CS-FS	DIT
Haydn	Rolling in foaming billows (The Creation)	L	C-F	†
-----	With joy th' impatient husbandman (The Seasons)	L	B-E	†
Jensen	Margreta	M	F-F	PET
Mahler	Ging heut Morgen uebers Feld	M	A-FS	INT
-----	Ich hab' ein gluehend Messer	M	BF-GF	WEI
-----	Lieder eines fahrenden Gesellen	M		INT
Mendelssohn	An die Entfernte	M	F-F	
-----	Ich bin ein vielgereister Mann (Heimkehr aus der Fremde)	ML		DIT
-----	Is not His word like a fire? (Elijah)	M	B-F	†
-----	Jagdlied	HL	BF-EF	†
Mozart	Der Vogelfaenger bin ich ja (Die Zauberfloete)	L	D-E	†
Schubert	Am Feierabend	HL	BF-F	†
-----	Aufenthalt	HLM	A-F	†

(Schubert)	Das Fischermaedchen	L	A-EF	†
-----	Der Schiffer	LH	BF-A	†
-----	Der zuernende Barde			PET
-----	Die Forelle	MLH	EF-GF	†
-----	Die Post	HML	BF-EF	†
-----	Erstarrung	HL	D-F	†
-----	Fischerweise	L	C-D	†
-----	Fruehlingssehnsucht	HL	B-E	
-----	Heidenroeslein			
-----	Mein!	HL		†
-----	Mut	HL		†
-----	Ueber Wildemann			PET
-----	Wohin?	HL	B-E	†
Schumann	Auftraege	HL	C-E	†
-----	Der Husar, trara!			
-----	Er ist's	HL	BF-EF	†
-----	Im Walde	HL	A-D	†
-----	Schoene Wiege meiner Leiden	HL	C-EF	†
-----	Waldesgespraech	HL	A-FS	†
-----	Wanderlied	HL	A-E	†
-----	Widmung	HL	BF-F	†
Strauss	Caecilie	MH	E-B	†
-----	Fuer fuenfzehn Pfennige			†
-----	Heimliche Aufforderung	HL	B-E	†
-----	Schlechtes Wetter			†
Weber	Reigen			PET
Wolf	Ach, im Maien	HL	C-E	†
-----	Auf dem gruenen Balkon	HL		†
-----	Auf einer Wanderung	HL		†
-----	Begegnung	M	EF-GF	PET
-----	Das Koehlerweib ist trunken			PET
-----	Der Feuerreiter			†
-----	Der Rattenfaenger	HL		†
-----	Der Soldat 1	LH	E-FS	†
-----	Ein Staendchen euch zu bringen	HL		†
-----	Er ist's	H	D-G	†
-----	Fussreise	HL	D-E	†
-----	Nimmersatte Liebe	LH	CF-AF	†
-----	Seemanns Abschiedslied	H	C-A	†
-----	Trunken muessen wir alle sein	M	ES-FS	†

Italian Songs and Arias Employing Spirited Singing

Baritone

Bononcini	L'esperto nocchiero (Astarte)	HL	B-E	†
Carissimi	Filli, non t'amo più	HL	B-D	†
-----	Vittoria, mio core	HLM	B-E	†
Cavalli	Donzelle fuggite	HL	C-EF	†
Cimara	Canto di primavera		D-G	FRL
Donaudy	Spirate, pur spirate			RIC
Durante	Danza, danza fanciulla gentile	HM	BF-F	†
Falconieri	Non più d'amore	HL	C-D	DIT
-----	Nudo arciero	HL	AF-AF	DIT
Gaffi	Luci vezzose	HL	D-E	DIT
Handel	Furibondo spira (Partenope)			KIS
-----	Si, tra i ceppi (Berenice)	L	B-D	†
-----	Volate più dei venti (Muzio Scevola)			MUP
Legrenzi	Che fiero costume	HML	C-D	†
Leoncavallo	Mattinata	MLH	C-AF	†
Mascagni	Il cavallo scalpita (Cavalleria Rusticana)			GSC
Mozart	Aprite un po quegl' occhi (Le Nozze di Figaro)			RIC
-----	Finch' han dal vino (Don Giovanni)	L	D-EF	†
-----	Non più andrai (Le Nozze di Figaro)	L	C-E	†
Paradies	M'ha preso alla sua ragna	M	EF-F	GSC
Pergolesi	Son imbrogliato io già (La Serva Padrona)	L		RIC
Respighi	Pioggia			BON
Rontani	Or ch'io non segno più	HL	CS-E	DIT
Scarlatti, A.	Chi vuole innamorarsi	HL	D-EF	DIT
-----	Già il sole dal Gange	LH	EF-F	GSC
Scarlatti, D.	Consolati e spara amante	L	BF-E	GSC
Tosti	The last song	HL		RIC
Verdi	Cortigiani, vil razza (Rigoletto)			GSC
Wolf-Ferrari	Aprila, o bella (Jewels of the Madonna)	HL	D-FS	GSC

Miscellaneous Songs Employing Spirited Singing

Baritone

Dvořák	I will sing new songs of gladness	HL		†
Falla	El paño moruno	HL		AMP
-----	Seguidilla murciana	HL		AMP
-----	Siete canciones	HL		AMP
Grieg	Good morning			†
-----	Hunter's song	L	DS-E	GSC
-----	Vaer hilset, I Damer	M	D-F	HAN
Koeneman	When the King went forth to war	ML	A-E	CHE
Mussorgsky	Siege of Kazan (Boris Godunoff)	L	F-E	GSC
Rachmaninoff	Floods of spring	HL		DIT
-----	God took away from me			GSC
-----	Oh, no, I pray, do not depart	H		DIT
Sandoval	Sin tu amor	H	E-G	GSC
Tchaikovsky	At the ball	MH		GSC
-----	Don Juan's serenade	HLM	B-E	GSC

Songs and Arias Employing Staccato

Baritone

Beethoven	Bitten			†
Fourdrain	Carnaval	M	C-F	RIC
Mozart	Se vuol ballare (Le Nozze di Figaro)	L		†
Mussorgsky	The song of the flea	L	AS-G	GSC
Paxson	Laughing song	M	C-F	CFI
Scarlatti, A.	Rugiadose odorose (Il Pirro e Demetrio)	HL	D-E	DIT
Schubert	Der Juengling an der Quelle	LH	E-A	†
Sibella	La Girometta	HML	D-E	GSC

American and British Songs
of Popular Appeal

Baritone

Andrews	Sea fever	L	A-D	GSC
Arden and Wille	Roses in your hair	ML	C-EF	ROW
Beach	Ah, love but a day			ASC
Bond	Still unexprest	HL	C-C	BOS
Bone and Fenton	Captain Kidd	MH	B-G	CFI
Brahe	Bless this house	HML	A-EF	BOO
Brown	Your song from paradise	LMH	D-G	BOO
Burleigh	Jean	HML		PRE
Cadman	The builder	HML	B-D	FLA
Chanler	I rise when you enter	M	CS-G	GSC
Charles	The house on a hill	LH	D-G	GSC
-----	When I have sung my songs	HM	BF-EF	GSC
-----	The green eyed dragon	M	BF-E	BOH
Clarke	Shy one	HL	BF-G	BOH
-----	The blind ploughman	HML	C-D	CHA
Coates	Sea rapture	MH	E-G	CHA
-----	Stone cracker John	L		BOO
Cowen	Border ballad	LM	D-E	BOO
Crouch	Kathleen Mavourneen	HL	A-E	CFI
Curran	Life	HM	BF-F	GSC
Damrosch	Danny Deever	L	A-F	PRE
Del Riego	Homing	HML	BF-E	CHA
-----	O dry those tears	LMH	E-GS	CHA
-----	Shadow march			CHA
De Rose	I heard a forest praying	MH	EF-GF	CHA
-----	Wagon wheels			SHA
D'Hardelot	I know a lovely garden			CHA
Dichmont	Ma little banjo	ML	E-CS	GSC
Dobson	Cargoes	ML	C-EF	GSC
Donaldson	My buddy			REM
Dougherty	Everyone sang			
Edwards	By the bend of the river	HML	C-E	GSC
-----	Can this be summer			
-----	Into the night	HML	C-DF	GSC
Enders	Hangman, hangman	M	C-E	GSC
Fenner	Night song	L	BF-EF	FEN
Fisher	At Tankerton Inn	LM	B-G	BOO
-----	Tavern song			BOO
Forsyth	The bell man			DIT
Foster	My journey's end	HLM	DF-G	GSC
Foster, S.C.	Gentle Annie			BOS

111

Fox	The hills of home	HML	BF-DF	CFI
German	Rolling down to Rio	ML	G-D	NOV
Glover	Rose of Tralee	LMH	E-G	MOV
Guion	Mam'selle Marie	M	D-E	GSC
-----	When the work's all done this fall	L	B-D	CFI
Hageman	Don Juan Gomez	M		GAL
Harmati	Bluebird of happiness			HAR
Head	When I think upon the maidens	LM	D-G	BOO
Hely-Hutchinson	Old mother Hubbard	HL	B-E	CFI
Hughes	Old mother Hubbard			CRA
Huhn	Invictus	ML	BF-DF	ASC
Kern	The last time I saw Paris			CHA
Kountz	Prayer of the Norwegian child	ML	C-C	GSC
La Forge	Song of the open	MH	EF-AF	DIT
-----	To a messenger	HLM	CF-G	GSC
Leoni	Tally-ho!			GSC
Lehmann	Myself when young	LL	A-E	GSC
Levitzki	Do you remember?	HML	BF-EF	GSC
Lohr	The little Irish girl	HLM	C-E	CHA
Mac Gimsey	Down to de river	M	B-G	CFI
-----	Egg-a-bread			MCG
-----	Jeri Jericho	M	C-G	CFI
-----	Jonah and the whale	M	BF-EF	CFI
-----	Thunderin' wonderin'	L	C-D	CFI
-----	To my mother	HML	C-C	CFI
Malotte	Blow me eyes	MH	C-G	GSC
-----	For my mother	HLM	BF-EF	GSC
-----	Mister Jim	M	D-F	GSC
-----	Sing a song of sixpence	M	C-F	GSC
-----	Song of the open road			ABC
Mana-Zucca	I love life	LM	F-F	PRE
-----	Nichavo	HLM	F-G	JCH
-----	The big brown bear	HML	C-F	GSC
Manning	In the Luxembourg gardens	HML	BF-D	GSC
-----	Shoes	M	EF-F	GSC
Margetson	Tommy, lad	HML	A-D	BOH
Marshall	I hear you calling me	LMH	G-A	BOO
Martin	Come to the fair	HML	D-D	BOO
Mason	A grain of salt	L	A-D	GSC
-----	I ain't afeared o' the Admiral	L	A-E	GSC
-----	The constant cannibal maiden	L	C-FS	GSC
McGill	Duna	HML	BF-D	BOO
Molloy	The Kerry Dance	LH	C-G	GSC

Moya	The song of songs	LM	D-F	CHA
Murray	She shall have music	M	A-G	CHA
Nevin	The Rosary	HML	C-D	BOS
Oberbrunner	Giuseppe, da barber	HML	E-E	GSC
Olcott	Mother Machree	LMH	F-A	WIT
Paxson	Laughing song	M	C-F	CFI
Posford	At the Balalaika	L	BF-EF	FEI
Quilter	Drink to me only	LMH	GF-GF	BOH
Rasbach	Overtones	HL	B-D	GSC
-----	Trees	LMH	CS-GS	GSC
Rogers	At parting	LH	CS-FS	GSC
Ronald	Prelude	HML	B-D	ENO
Russell	Children of men	HL	EF-F	FLA
-----	Fulfillment	LH	EF-GF	BOS
-----	Where the river Shannon flows	HML	C-D	WIT
Sacco	Brother Will, brother John	M	C-F	GSC
Sachs	Grandma			FLA
Sanderson	Captain Mac	ML	G-E	BOO
-----	Friend o' mine	HHM		BOO
-----	Laughing cavalier	LM	BF-F	BOO
-----	Shipmates of mine	LL	G-D	BOO
-----	Susan is her name	LM	D-E	BOH
-----	The company Sergeant Major			BOH
-----	Until	LMH	E-A	BOO
Schuman	Holiday song	M	C-F	GSC
Scott	Think on me	HML	D-EF	GAL
Somervell	A kingdom by the sea	ML	DF-F	BOO
Speaks	In May time	HL	D-E	JCH
-----	Morning	HML	BF-D	GSC
-----	On the road to Mandalay	HL	BF-F	PRE
-----	Sylvia	HML	AF-DF	GSC
Stanford	The bold unbiddable child	ML	B-DF	STB
-----	The little admiral	L	C-G	STB
Stickles	The open road			DIT
Stothart	Cuban love song	L	BF-G	ROB
-----	Ride cossack ride			FEI
-----	Rogue song			ROB
-----	The song of the shirt	L	A-E	ROB
-----	When I'm looking at you	F	C-F	ROB
Strelezki	Dreams	LMH	B-A	GSC
Suesse	Another mile			WOR
-----	The night is young and you're so beautiful	M	B-E	WOR
Sullivan	The lost chord	HL	C-F	GSC
Taylor	A song for lovers	MH	D-F	JFI
Torrence	Smilin' Kitty O'Day	ML	CS-D	BOO
Tours	Mother o' mine	HML	C-D	CHA

Tyson	Noon and night	LH	F-AF	GSC
Weaver	The Abbot of Derry	HL	B-EF	GSC
Wolfe	Betsy's boy	HL	A-E	GSC
-----	Bone come-a-knittin'			FLA
-----	De glory road	L	A-F	GSC
-----	Gwine to Hebb'n	LM	B-E	GSC
-----	Sailormen	HM	D-FS	GSC
-----	Short'nin' bread	LHM	D-D	FLA
-----	Spring plowing	LHM	CS-FS	GSC
-----	Who's gonna mourn for me	LMH	D-A	ROB
Wood	Do you know my garden	MH	EF-G	CHA
-----	I look into your garden	LMH	F-AF	CHA
Woodford-Finden	Kashmiri song			BOO
-----	Will the sun never set?			

(See also Humorous Songs, Negro Spirituals,
Folk Songs, Operetta Songs and Opera Arias.)

Miscellaneous Songs of Popular Appeal

Baritone

Alvarez	La partida	HL	DS-E	GSC
Bach-Gounod	Ave Maria			†
Berger	They all dance the samba	M	A-FS	GSC
Billi	E canta il grillo	HM		RIC
Bizet	Agnus Dei	HLM	C-AF	†
Brogi	Venitian vision	M	D-F	RIC
Buzzi-Peccia	Lolita			RIC
Cardillo	Core'ngrato			RIC
Cimara	Canto di primavera		D-G	FRL
De Curtis	Tu, ca nun chaigne			
Denza	Occhi de fata	HML		RIC
-----	Se	H	E-AF	GSC
Donaudy	O del mio amato ben	M	EF-F	RIC
Dvořák	Goin' home			DIT
-----	Songs my mother taught me	HM	E-E	†
Franz	Dedication	HML	BF-C	†
Freire	Ay, ay, ay	LH		RIC
Gounod	Au printemps	LMH	DF-AF	GSC
-----	Sérénade	LMH	D-A	GSC
Grieg	A dream			†
-----	I love thee	HML	E-F	†
Hubay	Hejre kati			BRE
Lara	Granada			SOU
Leoncavallo	Mattinata	MLH	C-AF	GSC

114

Massenet	Elégie	LM	C-GF	GSC
Mattei	Non è ver	HML		DIT
Mendelssohn	On wings of song			†
Messager	Long ago in Alcala	M		CHA
Mussorgsky	The evening prayer	M	C-E	GSC
Rachmaninoff	To the children	MH	F-G	DIT
Ravel	Dansant l'amique			
Rossini	La danza	MH	E-A	†
Sadero	Amuri, Amuri	M		CHE
Saint-Saëns	Danse macabre	L	BF-EF	AXE
Schubert	An die Musik	HL	A-DS	†
-----	Ave Maria	LMH	F-F	†
-----	Hark! hark! the lark	LMH	F-G	†
-----	Staendchen			
Schumann	Widmung	HL	BF-F	†
Sibella	La Girometta	HML	D-E	GSC
Sjoeberg	Visions	MH	F-AF	GAL
Straus	Song in my heart	M	C-G	GSC
Tchaikovsky	None but the lonely heart	HLM	C-F	DIT
-----	Pilgrim's song	HLM	B-E	GSC
Tosti	À vucchella	LH	F-G	RIC
-----	Marechiare	M	D-FS	GSC
-----	The last song	HL		RIC
Veláquez	Bésame mucho	M	CS-D	SOU
Yradier	La paloma	HL	BF-EF	GSC

(See also Humorous Songs, Negro Spirituals,
Folk Songs, Operetta Songs and Opera Arias.)

Arias From American Operas

Baritone

Dello Joio	The creed of Pierre Cochon (The Triumph of Joan)			
Gershwin	A woman is a sometime thing (Porgy and Bess)			GER
-----	I got plenty o' nuttin' (Porgy and Bess)	L	B-D	CHA
-----	It ain't necessarily so (Porgy and Bess)			CHA
Gruenberg	Standin' in de need of prayer (Emperor Jones)			CSC
Hanson	Oh, 'tis an earth defiled (Merry Mount)			HAR
Taylor	Nay, Maccus, lay him down (The King's Henchman)			JFI

| (Taylor) | The Colnel's air (Peter Ibbetson) | | | JFI |
| Thomson | Saint Ignatius' vision (Four Saints in Three Acts) | | | BRO |

Arias from British Operas

Baritone

Arne, T.	Preach not me your musty rules (Comus)	HML		ROW
Balfe	The heart bowed down (The Bohemian Girl)			†
Gay	If the heart of a man (The Beggar's Opera)			BOO
-----	In the days of my youth (The Beggar's Opera)			BOO
German	The English rose (Merrie England)			
Handel	Hear me, ye winds and waves (Scipione)	ML	G-EF	BOO
-----	Silent worship (Tolomeo)	LM	D-E	CUR
Purcell	I attempt from love's sickness to fly (The Indian Queen)	MH	CS-E	†
-----	Music for a while (Oedipus)	LH		SC
Sullivan	Ho, Jolly Jenkin (Ivanhoe)	LM	C-F	CHA

Arias From French Operas

Baritone

Berlioz	Chanson de la puce (La Damnation de Faust)			CST
-----	Inutiles regrets (Les Troyens à Carthage)	MH	E-C	CHO
-----	Sérénade de Mephisto (La Damnation de Faust)			DIT
-----	Voici des roses (La Damnation de Faust)			CST
Bizet	Chanson du Toreador (Carmen)	HL	BF-F	†
-----	L'orage s'est calmé (Les Pêcheurs des Perles)			CHO
-----	Quand la flamme de l'amour (Le Jolie Fille de Perth)			CHO

116

Charpentier	Les pauvre gens peuvent- ils être heureux? (Louise)			HEU
Debussy	Faites silence! Ecoutez tous! (L'Enfant Prodigue)			
Delibes	Lakmé, ton doux regards (Lakmé)			HEU
Gluck	Air d'Agamemnon (Iphigenie en Aulide)			LEM
-----	C'est en vain que l'enfer compte (Alceste)			†
-----	Un ruisselet bien clair (La Rencontre Imprévue)			LEM
Gounod	Avant de quitter ces lieux (Faust)	HM	DF-F	†
-----	Ballade de la reine Mab (Roméo et Juliette)			JCH
Grétry	Nièces, neuveux (Les Deux Avares)			JOB
-----	O Richard, ô mon Roi (Richard Coeur-De-Lion)	L	BF-G	LEM
-----	Songe enchanteur (Anacréon)			LEM
Lully	Air de Cadmus (Cadmus et Hermione)			ROU
-----	Air de Mecure (Persée)			
-----	Air des Songes (Persée)			
-----	Bois épais (Amadis)	ML	C-EF	†
-----	Il faut passer (Alceste)			LEM
Massenet	Chanson de la Touraine (Panurge)	M	EF-EF	HEU
-----	Dors ô cité perverse (Hérodiade)			
-----	Promesse de mon avenir (Le Roi de Lahore)	L	DF-GF	GSC
-----	Salomé, Salomé (Hérodiade)			GSC
-----	Vision fugitive (Hérodiade)	LM	C-GF	GSC
-----	Voila donc la terrible cité (Thaïs)			
Mehul	Femme sensible (Ariodant)			
Messager	La maison grise (Fortuno)			CHO
Meyerbeer	Adamastor, roi des vagues profondes (L'Africaine)	L	D-E	GSC
-----	Fille des rois (L'Africaine)			BRO
-----	Nonnes qui reposez (Robert le Diable)			GSC
-----	Se vendicata assai (Dinorah)	M	DF-GF	BRO
Offenbach	J'ai des yeux (Tales of Hoffman)			GSC
-----	Scintille diamant (Tales of Hoffman)	M		GSC

117

Rameau	A l'amour rendez les armes			CHO
	(Hippolyte et Aricie)			
-----	Air of Theseus			CHE
	(Hippolyte et Aricie)			
-----	Dans ces doux asiles			LEM
	(Castor et Pollux)			
-----	Invocation et hymne au soleil			LEM
	(Les Indes Galantes)			
Reyer	Et toi Fréia (Sigurd)			HEU
Saint-Saëns	Qui donc commande			GSC
	(Henry VIII)			
Spontini	Dans le sein d'un ami			PET
	(La Vestale)			
Thomas	Chanson bachique (O vin dissipe)			GSC
	(Hamlet)			
-----	Comme une pâle fleur			HEU
	(Hamlet)			

Arias From German Operas

Baritone

Humperdinck	Peter's song				SC
	(Haensel und Gretel)				
-----	Spielmann's air				
	(Die Koenigskinder)				
Korngold	Pierrot's dance song				AMP
	(The Dead City)				
Lortzing	Es wohnt am Seegestade (Undine)				
Mendelssohn	Ich bin ein vielgereister Mann	ML			DIT
	(Heimkehr aus der Fremde)				
Mozart	Air d'Alazim (Zaïde)				INT
-----	Der Vogelfaenger bin ich ja	L	D-E		†
	(Die Zauberfloete)				
-----	Ein Maedchen oder Weibchen				†
	wuenscht (Die Zauberfloete)				
-----	Invocation to the sun				
	(King Thamos in Egypt)				
Wagner	Als du in kuehnem Sange				†
	(Tannhaeuser)				
-----	Blick' ich umher	M	B-EF		†
	(Tannhaeuser)				
-----	Darf ich die Antwort sagen				
	(Tristan und Isolde)				
-----	Die Frist ist um (Der Fliegende				†
	Hollaender)				
-----	Durch dich musst' ich	H	B-F		GSC
	verlieren (Lohengrin)				

(Wagner)	Koenig's Gebet (Lohengrin)	M	F-EF	GSC
-----	Leb' wohl, du kuehnes, herrliches Kind (Die Walkuere)	L	B-E	†
-----	O du, mein holder Abendstern (Tannhaeuser)	L	BF-E	†
-----	O Himmel, lass dich jetzt erflehen (Tannhaeuser)			GSC
-----	Wahn! Wahn! ueberall Wahn! (Die Meistersinger)	L	A-E	†
-----	Was duftet doch der Flieder (Die Meistersinger)			
-----	Wohl wusst' ich hier sie im Gebet zu finden (Tannhaeuser)			GSC
Weber	Wo berg' ich mich (Euryanthe)			†

Arias From Italian Operas

Baritone

Bellini	Ah! per sempre (I Puritani)			RIC
Cilea	Come due tizzi accesi (L'Arlesiana)			SON
-----	Ecco il monologo (Adriana Lecouvreur)			SON
Diaz	O splendore infinito (Benvenuto)	L	A-F	GRU
Donizetti	A tanto amor (La Favorita)			BRO
-----	Ambo nati in questa valle (Linda di Chamounix)			RIC
-----	Bella siccome un angelo (Don Pasquale)			BRO
-----	Cruda funesta smania (Lucia di Lammermoor)			BRO
-----	Vien, Leonora a piedi tuoi (La Favorita)			BRO
Franchetti	Ferito prigionier (Germania)			RIC
Giordano	Nemico della patria (Andrea Chenier)	L	B-FS	SON
Leoncavallo	Prologue (I Pagliacci)	M	BF-A	CFI
-----	Zaza, piccola zingara (Zaza)			SON
Mascagni	Il cavallo scalpita (Cavalleria Rusticana)			GSC
Montemezzi	Suonata è l'ora (L'Amore dei Tre Re)			RIC
Monteverdi	Ahi, troppo è duro (Il Balletto delle Ingrate)	HL	C-EF	DIT
-----	Lasciatemi morire (Arianna)	ML	D-D	†

(Monteverdi)	Qual honor (Orfeo)			BRO
Mozart	Aprite un po quegl' occhi (Le Nozze di Figaro)			†
-----	Deh vieni alla finestra (Don Giovanni)	L	D-E	†
-----	Finch' han dal vino (Don Giovanni)	L	D-EF	†
-----	Ho capito, Signor (Don Giovanni)			
-----	Non più andrai (Le Nozze di Figaro)	L	C-E	†
-----	Se vuol ballare (Le Nozze di Figaro)	L		†
Pergolesi	Son imbrogliato io già (La Serva Padrona)	L		RIC
Ponchielli	O monumento (La Gioconda)			RIC
-----	Pescator, affonda l'esca (La Gioconda)			RIC
Puccini	Minnie, dalla mia casa son partito (La Fanciulla del West)			RIC
-----	Se la giurata fede (Tosca)	M	DF-F	RIC
-----	Scorri fiume eterno (Il Tabarro)			RIC
Rossini	Largo al factotum (Il Barbiere di Siviglia)	L	D-G	†
Verdi	Alla vita che t'arride (Un Ballo in Maschera)			RIC
-----	Cortigiani, vil razza (Rigoletto)			GSC
-----	Credo (Otello)	M	AS-FS	JCH
-----	Di provenza il mar (La Traviata)	M	DF-GF	GSC
-----	Egli è salvo! (La Forza del Destino)			RIC
-----	Era la notte (Otello)			GSC
-----	Eri tu (Un Ballo in Maschera)	M	A-G	
-----	Ford's monologue (E sogno) (Falstaff)			RIC
-----	Il balen del suo sorriso (Il Trovatore)	M	A-G	†
-----	Il mio sangue (Luisa Miller)			RIC
-----	In braccio alle dovizie (I Vespri Siciliani)			RIC
-----	L'onore! ladri! (Falstaff)			RIC
-----	Le menaccie fieri accenti (La Forza del Destino)			RIC
-----	O de' verd' anni miei (Ernani)			RIC

(Verdi)	O vecchio cor, che batti (I Due Foscari)			RIC
-----	Pari siamo (Rigoletto)			GSC
-----	Per me giunto (Don Carlos)			RIC
-----	Quand' ero paggio (Falstaff)	MH	DS-AF	RIC
-----	Urna fatale (La Forza del Destino)			RIC
Wolf-Ferrari	Aprila, o bella (Jewels of the Madonna)	HL	D-FS	GSC

Miscellaneous Opera Arias

Baritone

Borodin	No sleep, no rest (Prince Igor)			BOO
Kodaly	I am going to plow the Emperor's courtyard (Hary Janos)			
-----	Red apple (Hary Janos)			
Mussorgsky	Monologue and Hallucination Scene (Boris Godunoff)			BES
-----	Shaklovitov's aria (Khovantchina)			
-----	Siege of Kazan (Boris Godunoff)	L	F-E	GSC
-----	Song of the parrot (Boris Godunoff)			DIT
Rimsky-Korsakov	Song of the Venetian guest (Sadko)			BRO
Rubinstein	The demon's song (The Demon)			
Tchaikovsky	Onegin's aria (Eugene Onegin)			GSC
-----	Prince Yeletsky's aria (Pique Dame)			GSC
-----	Who can compare? (Iolanthe)			

Arias From Oratorios and Latin Works

Baritone

Bach, J.S.	Consider, O my soul (St. John Passion)			†
-----	Mighty Lord (Christmas Oratorio)			

(Bach, J.S.)	My darkened heart (Christmas Oratorio)			
Berlioz	Le repos de la Ste. Famille (L'Enfance du Christ)	MH		CST
Dubois	God, my father (Seven Last Words)			GSC
Dvořák	Give ear, ye people (St. Ludmilla)			
-----	I was not deceived (St. Ludmilla)			
Elgar	I am the good shepherd (Light of Life)			NOV
Handel	But who may abide (The Messiah)	L	G-E	†
-----	Chi sprezzando il somo bene (La Passione)			
-----	Defend her! Heaven (Theodora) Edited and set for strings			STB
-----	Let me wander not unseen (L'Allegro)	M	D-G	†
-----	Loathsome urns disclose your treasure (Triumph of Time and Truth)			DIT
-----	More sweet is that name (Semele)			
-----	O ruddier than the cherry (Acis and Galatea)	L	G-F	DIT
-----	O sleep why dost thou leave me (Semele)	H	DS-GS	†
-----	Revenge, Timotheus cries (Alexander's Feast)	L	G-D	†
-----	See, the conqu'ring hero comes (Judas Maccabaeus)			†
-----	See the raging flames arise (Joshua)			†
-----	Shall I in Mamre's fertile plain (Joshua)	L	G-EF	DIT
-----	Tears such as tender fathers shed (Deborah)	L		†
-----	The people that walked in darkness (The Messiah)			†
-----	The trumpet shall sound (The Messiah) Trumpet	L		†
-----	Thy glorious deeds (Samson)	M	C-F	†
-----	Wher'er you walk (Semele)	HML	C-D	†
-----	Why do the nations (The Messiah)	L	B-E	†
Haydn	Now heav'n in fullest glory shone (The Creation)	L		†
-----	Rolling in foaming billows (The Creation)	L	C-F	†

(Haydn)	With joy th' impatient husbandman (The Seasons)	L	B-E	GSC
Mendelssohn	But the mountains shall depart (Elijah)			
-----	For know ye not (Saint Paul)			
-----	Is not His word like a fire (Elijah)	M	B-F	†
-----	It is enough (Elijah)	L	A-E	†
-----	Lord God of Abraham (Elijah)	L	B-E	†
-----	O God, have mercy (Saint Paul)	L	B-D	†
Sullivan	Honor the Lord with they substance (The Prodigal Son)			

Cantata Arias

Baritone

Bach, J.S.	Doch weichet, ihr tollen vergeblichen (Cantata 8) Flute			NOV
-----	Gleich wie die wilden Meereswellen (Cantata 178) Violin			
-----	Good fellows be merry (The Peasant Cantata)			†
-----	Hier in meines Vaters staette (Cantata 32) Violin			
-----	Sheep may safely graze (Cantata 208) 2 Flutes and continuo	LM	EF-GF	GAL
-----	So oft ich meine Tabakspfeife (The Coffee Cantata)			BRH
-----	Wie will ich lustig lachen (Cantata 205)			OXF
Handel	Have mercy, Lord (Te Deum)	HM		†
Mussorgsky	Oriental chant (Josua Navine Cantata)	ML	BF-E	GSC
Pasquini	Air in Riva del Giordano (Erminia)			
Tchaikovsky	Prayer (Moscow Cantata)	M	A-GF	GAL

Operetta, Musical Comedy
or Show Songs

Baritone

Arlen	My shining hour			MOR
	(The Sky's the Limit)			
Berlin	The girl that I marry			BER
	(Annie Get Your Gun)			
-----	White Christmas			BER
	(Holiday Inn)			
Brown	Singing in the rain			ROB
	(Hollywood Review)			
-----	You are my lucky star			ROB
	(Broadway Melody of 1936)			
Coward	Dear little cafe			HAR
	(Bitter Sweet)			
-----	I'll see you again	M	C-F	HAR
	(Bitter Sweet)			
-----	Imagine the Duchess's feelings			CHA
	(Conversation Piece)			
-----	Tokay (Bitter Sweet)			HAR
Forrest- Grieg	Strange music			CHA
	(Song of Norway)			
Friml	Donkey Serenade			WIT
	(The Firefly)			
-----	Gather the rose			MLS
	(The White Eagle)			
-----	Give me one hour			MRT
	(The White Eagle)			
-----	Ma belle			HAR
	(The Three Musketeers)			
-----	March of the musketeers			HAR
	(The Three Musketeers)			
-----	Only a rose			GSC
	(The Vagabond King)			
-----	Rose Marie (Rose Marie)	M	EF-G	HAR
-----	Song of the vagabond	M	C-F	FAM
	(The Vagabond King)			
-----	The mounties (Rose Marie)			HAR
Gershwin	Love walked in			CHA
	(Goldwyn Follies 1938)			
-----	Song of the Flame			CHA
	(Song of the Flame)			
-----	Soon (Strike Up the Band)			BRO
-----	Swanee (Sinbad)			CHA
Henderson	The thrill is gone			CRF
	(Scandals of 1931)			

Herbert	Absinthe frappe (It Happened in Nordland)			WIT
-----	Ah! sweet mystery of life (Naughty Marietta)	LMH	A-A	WIT
-----	Every day is ladies' day with me (The Red Mill)			WIT
-----	Free trade and a misty moon (Eileen)			WIT
-----	Good-a-bye, John (The Red Mill)			WIT
-----	Gypsy love song (The Fortune Teller)	LHM	C-E	WIT
-----	I'm falling in love with someone (Naughty Marietta)			WIT
-----	I want what I want when I want it (Mlle. Modiste)			WIT
-----	I wish I was an island in an ocean of girls (Princess Pat)			WIT
-----	Neapolitan love song (Princess Pat)			WIT
-----	'Neath the southern moon (Naughty Marietta)			
-----	The love of the Lorelei (The Debutante)			GSC
-----	Thine alone (Eileen)			WIT
-----	Tramp, tramp, tramp (Naughty Marietta)			WIT
Hirsch	Learn to smile (The O'Brien Girl)			VIC
Howard	I wonder who's kissing her now (The Prince of Tonight)			BMI
Kalman	Play gipsies, dance gipsies (Graefin Mariza)			HAR
Kern	Any moment now (Can't Help Singing)			HAR
-----	Look for the silver lining (Sally)			CHA
-----	Lovely to look at (Roberta)			CHA
-----	More and more (Can't Help Singing)			CHA
-----	Ol' man river (Show Boat)	LM	BF-G	HAR
-----	The song is you (Music in the Air)	M	C-F	HAR
-----	They didn't believe me (Girl From Utah)			HAR
-----	Try to forget (The Cat and the Fiddle)			HAR
Kreisler	You are free (Apple Blossoms)			HAR
Kirsch	The love nest (Mary)			HAR

Lehar	Yours is my heart alone (The Land of Smiles)			HAR
Loewe	I talk to the trees (Paint Your Wagon)			
-----	There but for you go I (Brigadoon)			FOX
Luders	Fall in (The Prince of Pilsen)			WIT
-----	Message of the violet (The Prince of Pilsen)			WIT
Monsigny	Adieu, chère Louise (Le Déserteur)			JOB
Porter	All thru the night (Anything Goes)			BRO
-----	Begin the Beguine (Jubilee)	L	BF-F	HAR
-----	Blow, Gabriel, blow (Anything Goes)			BRO
-----	Brush up your Shakespeare (Kiss Me Kate)			HAR
-----	I get a kick out of you (Anything Goes)			BRO
-----	Night and Day (Gay Divorcee)	M	BF-EF	HAR
-----	So in love (Kiss Me Kate)			CHA
Rodgers	Getting to know you (The King and I)			BRO
-----	Hello young lovers (The King and I)			BRO
-----	If I love you (Carousel)			WIL
-----	June is bustin' out all over (Carousel)			WIL
-----	Kansas City (Oklahoma)			WIL
-----	Mountain greenery (The Garrick Gaities)			HAR
-----	Oh, what a beautiful morning (Oklahoma)			WIL
-----	Soliloquy (Carousel)			CHA
-----	Some enchanted evening (South Pacific)	M	C-E	CHA
-----	The surrey with the fringe on the top (Oklahoma)			WIL
-----	Where or when? (Babes in Arms)			CHA
-----	You are never away (Allegro)			BRO
-----	You'll never walk alone (Carousel)			WIL
-----	Younger than springtime (South Pacific)			WIL

Romberg	Auf Wiedersehen (The Blue Paradise)	HL		GSC
-----	Lover come back to me (New Moon)	H	D-G	HAR
-----	Once to every heart (Blossom Time)			FEI
-----	One alone (The Desert Song)			HAR
-----	Senorita (Girl of the Golden West)	M		FEI
-----	Soldiers of fortune (Girl of the Golden West)	M		FEI
-----	Stouthearted men (New Moon)	L	C-F	HAR
-----	Sun up to sundown (Girl of the Golden West)			FEI
-----	The desert song (The Desert Song)			HAR
-----	The fireman's bride (Up in Central Park)	M	D-EF	WIL
-----	The Riff song (The Desert Song)	L	D-G	HAR
-----	Wanting you (New Moon)			BRO
-----	When I grow too old to dream (The Night is Young)	HLM	C-G	ROB
-----	Who are we to say? (Girl of the Golden West)	M		FEI
-----	Zing, zing, zoom, zoom (Up in Central Park)			ROB
Schwartz	I'll never leave you (Prince Charming)			HAR
Sloane	What's the matter with the moon? (The Mocking Bird)			MAR
Spoliensky	Tell me tonight (Tell Me Tonight)			HAR
Straus	Life is a dream (The Prodigal)			ROB
-----	My hero (The Chocolate Soldier)	H	D-G	WIT
Strauss, J.	Ach wie so herrlich (Eine Nacht in Venedig)			
-----	Als flotter Geist, doch frueh verwaist (The Gypsy Baron)			CRZ
-----	Ja, das Schreiben und das Lesen (The Gypsy Baron)			CRZ
-----	Love can be dreamed (The Gypsy Baron)			GSC
-----	Mine alone (The Gypsy Baron)			CRZ

127

(Strauss, J.)	Open road, open sky (The Gypsy Baron)			GSC
Sullivan	The Lord Chancellor's insomnia (Iolanthe)			
-----	Tit willow (The Mikado)			GSC
-----	When I was a lad (H. M. S. Pinafore)			GSC
Tierney	Ranger's song (Rio Rita)			FEI
-----	Rio Rita (Rio Rita)	M	C-F	FEI
Weill	Soliloquy (Lost in the Stars)			BRO
Youmans	Drums in my heart (Through the Years)			HAR
-----	Great day (Great Day)	M	EF-F	MLR
-----	Hallelujah! (Hit the Deck)	L	BF-F	HAR
-----	Tea for two (No, no Nanette)			HAR
-----	Without a song (Great Day)	HLM	BF-F	MLR
Zeller	Lass dir zeit (Der Kellermeister)			
-----	Sei nicht boes! (Der Obersteiger)			

Song Cycles (Or Groups of Songs)

Baritone

Babin	Beloved stranger	L		AUG
Barber	Three songs for voice and piano, Op. 10			GSC
Beethoven	An die ferne Geliebte	HL	C-E	†
-----	Sechs geistliche Lieder			
Berger	Four sonnets Piano or string quartet	M	A-G	GSC
Bloch	Poèmes d'automne	M	B-G	GSC
Brahms	Romanzen auz Magelone			†
-----	Vier ernste Gesaenge			†
-----	Zigeunerlieder			
Copland	Old American songs			
Cornelius	Six Christmas songs	HL		BOS
Debussy	Le promenoir des deux amants			DUR
-----	Trois ballades de Francois Villon			DUR
-----	Trois chansons de France			DUR
Dougherty	Five sea chanties	L	A-EF	GSC
Dvořák	Biblical songs	HL		AMP
-----	Gypsy songs	LH	D-A	AMP

Falla	Siete canciones	HL		AMP
Fauré	L'horizon chimérique	M		DUR
-----	La bonne chanson	HL		INT
-----	Poème d'un jour			HAM
Finzi	Earth and air and rain (10 songs)			OXF
Griffes	Five poems of ancient China and Japan	M	AS-EF	GSC
Honegger	Trois chansons String quartet and flute			SEN
Kilpinen	Lieder un den Tod	M		AMP
-----	Spielmannslieder			
Mahler	Kindertotenlieder	L	G-GF	INT
-----	Lieder eines fahrenden Gesellen	M		INT
Mason	Nautical lays of a landsman	L	A-E	GSC
-----	Russians (Song cycle)			
Milhaud	Quatre chants hébraïques			
Mussorgsky	Songs and dances of death			INT
-----	Sunless			CHE
-----	The nursery	M	C-G	INT
Niles	Five gambling songs	M		GSC
Poulenc	Banalités			AMP
-----	Chansons Gaillardes	L		HEU
-----	Chansons villageoises	M	C-G	ESC
-----	Le bestiaire String quartet, flute, clarinet and bassoon	M		AMP
-----	Métamorphoses			SAL
-----	Tel jour, telle nuit	M	B-A	DUR
-----	12 Poems of Guillaume Appollinaire			ESC
Powell	Five Virginian folk songs			JFI
Ravel	Chansons madécasses Flute, cello and piano			DUR
-----	Don Quichotte à Dulcinée	HM	A-F	DUR
-----	Histoires naturelles			DUR
-----	Quatre chants populaires	M		DUR
Schubert	Die schoene Muellerin	HL		†
-----	Die Winterreise			†
-----	Gesaenge des Harfners, 1, 2 and 3			PET
Schumann	Der arme Peter	HL	B-G	†
-----	Dichterliebe			†
-----	Liederkreis			
-----	Vier Husarenlieder	L	D-EF	BRH
Somervell	Maud			BOH
Strauss	Drei Liebeslieder			PET
Stravinsky	Trois histoires pour enfants			CHE

Vaughan				
Williams	Songs of travel			BOH
-----	The house of life			ASH
Wolf	Harfenspieler Lieder (1, 2 and 3)			
-----	Michelángelo Lieder			†
Woodford-				
Finden	Indian love lyrics			BOO

Solo Cantatas

Baritone

Bach, J. S.	Ich habe genug (Cantata 82)			
	Oboe, strings and continuo			
Foss	Song of anguish			
Handel	Dalla guerra amorosa			
Pergolesi	Salve Regina			
Propora	Salve Regina			
Rameau	La Musette			
Stradella	Se amor m'annoda	L	BF-F	
Telemann	Kleine Kantate			
	(Von Wald und Au)			

(See Solo Cantatas of Pergolesi, Handel and
Scarlatti, Kirchenkantaten of Buxtehude and
Symphoniae Sacrae of Schuetz.)

Concert Arias

Baritone

Mozart	Io ti lascio, o cara, addio	L	BF-D	AUG
-----	Mentre ti lascio	L		BOO

Christmas Songs

Baritone

Adam	O holy night	LMH	EF-G	†
Andrews	I heard the bells on	L	A-E	GAL
	Christmas day			
Bach, J. S.	Mighty Lord (Christmas Oratorio)			
-----	My darkened heart			
	(Christmas Oratorio)			
-----	So appears Thy natal day	L		GAL
Berlin	White Christmas			BER
	(Holiday Inn)			

Berlioz	Le repos de la Ste. Famille (L'Enfance du Christ)	MH		CST
Branscombe	Hail ye time of holidays			
Chaminade	Christmas carol of the birds	MH	D-A	GSC
De Koven	The white Christ	L	C-D	GSC
Dickinson	Joseph, tender Joseph	M		GRA
Dunhill	To the Queen of Heaven	M	C-G	GSC
Eakin	What of that midnight long ago	M	D-F	GAL
Elmore and Reed	Come all ye who weary	L	C-C	JFI
Evans	The Virgin had a baby	L	C-EF	BOH
Fauré	Noël	LH	EF-AF	GSC
Grieg	Christmas song			AUG
Harris	The feast of Christmas	M	C-F	OXF
Head	The three mummers			BOO
Jewell	The vision of the shepherds	HL	A-D	ASC
Kountz	The sleigh	HL	D-FS	GSC
Kramer	Dark and wondrous night	HML	C-E	DIT
Lynn	Gently little Jesus	L	BF-BF	DIT
Mac Gimsey	A new Christmas morning hallelujah	M	DF-F	CFI
Martin	The Holy Child	HML	G-G	ENO
Massenet	Légende de la sauge (Jongleur de Notre-Dame)	M	CS-F	HEU
Matthews	Voices of the sky	HL	BF-D	GSC
Mc Kinney	The Holy Mother sings	MH	AF-AF	JFI
Murphy	O little town of Bethlehem	M	D-F	SUM
Neidlinger	The birthday of a King	LMH	C-F	GSC
-----	The manger cradle	L	EF-F	GSC
Niles	The cherry tree			GSC
Prokoff	Christmas cradle song	LM	D-E	CHA
Rodney	A dream of Bethlehem	MML	G-DF	ENO
Russell	Child Redeemer	HL		GAL
Schubert	Ave Maria	LMH	F-F	†
-----	They sang that night in Bethlehem	LMH	EF-EF	GSC
Taylor	Christmas folk song	L	BF-EF	GRA
Thiman	In the bleak midwinter	L	A-E	NOV
Trunk	The Christ child in the manger	HM		AMP
Walsh	Christmas story			REM
West	It came upon a midnight	MM	E-FS	SUM
Wild	The Christ child	M	EF-EF	CFI
Wolf	Schlafendes Jesuskind	HL	AS-F	†

Easter Songs

Baritone

Bach, J.S.	Jesus from the grave is risen	M	F-EF	CFI
Curran	Crucifixion			
Dennee	Easter song	HM	B-F	ASC
Dubois	God, my father (Seven Last Words)			GSC
Guion	At the cry of the first bird	H	D-G	GSC
Hageman	Christ went up into the hills	LH	EF-AF	CFI
Handel	The trumpet shall sound (The Messiah) Trumpet	L		†
Huhn	Christ is risen	HM	C-E	ASC
Kountz	Palm Sunday	HL		GAL
La Forge	Before the Crucifix	HML	BF-EF	GSC
Mac Farlane	On wings of living light	MH	D-G	GSC
Mac Gimsey	I was there when they crucified my Lord	HL		CFI
O'Hara	There is no death	LMH	EF-AF	CHA
Rachmaninoff	Christ is risen	LM	D-F	GAL
Schubert	Ave Maria	LMH	F-F	†
Scott	Angels roll the rock away	MH	E-G	HUN
Tchaikovsky	A legend	M	D-E	GSC
Turner	Hail your risen Lord	HL	C-D	GSC
Vaughan Williams	Easter			GAL
Wolf	Herr, was traegt der Boden	HL	B-DS	†
Yon	Christ triumphant	MH	E-A	JFI
-----	O faithful Cross	HM	C-EF	JFI
-----	Our Paschal joy	LH	AF-AF	JFI

Patriotic Songs

Baritone

Bone and Fenton	Prayer for a waiting world	L		CFI
Bowles	An American hero	M	E-E	AXE
Candlyn	O God of armies	L	DF-DF	GRA
Chadwick	He maketh wars to cease	ML		ASC
De Koven	Recessional			
Dix	The trumpeter	HML	A-C	BOH

Dungan	Eternal life	HL		PRE
Foster, F.	The Americans come	MH	F-BF	JFI
Handel	Arm, arm ye brave (Judas Maccabaeus)	L	B-E	†
Lester	Greater love hath no man	LH	B-E	CFI
O'Hara	Guns	M	C-F	DBH
-----	There is no death	LMH	EF-AF	CHA

Sacred Songs

Baritone

Bach, J.S.	Draw near to me	HML		GSC
Beethoven	The worship of God in nature			
Bizet	O Lord be merciful	HL		GSC
Bone and Fenton	First Psalm	LM	DF-F	CFI
-----	Thy word is a lamp	LH	C-F	ROW
Brown	The twenty-third Psalm	LH		GRA
-----	What are these which are arrayed	HLM	C-F	ASC
Browning	For I am persuaded	LM	DF-G	CFI
-----	The beatitudes	HM	C-F	CFI
Buck	Fear not ye, O Israel	HLM		GSC
Campbell-Tipton	I will give thanks unto the Lord	LMH	DF-AF	GSC
Candlyn	God that madest earth and heaven	M	C-F	GRA
Chadwick	A ballad of trees and the Master	HML	A-F	DIT
Charles	Incline Thine ear	HL	BF-D	GSC
Clokey	God is in everything	LH	D-G	JFI
Davis	Be ye kind, one to another	L		GAL
-----	Let not your heart be troubled	HML		WOO
-----	Trust in the Lord	MH	CS-G	GAL
Dvořák	God is my shepherd			AMP
-----	Hear my prayer, O Lord			AMP
-----	Turn Thee to me			AMP
Edmunds	Praise we the Lord	HL	D-D	ROW
Faure	The palms	HM	C-EF	DIT
Franck	O Lord most holy	LM	A-FS	BOS
Goodhall	The mountain	M	D-E	GSL
Green	Praised be the Lord	M	C-F	OXF
Guion	Prayer	HL		GSC
-----	The cross bearer	HM	B-DS	GSC
Handel	Thanks be to Thee	M	CS-E	†

133

Hinchliffe	Tranquillity	M	E-F	CFI
Holst	The heart worships	ML	BF-D	STB
Knapp	Open the gates of the temple	HML	A-D	PON
La Forge	They that trust in the Lord	HL	BF-EF	GAL
-----	What shall I render unto the Lord?	HL	C-D	GSC
Lederer	Psalm 104	L	A-E	CFI
Liddle	How lovely are Thy dwellings	HML		BOS
Mac Dermid	In my Fathers house are many mansions	HML		FRS
-----	Ninety first Psalm	HLM		FRS
Mac Gimsey	Think on these things	LM	BF-EF	CFI
Malotte	The beatitudes	LH	E-G	GSC
-----	The Lord's Prayer			
-----	The twenty-third Psalm	HLM	C-F	GSC
Mc Feeters	A Psalm of praise	M		CFI
Mc Gill	Thine eternal peace	HL	A-CS	GSC
Mendelssohn	But the mountains shall depart (Elijah)			
-----	For know ye not (Saint Paul)			
-----	Lord God of Abraham (Elijah)	L	B-E	†
-----	O God, have mercy (Saint Paul)	L	B-D	†
Noble	Souls of the righteous	M		GRA
O'Connor-Morris	Fill thou my life, O Lord	L	BF-EF	CFI
Rorem	Song of David	M		AMP
Sanderson	Green pastures	HL	BF-EF	BOO
Schubert	The Omnipotent			
-----	To the Infinite			
Scott	Consider the lilies	HL	C-E	GSC
-----	Ride on, ride on	HML		FLA
Speaks	The Lord is my light	HML		GSC
-----	Thou wilt keep him in perfect peace	HML		GSC
Stevenson	I sought the Lord	HL	D-F	DIT
-----	Praise	M	F-F	CFI
Stickles	Saith the Lord	LH	D-F	CHA
Sullivan	Honor the Lord with thy substance (The Prodigal Son)			
Tchaikovsky	Lord Almighty God (Moscow Cantata)	M		GRA
-----	Pilgrim's song	HLM	B-E	GSC
Thiman	My master hath a garden	HL		NOV
Thompson	My Master hath a garden	M		ECS
Van de Water	The penitent	HM		DIT

(Van de Water)	The publican	HL	C-E	DIT
Weaver	Build thee more stately mansions	M	C-E	GAL
Wolf	Morning prayer (Morgenstimme)			
-----	Prayer (Gebet)			

Wedding Songs

Baritone

Barnby	O perfect love	M	C-G	DIT
Beethoven	Ich liebe dich	HL	BF-DF	†
Bond	I love you truly			BOS
Clough-Leighter	Possession	MH	DF-AF	GSC
De Koven	Oh promise me (Robin Hood)	HML	C-D	†
Delius	So white, so soft, is she	LH	B-FS	BOH
D'Hardelot	Because	MH	E-G	CHA
Diggle	A wedding prayer	HM	EF-F	GSC
Franck	O Lord most holy	LM	A-FS	BOS
Geehl	For you alone			SHU
Grieg	I love thee	HML	E-F	†
La Forge	How much I love you	HM	DF-F	GSC
Lippe	How do I love thee?			BOS
Marx	Hat dich die Liebe beruehrt	MH	EF-BF	AMP
Sacco	With this ring	M	F-F	BVC
Schubert	Du bist die Ruh	LMH	EF-AF	†
-----	Ungeduld	HML		†
Schumann	Widmung	HL	BF-F	†
Sharp	Possession	MH	D-A	DIT
Sowerby	O perfect love	MH	EF-AF	GRA
Strauss	Ich liebe dich			†
Thiman	The God of love my Shepherd is	ML	A-D	NOV
Youmans	Through the years (Through the Years)	HML	A-F	MLR

Songs and Arias With Added Accompanying Instrument

Baritone

Bach, J.S.	Gleich wie die wilden Meereswellen (Cantata 178) Violin			

(Bach, J.S.)	Hier in meines Vaters Staette (Cantata 32) Violin			AUG
Barber	Dover Beach String quartet	M	BF-F	GSC
Berger	Four sonnets Piano or string quartet	M	A-G	GSC
Chausson	Le colibri Violin or cello	M	F-GF	BOS
Curran	Nocturne Violin	HML	B-DS	GSC
Handel	Defend her! Heaven (Theodora) Edited and set for strings			STB
-----	The trumpet shall sound (The Messiah) Trumpet	L		†
Honegger	Chanson (Ronsard) Flute and string quartet			SEN
-----	Trois chansons String quartet and flute			SEN
Kramer	Pleading String quartet	LH	D-GF	JFI
Mana-Zucca	Rachem Trumpet	HML		CHA
Milford	So sweet love seemed Cello	HL	D-D	GRA
Peterkin	A curse on a closed gate Voice and viola	M	D-E	OXF
Poulenc	Le bestiaire String quartet, flute, clarinet and bassoon	M		AMP
Ravel	Chansons madécasses Flute, cello and piano			DUR

American Recital Songs

Bass

Athay	City streets	M	E-EF	CFI
Bacon	A clear midnight			NEM
-----	Brady			BOO
Barber	I hear an army	LH	D-AF	GSC
-----	Nocturne	HM	CS-FS	GSC
-----	Rain has fallen	HM	D-E	GSC
-----	With rue my heart is laden	HL	CS-D	GSC
Bauer	Songs in the night	HL	A-C	GSC
Billings	David's lamentation			BIR
Binder	Abraham Lincoln walks at midnight			
Boyd	Cape Horn gospel	L	BF-D	GAL
Braine	Dawn awakes	HML	A-D	ASC

Cadman	Service	HML	BF-D	FLA
Campbell-Tipton	The crying of water	LH	FS-GS	GSC
Carpenter	Dansons la gigue	M	B-E	GSC
-----	Don't ceare	M	C-D	GSC
-----	Go, lovely rose	M	DF-EF	GSC
-----	Looking glass river	M	B-D	GSC
-----	The cock shall crow	M	B-E	GSC
-----	The day is no more	M	GS-DS	GSC
-----	The green river	M	B-E	GSC
-----	To one unknown	M	A-DS	GSC
Chanler	The policeman in the park	L		GSC
Charles	Sweet song of long ago	HML	A-D	GSC
-----	When I have sung my songs	HM	BF-EF	GSC
Coombs	Her rose	HL	D-C	GSC
Deis	Reflection	HM	B-F	
Dougherty	Blow ye winds	L	C-D	GSC
-----	Declaration of independence	L	C-C	GSC
-----	Loveliest of trees	HM	C-E	BOH
Dreier	They call me vagabond			
Duke	Calvary	L	G-F	CFI
-----	Deep sea mood			
-----	Here in this spot with you	M	B-F	GSC
-----	Loveliest of trees	L	C-D	GSC
-----	Richard Cory	L	A-EF	CFI
Dungan	Down the wild song	HL	AF-F	CFI
Edmunds	Billy boy	ML	BF-EF	ROW
Farwell	These saw visions			GAL
Foote	I'm wearing awa'	HL		ASC
Ganz	A woman's last word	HL	BF-F	GRA
Golde	Calls	HL	BF-EF	GSC
Griffes	An old song resung	LM	EF-F	GSC
Harris	Agatha Morley	M	C-D	CFI
Haubiel	Terry, my son	M		CMP
Hawley	Ah, 'tis a dream	L	G-C	JCH
Huhn	Cato's advice	L	G-C	GSC
Ives	Charlie Rutlage	M		ARR
-----	General William Booth enters into Heaven			
Kramer	Minnelied	M	C-E	JFI
La Forge	To a messenger	HLM	CF-G	GSC
Levitzki	Do you remember?	HML	BF-EF	GSC
Mac Gimsey	Thunderin' wonderin'	L	C-D	CFI
-----	Trouble	ML	C-D	CFI
Malotte	Upstream	M	C-F	GSC
Mana-Zucca	Thy will be done			CNG
Manning	In the Luxembourg gardens	HML	BF-D	GSC
Mason	A prophet	M	BF-GF	GSC

(Mason)	A sea dirge			WIT
Mc Gill	O sleep	L	A-CS	GSC
Mead	The wanderer	LMH	D-A	CFI
Metcalf	At nightfall	HML	C-DF	ASC
Miller	Boats of mine	HML	BF-EF	FLA
Naginski	The ship starting	M	BF-B	GSC
Paxson	Dusk at sea	HL	A-EF	GSC
Pinsuti	Bedouin love song	HL	FS-DS	GSC
Robinson	Joe Hill			MRR
Rogers	The last song	MLH	E-AF	GSC
Sachs	The three riders	M	C-F	GSC
Schuman	Holiday song	M	C-F	GSC
Singer	This want of you	L	E-FS	BOH
Sonneck	To Helen	M	B-F	GSC
Speaks	Shepherd, see thy horse's foaming mane			FLA
Still	If you should go			LEE
Swanson	Pierrot	L	B-D	WTR
-----	The valley	L	BF-DF	LEE
Taylor	Captain Stratton's fancy	L	CS-F	JFI
Thompson	Velvet shoes	M	C-E	ECS
Thomson	Dirge	M	D-F	GSC
Tyson	Noon and night	LH	F-AF	GSC

British Recital Songs

Bass

Aiken	Sigh no more	HML		STB
Anon	False Phillis			
Arne, T.	By the gaily circling glass	L		DIT
-----	Now Phoebus sinketh in the west			GSC
-----	Why so pale and wan?			GSC
Bantock	Silent strings	MH	F-G	BOO
Berners	Dialogue between Tom Filuter and his man	M	D-F	CHE
Boyce	Rail no more ye learned asses	L	G-D	OXF
-----	The song of Momus to Mars	M	BF-EF	CFI
Campion	Follow thy fair sun			STB
-----	There is a garden in her face			DIT
Coleridge-Taylor	She rested by the broken brook	HL		DIT
Dibdin	Blow high, blow low			POT

Dowland	Shall I sue?			STB
Dunhill	The cloths of Heaven	LM	EF-G	STB
Ford	Since first I saw your face			DIT
Forsyth	The bell man			DIT
German	My song is of the sturdy north	ML		CHA
------	Rolling down to Rio	ML	G-D	NOV
Gibbs	Five eyes	HL	D-D	BOS
------	The ballad of Semmerwater	L	AF-EF	CUR
------	Toll the bell			
Goossens	Melancholy	M		CHE
Handel	Droop not young lover		G-E	
------	The birds no more shall sing			
Harrison	I hear an army			CRA
Harty	Homeward	L	C-E	NOV
Head	Money Oh!			
------	Sweet chance that led my steps abroad	LM	C-F	BOH
------	The ships of Arcady	ML	BF-EF	BOH
------	When I think upon the maidens	LM	D-G	BOO
Hely-Hutchinson	Old mother Hubbard	HL	B-E	CFI
Holst	Creation			GSC
------	The heart worships	ML	BF-D	STB
------	The Sergeant's song			ASH
Jones	Love is a babble			STB
Keel	Trade winds	HL	BF-EF	BCH
Lawes	I am confirmed			BOO
Leveridge	The beggar's song	L	G-D	BOO
Longsteffe	When the Sergeant Major's on parade			CHA
Milford	So sweet love seemed Cello	HL	D-D	GRA
Munro	My lovely Celia			BIR
Parry	Why so pale and wan, fond lover	L		NOV
Purcell, E.	Passing by	HM	D-D	DIT
Purcell, H.	Arise, ye subterranean winds			GSC
------	Evening hymn	M	C-F	OXF
------	If music be the food of love	M	D-G	BOO
------	I'll sail upon the dog star	HL	A-E	†
Quilter	It was a lover and his lass	HL	CS-E	BOO
------	Music and moonlight	L	C-EF	CUR
------	Now sleeps the crimson petal	LMH	EF-GF	BOO
------	O mistress mine	HML		BOO
------	Take, o take those lips away			BOO
Rosseter	When Laura smiles	LM	D-E	STB

139

Russell	Poor man's garden	HML	A-D	BOO
Sanderson	Quiet	ML	AF-EF	BOH
Scott	Song of London	M	BF-E	ELK
Shaw	Song of the Palanquin bearers	E-F		CUR
Singer	This want of you	L	E-FS	BOH
Stanford	A soft day	ML	DF-DF	STB
-----	Faith			BOH
-----	Farewell	M	BF-E	STB
-----	She is far from the land			
-----	Windy nights			
Stephenson	Love is a sickness	HML	C-D	BOO
Taylor	The banks o' Doon	ML		JFI
-----	The wind mill	M		OXF
Toye	The inn	L	C-E	CUR
Vaughan Williams	Four nights	L	AF-EF	OXF
-----	How can the tree but wither?			OXF
-----	The roadside fire	HML	BF-EF	BOO
-----	The water mill	L	C-D	OXF
Warlock	Good ale			AUG

French Recital Songs

Bass

Bruneau	L'heureux vagabond	LH	EF-G	GSC
Chausson	Le colibri Violin or cello	M	F-GF	BOS
-----	Le temps des lilas	MH	D-GS	†
Debussy	Beau soir	LH	C-FS	†
-----	Colloque sentimental			DUR
-----	La mer est plus belle	HL		†
-----	Le faune			DUR
-----	Le temps a laissié son manteau			DUR
Duparc	Chanson triste	MH	FS-AF	†
-----	La vague et la cloche			ROU
-----	Lamento	ML	EF-EF	†
-----	Le manoir de Rosamunde	HL	B-F	BOS
-----	L'invitation au voyage	HM	E-F	†
-----	Phidylé	MH	EF-AF	BOS
Dupont	Les boeufs			SAL
Fauré	Après un rêve	HM	C-F	†
-----	Automne	MH	D-FS	GSC
-----	Dans les ruines d'une abbaye	M	E-FS	†
-----	Fleur jetée	HM	BF-FS	†
-----	Le parfum impérissable	LH	GF-GF	
-----	Les berceaux	LMH	BF-G	†

(Fauré)	Nocturne	H	F-A	MAR
-----	Prison	LH		MAR
-----	Rencontre	H	EF-AF	†
-----	Sérénade toscane	MH	G-AF	HAM
Ferrari	Le lazzarone			
-----	Le miroir	M	E-F	GSC
Fourdrain	Promenade au mule			
Garat	Dans le printemps de mes années	M		DUR
Georges	Le flibustier			
Gounod	Au printemps	LMH	DF-AF	GSC
-----	Au rossignol	LMH	D-G	CHO
-----	Que les songes heureux			GSC
Hahn	D'une prison	L	BF-EF	HEU
-----	Je me metz en vostre mercy			HEU
-----	L'heure exquise	M	DF-F	†
-----	Offrande	M	D-D	†
-----	Paysage	MH	EF-G	HEU
-----	The gay vagabond			
-----	Trois jours de vendange	M		HEU
Holmès	Au pays	HM	C-F	CFI
Honegger	Chanson (Ronsard) Flute and string quartet			SEN
-----	Psalm 34 (I will bless the Lord at all times)			SAL
-----	Psalm 130 (Mimaamaquim)			SAL
-----	Psalm 138 (I will give Thee thanks with my whole heart)			SAL
Hue	J'ai pleuré en rêve	HL	D-E	BOS
Ibert	Chanson de la mort			
Indy	Madrigal			DIT
Lenormand	Quelle souffrance	HM	AF-F	HAM
Martini	Plaisir d'amour	M	BF-EF	GSC
Milhaud	Le chant du veilleur			
Paladilhe	Les trois prières			
Pessard	L'adieu du matin	ML	BF-D	GSC
Poulenc	Chanson à boire	L	B-E	HEU
-----	Fêtes galantes			SAL
-----	Invocation aux Parques			HEU
-----	La belle jeunesse	L	D-F	HEU
-----	Madrigal			
-----	Sérénade			
Ravel	Ronsard à son âme	L	CS-E	DUR
Saint-Saëns	Danse macabre	L	BF-EF	AXE
-----	Les pas d'armes du Roi Jean	HML	A-F	RIC
Severac	Les hiboux			ROU
Widor	Je ne veux pas autre chose	HL	C-EF	HAM

Bass

Beethoven	Adelaide	HML	BF-E	†
-----	An die Geliebte	M	E-E	†
-----	Auf dem Huegel sitz' ich spaehend			†
-----	Aus Goethes Faust			
-----	Der Kuss			†
-----	Der Wachtelschlag			†
-----	Die Ehre Gottes	HL	AF-EF	†
-----	Die Liebe des Naechsten			
-----	Diese Wolken in den Hoehen			†
-----	God is my song			
-----	Ich liebe dich	HL	BF-DF	†
-----	In questa tomba	ML	A-CS	†
-----	Vom Tode	L	A-EF	GSC
-----	Wonne der Wehmut			†
Brahms	Am Sonntag Morgen	L	CS-FS	†
-----	An die Nachtigall	H	DS-G	†
-----	Auf dem Kirchhofe	HL	BF-EF	†
-----	Botschaft	HL	D-F	†
-----	Dein blaues Auge	MH	BF-G	†
-----	Denn es gehet dem Menschen	HL		†
-----	Der Ueberlaeufer			†
-----	Die Mainacht	HL	BF-FF	†
-----	Ein Sonett			†
-----	Ein Wanderer	LH	E-AF	†
-----	Erinnerung	H	E-G	†
-----	Feldeinsamkeit	HL	C-EF	GSC
-----	Ich wandte mich und sahe an	HL		†
-----	In Waldeseinsamkeit	H	ES-G	†
-----	Kein Haus, keine Heimat	HL	D-D	†
-----	Maienkaetzchen	L	D-E	†
-----	Meine Liebe ist gruen	MLH	ES-A	†
-----	Minnelied	MHL	C-EF	†
-----	Mit vierzig Jahren	HL	FS-D	†
-----	Nachtigall	MHL	BF-FS	†
-----	Nicht mehr zu dir zu gehen			†
-----	O kuehler Wald	MH	A-F	†
-----	O liebliche Wangen	MLH	E-G	†
-----	O wuesst' ich doch den Weg zurueck	H	E-FS	†
-----	Ruhe Suessliebchen	HL	BS-E	†
-----	Sandmaennchen	LH	F-G	†
-----	Sapphische Ode	HML		†

(Brahms)	Sonntag	H	D-G	†
-----	Staendchen	HL	BF-E	†
-----	Steig' auf, geliebter Schatten	HL	BF-EF	†
-----	Tambourliedchen			†
-----	Treue Liebe	LMH	DS-E	†
-----	Unbewegte laue Luft			†
-----	Unueberwindlich			†
-----	Vergebliches Staendchen	LMH		†
-----	Verrat	HL	FS-EF	GSC
-----	Von ewiger Liebe	LMH	B-AF ⌐	†
-----	Vor dem Fenster			†
-----	Wenn ich mit Menschen			†
-----	Wie bist du meine Koenigin	HL	C-E	†
-----	Wie Melodien zieht es	HL	A-E	†
-----	Wie rafft ich mich auf			†
-----	Wir wandelten	LH	EF-GF	†
Franz	Es ragt ins Meer der Runenstein	HL	G-F	†
-----	For music	ML	C-D	†
-----	Im Herbst	HM	A-F	†
-----	Mutter, o sing mich zur Ruh	HL	E-G	†
Handel	Dank sei Dir, Herr	M	CS-E	†
Haydn	The spirit's song	M	B-GF	†
-----	The wanderer			
Liszt	Die Lorelei	LH	BF-BF	†
-----	Ueber allen Gipfeln ist Ruh			DUR
Loewe	Der heilige Franziskus	L	A-E	SC
-----	Der Noeck			SC
-----	Der selt'ne Beter			SC
-----	Die Uhr	HML	AF-EF	†
-----	Edward	HL	F-E	†
-----	Friedericus Rex			SC
-----	Odins Meeresritt			SC
-----	Tom der Reimer			HSC
Mozart	An Chloe	LH	EF-AF	
-----	Die Verschweigung			
-----	Warnung	HM	C-D	
Pfitzner	Der Gaertner			
-----	Ist der Himmel im Lenz so blau			
Schubert	Am Bach im Fruehling			PET
-----	Am Meer	HML	B-D	†
-----	An die Leier	LM	BF-F	†
-----	An Schwager Kronos	HL	G-E	†
-----	An Silvia			†
-----	Aufenthalt	HLM	A-F	†
-----	Aus Heliopolis			PET

(Schubert)	Ave Maria	LMH	F-F	†
-----	Das Wirtshaus	HL	C-D	†
-----	Der Atlas	HL	BF-F	†
-----	Der Doppelgaenger	HL	G-D	†
-----	Der Erlkoenig	HML	A-E	†
-----	Der Goldschmiedsgesell			PET
-----	Der Juengling an der Quelle	LH	E-A	†
-----	Der Juengling auf dem Huegel	L	G-F	†
-----	Der Kampf			PET
-----	Der Leiermann	ML	C-D	†
-----	Der Lindenbaum	HL	A-D	†
-----	Der Schiffer	LH	BF-A	†
-----	Der stuermische Morgen	HL		
-----	Der Wanderer	HML	FS-D	†
-----	Der Wegweiser	L	D-EF	†
-----	Der Zwerg	M	A-GF	PET
-----	Der zuernende Barde			PET
-----	Die Allmacht	HML	G-E	†
-----	Die Forelle	MLH	EF-GF	†
-----	Die Kraehe	HL	A-E	†
-----	Die Post	HML	BF-EF	†
-----	Die Stadt	HL	A-E	†
-----	Fahrt zum Hades	HL	G-DF	PET
-----	Fischerweise	L	C-D	†
-----	Fruehlingsglaube	M	EF-F	†
-----	Gebet waehrend der Schlacht	M	CS-E	†
-----	Gruppe aus dem Tartarus	L	CS-EF	†
-----	Gute Nacht	LH	C-FS	†
-----	Heidenroeslein			
-----	Ihr Grab			PET
-----	Il modo di prender moglie			
-----	Il traditor deluso			
-----	Im Abendrot	HL	C-D	†
-----	Kriegers Ahnung	HL	G-EF	†
-----	L'incanto degli occhi			
-----	Lachen und Weinen	HL	C-EF	†
-----	Mein!	HL		†
-----	Mut	HL		†
-----	Rastlose Liebe	M	B-F	†
-----	Sei mir gegruesst	LH	G-G	†
-----	Seligkeit			
-----	Staendchen	MH	B-E	†
-----	Tischlied			PET
-----	Totengraebers Heimweh	HL	G-EF	†
-----	Ungeduld	HML		†
-----	Wohin?	HL	B-E	†

Schuetz	Aus dem 119th Psalm			
-----	Herr, nun laessest Du Deinen Diener			BAR
Schumann	An den Sonnenschein	HL	A-D	†
-----	Der Soldat			
-----	Die beiden Grenadiere			
-----	Die Lotusblume	HLM	BF-F	†
-----	Du bist wie eine Blume	HM	F-EF	†
-----	Fruehlingsfahrt	HL	B-E	†
-----	Ich grolle nicht	HL	BF-D	†
-----	Im Rhein, im heiligen Strome	HM	D-F	
-----	Im Walde	HL	A-D	†
-----	Lieb' Liebchen	HL	B-E	†
-----	Romanze	HL	C-E	GSC
-----	Wanderlied	HL	A-E	†
-----	Wenn ich in deine Augen seh'	HL	EF-FF	†
-----	Wer nie sein Brot			†
-----	Widmung	HL	BF-F	†
Strauss	Breit ueber mein Haupt	LH	GF-AF	HSC
-----	Caecilie	MH	E-B	†
-----	Der Einsame			†
-----	Die Nacht	HL		†
-----	Freundliche Vision	HL	C-F	†
-----	Heimliche Aufforderung	HL	B-E	†
-----	Im Spaetboot			
-----	Madrigal	LH	EF-GF	
-----	Mit deinen blauen Augen	LH	C-GS	†
-----	Morgen	HML	E-F	†
-----	Nachtgang			†
-----	Ruhe meine Seele			†
-----	Staendchen	HM	A-FS	†
-----	Traum durch die Daemmerung	HML	BF-EF	†
-----	Wie sollten wir geheim sie halten	LH	D-A	
-----	Zueignung	HL	CS-FS	†
Wolf	Abschied			†
-----	Alles endet, was entstehet	HL	F-C	†
-----	Anakreons Grab	HL	D-D	†
-----	An die Geliebte			†
-----	Auf einer Wanderung	HL		†
-----	Biterolf	HL	D-F	†
-----	Cophtisches Lied, 1			†
-----	Der Freund	HM	BF-E	PET
-----	Der Gaertner	HL		†
-----	Der Musikant	HL	CS-D	†
-----	Der Rattenfaenger	HL		†

(Wolf)	Der Schreckenberger			†
-----	Der Soldat, 1	LH	E-FS	†
-----	Der Tambour	HL		†
-----	Er ist's	H	D-G	†
-----	Fuehlt meine Seele	L	A-D	†
-----	Fussreise	HL	D-E	†
-----	Gesang Weylas	HL	DF-F	†
-----	Gesegnet sei das Gruen	HL		†
-----	Gesegnet sei, durch den die Welt	HL		†
-----	Heb' auf dein blondes Haupt	HL	G-DF	†
-----	In der Fruehe	HL	C-C	†
-----	Nun lass uns Frieden schliessen	HL		†
-----	Nun wandre, Maria	HL	EF-D	†
-----	Prometheus			PET
-----	Seemanns Abschiedslied	H	C-A	†
-----	Trunken muessen wir alle sein	M	ES-FS	†
-----	Ueber Nacht	LH	D-G	†
-----	Um Mitternacht	HL	G-EF	†
-----	Und steht ihr frueh am Morgen auf			†
-----	Verborgenheit	HL	B-E	†
-----	Wenn du zu den Blumen gehst	HL	B-EF	†
-----	Wohl denk' ich oft	M	C-EF	†
Wolff	Ewig			
-----	Sommernacht			

Italian Recital Songs

Bass

Bassani	Dormi, bella, dormi tu	L	EF-F	GSC
Bononcini	L'esperto nocchiero (Astarte)	HL	B-E	†
-----	Pupille nere			
Caccini	Amarilli, mia bella	ML	C-D	†
Caldara	Alma del core			GSC
-----	Come raggio di sol	HL	D-F	†
-----	Mirti, faggi			PET
-----	Sebben crudele	HML	E-DS	†
-----	Selve amiche, ombrose piante	HM	E-E	†
Carissimi	A morire!	ML	C-D	
-----	Filli, non t'amo più	HL	B-D	†
-----	No, no, non si speri!	HL	C-EF	†

(Carissimi)	Vittoria, mio core!	HLM	B-E	†
Castelnuovo-Tedesco	Ninna Nanna			
Cavalli	Beato chi può (Serse)			HEU
-----	Donzelle fuggite	HL	C-EF	†
Cesti	Che angoscia, che affanno (Il Pomo d'Oro)	HL	C-DF	DIT
-----	E dove t'aggiri (Il Pomo d'Oro)	HM	D-EF	DIT
-----	Intorno all'idol mio (Orontea)	MH	D-F	†
Cimara	Fiocca la neve	H	G-G	GSC
Coscia	Dormi, dormi			
Durante	Danza, danza fanciulla gentile	HM	BF-F	†
-----	Vergin, tutta amor	LM	C-EF	†
Falconieri	O bellissimi capelli	HL	B-D	†
-----	Vezzosette e care	M	CS-E	GSC
Frescobaldi	Se l'aura spira	HL	C-EF	DIT
Gagliano	Dormi, amore	HL	CS-E	DIT
Gasparini	Caro laccio, dolce nodo	M	EF-EF	GSC
Giordani	Caro mio ben	HML	B-D	†
Handel	Alma mia (Floridante)	HM	CS-E	†
--+--	Cara sposa (Radamisto)	M	CS-D	†
-----	Col raggio placido (Agrippina)			
-----	Del minnacciar del vento (Ottone)	L		†
-----	Ombra mai fu (Serse)	HM	BF-EF	†
-----	Si, tra i ceppi (Berenice)	L	B-D	†
Legrenzi	Che fiero costume	HML	C-D	†
Lotti	Pur dicesti, o bocca bella	LMH	E-FS	GSC
Marcello	Non m'è grave morir per amore	L	C-E	GSC
-----	Perchè mai non m'uccise il dolore			
Monteverdi	Addio di Seneca			
Paisiello	Nel cor più non mi sento	HL	C-EF	†
Pergolesi	Bella mia (Il Maestro di Musica)			GSC
-----	Nina	HL	CS-D	DIT
Peri	Invocazione di Orfeo (Euridice)	HL	E-CS	DIT
Pizzetti	L'annuncie			
Provenzale	La stellidaura vendicata (A. of Armidoro)			
Respighi	Nebbie			†
Rontani	Se bel rio	ML	D-C	†
Rosa	Star vicino	HL	D-E	†
Sadero	L'amor xe una pietanza	M		CHE

147

Sarti	Lungi dal caro bene (Armide)	HL	G-D	GSC
Scarlatti, A.	Chi vuole innamorarsi	HL	D-EF	DIT
-----	Già il sole dal Gange	LH	EF-F	GSC
----	La fortuna			BOS
-----	Rugiadose odorose (Il Pirro e Demetrio)	HL	D-E	DIT
Scarlatti, D.	Consolati e spara amante	L	BF-E	GSC
Sibella	La Girometta	HML	D-E	GSC
-----	Non ho parole	HL	C-F	GSC
Stradella	Per pietà (Il Floridoro)	HM	D-F	DIT
-----	Pietà, Signore	HM	C-F	
Torelli	Tu lo sai	HL	BF-F	†
Tosti	La serenata	HLM	D-EF	GSC
-----	Sogno			RIC
-----	The last song	HL		RIC
Zandonai	I due tarli	M		RIC

Russian Recital Songs

Bass

Borodin	Love			
Cui	Hunger song	LM	E-F	DIT
Dargomijshky	The old corporal			
Glazounoff	Song of Bacchus			
Gretchaninoff	Death			AMP
-----	My native land	L	C-EF	GSC
-----	Over the steppe	LM	C-G	GSC
-----	Voices of night			
-----	Wounded birch	HL	B-EF	†
Koeneman	When the King went forth to war	ML	A-E	CHE
Malashkin	O could I but express in song	LH		CHE
Mednikoff	The hills of Gruzia	H	DS-A	LAC
Mussorgsky	After the battle			GSC
-----	Death and the peasant			GSC
-----	Death the commander			
-----	Serenade			BES
-----	Song of the old man			
-----	Sphinx			BRH
-----	The banks of the Don			GSC
-----	The classic			BRH
-----	The grave			BRH
-----	The seminarian			GSC
-----	Trepak			BES
-----	Within four walls			CHE

Rachmaninoff	All things depart			BOO
-----	Floods of spring	HL		DIT
-----	How fair this spot	MH		GSC
-----	Oh, never sing to me again	H		BOO
-----	O thou billowy harvest field	HL	CS-E	GSC
-----	Spring waters	M	D-GS	CHE
-----	When yesterday we met			BOH
Revutzki	My beloved			
-----	The merry fiddler			
Rimsky- Korsakov	The prophet			
Rubinstein	Ballad			
-----	Do not weep my child			
-----	Gold rolls here below me			
-----	The prisoner			
Shostakovich	In the fields			
Tchaikovsky	At the ball	MH		GSC
-----	Be it a bright day			
-----	Don Juan's serenade	HLM	B-E	GSC
-----	Moment of fear			
-----	Pilgrim's song	HLM	B-E	GSC

Scandinavian Recital Songs

Bass

Grieg	A swan			†
-----	Autumnal gale	HL	A-F	CFI
-----	I love thee	HML	E-F	†
-----	Jeg lever et liv i laengsel	L	BF-E	HAN
-----	The old mother	ML	D-D	DIT
-----	The tryst			DIT
-----	Two brown eyes	LM	EF-F	GSC
Kilpinen	Elegia satakielle			
Palmgren	Var ar vägens mål?			HAN
Sibelius	Black roses	M	A-ES	AMP

Spanish Recital Songs

Bass

De Cola	Sarie Marías		
Nin	El canto de los pájaros		ESC
-----	Granadina		AMP
-----	Minué cantado		ESC
Obradors	El vito		

Miscellaneous Recital Songs

Bass

Bizet	Agnus Del	HLM	C-AF	
Chopin	The little ring	HL		GSC
Dvořák	Clouds and darkness			
-----	God is my shepherd			AMP
-----	I will sing new songs of gladness	HL		†
-----	Lord, Thou art my refuge and shield			AMP
-----	Songs my mother taugh me	HM	E-E	†
-----	Turn Thee to me			AMP
Franck	Panis angelicus	LM		
Haydn	O Jesus, Deus Pacis			
Sinadinos	The Eagle			

British Songs and Arias
For Opening Recitals

Bass

Blow	Music's the cordial of a troubled breast (Begin the Song)	L	D-E	PET
Boyce	The song of Momus to Mars	M	BF-EF	CFI
Handel	Hear me, ye winds and waves (Scipione)	ML	G-EF	BOO
-----	Silent worship (Tolomeo)	LM	D-E	CUR
-----	Wher'er you walk (Semele)	HML	C-D	†
Purcell	Arise, ye subterranean winds			GSC
-----	Evening hymn	M	C-F	OXF
-----	If music be the food of love	M	D-G	BOO
-----	Music for a while (Oedipus)	LH		SC
Wilson	When dull care			BOO

German Songs For Opening Recitals

Bass

Beethoven	Adelaide	HML	BF-E	†
-----	God is my song			
-----	Ich liebe dich	HL	BF-DF	†
Brahms	Ein Wanderer	LH	E-AF	†
-----	Nachtigall	MHL	BF-FS	†
Handel	Dank sei Dir, Herr	M	CS-E	†
Haydn	She never told her love	HL		DIT
Mozart	An Chloe	LH	EF-AF	
Schubert	Das Wandern	HLM	E-E	†
Wolf	Ueber Nacht	LH	D-G	†

Italian Songs and Arias
For Opening Recitals

Bass

Caccini	Amarilli, mia bella	ML	C-D	†
Caldara	Sebben crudele	HML	E-DS	†
Carissimi	Vittoria, mio core	HLM	B-E	†
Cavalli	Beato chi può (Serse)			HEU
-----	Donzelle fuggite	HL	C-EF	†
Cesti	Che angoscia, che affanno (Il Pomo d' Oro)	HL	C-DF	DIT
Durante	Vergin, tutta amor	LM	C-EF	†
Falconieri	O bellissimi capelli	HL	B-D	†
Handel	Cara sposa (Radamisto)	M	CS-D	†
-----	Confusa si miri (Rodelinda)	L	B-D	CFI
-----	Ombra mai fu (Serse)	HM	BF-EF	†
-----	Si, tra i ceppi (Berenice)	L	B-D	†
Lotti	Pur dicesti, o bocca bella	LMH	E-FS	GSC
Monteverdi	Ahi, troppo è duro (Il Balletto delle Ingrate)	HL	C-EF	DIT
Mozart	Mentre ti lascio	L		BOO
Paisiello	Nel cor più non mi sento	HL	C-EF	†
Peri	Invocazione di Orfeo (Euridice)	HL	E-CS	DIT
Rosa	Star vicino	HL	D-E	RIC
Sarti	Lungi dal caro bene (Armide)	HL	G-D	GSC
Scarlatti, A.	Già il sole dal Gange	LH	EF-F	GSC
Stradella	Per pietà (Il Floridoro)			
-----	Pietà, Signore	HM	C-F	GSC

American Songs For Closing Recitals

Bass

Barber	I hear an army	LH	D-AF	GSC
Charles	When I have sung my songs	HM	BF-EF	GSC
Copland	I bought me a cat			
-----	Old American songs			
Diack	Little Jack Horner			CFI
Dougherty	Everyone sang			
Foster	My journey's end	HLM	DF-G	GSC
La Forge	To a messenger	HLM	CF-G	GSC
Mac Gimsey	Jwri Jericho	M	C-G	CFI
-----	Land uv degradashun	M	BF-F	CFI
-----	Thunderin' wonderin'	L	C-D	CFI
Malotte	Blow me eyes	MH	C-G	GSC
-----	Song of the open road			ABC
-----	Upstream	M	C-F	GSC
Niles	The rovin' gambler	HL	BF-EF	GSC
Rogers	The last song	MLH	E-AF	GSC
Sachs	The three riders	M	C-F	GSC
Singer	This want of you	L	E-FS	BOH
Swanson	Pierrot	L	B-D	WTR
Taylor	Captain Stratton's fancy	L	CS-F	JFI
Wolfe	Who's gonna mourn for me?	LMH	D-A	ROB

(See also Negro Spirituals and Folk Songs.)

Miscellaneous Songs For Closing Recitals

Bass

Brahms	Feinsliebchen, du sollst nicht barfuss geh'n			†
-----	Meine liebe ist Gruen	MLH	ES-A	†
Cowen	Border ballad	LM	D-E	BOO
Durante	Danza, danza fanciulla gentile	HM	BF-F	†
German	My song is of the sturdy north	ML		CHA
Gretchaninoff	My native land	L	C-EF	GSC
Grieg	Jeg lever et liv i laengsel	L	BF-E	HAN
Head	When I think upon the maidens	LM	D-G	BOO

152

Hely-Hutchinson	Old Mother Hubbard	HL	B-E	CFI
Keel	Trade winds	HL	BF-EF	BOH
Lara	Granada			
Obradors	El vito			
Quilter	Over the mountains			BOS
Rachmaninoff	Floods of spring	HL		DIT
Schubert	Die Forelle	MLH	EF-GF	†
Sinadinos	The eagle			
Strauss	Staendchen	HM	A-FS	†
Vaughan Williams	The roadside fire	HML	BF-EF	BOO
Warlock	Yarmouth Fair	HL	B-E	CFI
Wilson	When dull care			BOO
Wolf	Er ist's	H	D-G	†

Atmospheric Songs and Arias

Bass

Barber	Rain has fallen	HM	D-E	GSC
Brahms	Steig' auf, geliebter Schatten	HL	BF-EF	†
Burleigh	Sometimes I feel like a motherless child	HML		RIC
Carpenter	Go, lovely rose	M	DF-EF	GSC
-----	Looking glass river	M	B-D	GSC
-----	The day is no more	M	GS-DS	GSC
-----	The green river	M	B-E	GSC
Charles	When I have sung my songs	HM	BF-EF	GSC
Cimara	Fiocca la neve	H	G-G	GSC
Delibes	Lakmé ton doux regards (Lakmé)			HEU
Dougherty	Loveliest of trees	HM	C-E	BOH
Duke	Loveliest of trees	L	C-D	GSC
Dunhill	The cloths of Heaven	LM	EF-G	STB
Elmore and Reed	Come all ye who weary	L	C-C	JFI
Ferrari	Le miroir	M	E-F	GSC
Forsyth	The bell man			DIT
Grieg	A swan			†
Hahn	D'une prison	L	BF-EF	HEU
-----	L'heure exquise	M	DF-F	†
-----	Paysage	MH	EF-G	HEU
Holmès	Au pays	HM	C-F	CFI
Holst	The heart worships	ML	BF-D	STB
Hughes	A Ballynure ballad	L	BF-D	BOH

Kramer	Minnelied	M	C-E	JFI
Lynn	Gently little Jesus	L	BF-BF	DIT
-----	The magic night of Christmas	M	D-D	DIT
Massenet	Chanson de la Touraine (Panurge)	M	EF-EF	HEU
Niles	I wonder as I wander	HL	BF-D	GSC
-----	Jesus, Jesus rest your head	HL	A-D	GSC
Quilter	Now sleeps the crimson petal	LMH	EF-GF	BOO
Robinson	Water boy	M	B-E	BOS
Sanderson	Quiet	ML	AF-EF	BOH
Schubert	Gute Nacht	LH	C-FS	†
Schumann	Im Walde	HL	A-D	†
Strauss	Die Nacht	HL		†
-----	Traum durch die Daemmerung	HML	BF-EF	†
Tyson	Noon and night	LH	F-AF	GSC
Vaughan Williams	Four nights	L	AF-EF	OXF
Wolf	Verborgenheit	HL	B-E	†

American Dramatic Songs

Bass

Barber	I hear an army	LH	D-AF	GSC
Campbell-Tipton	The crying of water	LH	FS-GS	GSC
Carpenter	The green river	M	B-E	GSC
-----	To one unknown	M	A-DS	GSC
Damrosch	Danny Deever	L	A-F	PRE
Duke	Calvary	L	G-F	CFI
-----	Here in this spot with you	M	B-F	GSC
Foster	My journey's end	HLM	DF-G	GSC
Griffes	An old song resung	LM	EF-F	GSC
Huhn	Cato's advice	L	G-C	GSC
-----	Invictus	ML	BF-DF	ASC
Ives	Charlie Rutlage	M		ARR
Mac Gimsey	Land uv degradashun	M	BF-F	CFI
Malotte	Song of the open road			ABC
Mana-Zucca	I love life	LM	F-F	PRE
Rogers	The last song	MLH	E-AF	GSC
Romberg	Stouthearted men (New Moon)	L	C-F	HAR
Schuman	Holiday song	M	C-F	GSC
Singer	This want of you	L	E-FS	BOH

Speaks	Shepherd, see thy horse's foaming mane			FLA
Taylor	Captain Stratton's fancy	L	CS-F	JFI
Wolfe	Who's gonna mourn for me	LMH	D-A	ROB

British Dramatic Songs and Arias

Bass

Arne, T.	Preach not me your musty rules (Comus)	HML		ROW
Cowen	Border ballad	LM	D-E	BOO
Del Riego	Homing	HML	BF-E	CHA
Dix	The trumpeter	HML	A-C	BOH
German	My song is of the sturdy north	ML		CHA
-----	Rolling down to Rio	ML	G-D	NOV
Grainger	Shallow brown	M	F-F	GSC
Handel	But who may abide (The Messiah)	L	G-E	†
-----	Why do the nations (The Messiah)	L	B-E	†
Harrison	I hear an army			CRA
Holst	The Sergeant's song			ASH
Purcell	Arise, ye subterranean winds			GSC
-----	I'll sail upon the dog star	HL	A-E	†
Sanderson	Shipmates of mine	LL	G-D	BOO
Sullivan	The lost chord	HL	C-F	GSC
Templeton	Wi' a hundred pipers	L	BF-EF	GSC

French Dramatic Songs and Arias

Bass

Berlioz	O misère des rois (L'Enfance du Christ)			CST
Bizet	Quand la flamme de l'amour (Le Jolie Fille de Perth)			CHO
Debussy	Colloque sentimental			DUR
Duparc	La vague et la cloche			ROU
-----	Le manoir de Rosamunde	HL	B-F	BOS
-----	Phidylé	MH	EF-AF	BOS
Fauré	Automne	MH	D-FS	GSC
-----	Fleur jetée	HM	BF-FS	†
-----	Prison	LH		†

Gounod	Au bruit des lourds marteaux (Philémon et Baucis)	L	AF-EF	†
Hahn	D'une prison	L	BF-EF	HEU
-----	Offrande	M	D-D	†
Holmès	Au pays	HM	C-F	CFI
Hue	J'ai pleuré en rêve	HL	D-E	BOS
Lenormand	Quelle souffrance	HM	AF-F	HAM
Massenet	Les grands mots (Manon)			GSC
Meyerbeer	Nonnes qui reposez (Robert le Diable)			GSC
Saint-Saëns	Danse macabre	L	BF-EF	AXE
-----	Les pas d'armes du Roi Jean	HML	A-F	RIC
Thomas	Le tambour major (Le Caid)			HEU

German Dramatic Songs and Arias

Bass

Beethoven	Ha! welch ein Augenblick (Fidelio)			†
-----	In questa tomba	ML	A-CS	†
Brahms	Am Sonntag Morgen	L	CS-FS	†
-----	Nicht mehr zu dir zu gehen			†
-----	Treue Liebe	LMH	DS-E	†
-----	Verrat	HL	FS-EF	†
-----	Von ewiger Liebe	LMH	B-AF	†
Franz	Im Herbst	HM	A-F	†
Liszt	Die Lorelei	LH	BF-BF	†
Loewe	Der selt'ne Beter			SC
-----	Edward	HL	F-E	†
-----	Odins Meeresritt			SC
Mendelssohn	Is not His word like a fire? (Elijah)	M	B-F	†
-----	It is enough (Elijah)	L	A-E	
Schubert	Am Meer	HML	B-D	†
-----	An Schwager Kronos	HL	G-E	†
-----	Aufenthalt	HLM	A-F	†
-----	Der Atlas	HL	BF-F	†
-----	Der Doppelgaenger	HL	G-D	†
-----	Der Erlkoenig	HML	A-E	†
-----	Der Lindenbaum	HL	A-D	†
-----	Der Schiffer	LH	BF-A	†
-----	Der Zwerg	M	A-GF	PET
-----	Die Allmacht	HML	G-E	GSC
-----	Die Kraehe	HL	A-E	†
-----	Die Stadt	HL	A-E	†

(Schubert)	Fahrt zum Hades	HL	G-DF	PET
-----	Gebet waehrend der Schlacht	M	CS-E	†
-----	Gruppe aus dem Tartarus	L	CS-EF	†
-----	Kriegers Ahnung	HL	G-EF	†
-----	Mut	HL		†
-----	Totengraebers Heimweh	HL	G-EF	†
Schumann	Der Soldat			
-----	Fruehlingsfahrt	HL	B-E	†
-----	Ich grolle nicht	HL	BF-D	†
-----	Wer nie sein Brot			†
Strauss	Caecilie	MH	E-B	†
-----	Madrigal	LH	EF-GF	
-----	Ruhe meine Seele			†
-----	Zueignung	HL	CS-FS	†
Wagner	Jerum! jerum! (Die Meistersinger)			†
-----	Leb' wohl, du kuehnes herrliches Kind (Die Walkuere)	L	B-E	†
-----	Pogners Anrede (Die Meistersinger)	L	A-F	†
Wolf	Der Freund	HM	BF-E	PET
-----	Der Rattenfaenger	HL		†
-----	Prometheus			PET
-----	Seemanns Abschiedslied	H	C-A	†
-----	Ueber Nacht	LH	D-G	INT

Italian Dramatic Songs and Arias

Bass

Boito	Son lo spirito (Mefistofele)	L	G-E	RIC
Donizetti	Vieni la mia vendetta (Lucrezia Borgia)			BRO
Durante	Vergin, tutta amor	LM	C-EF	†
Ponchielli	Si, morir ella de' (La Gioconda)			RIC
Respighi	Nebbie			†
Verdi	Ella giammai m'amò (Don Carlos)	L	A-E	RIC
-----	Infelice è tu credevi (Ernani)	L	GF-EF	GSC
-----	O tu Palermo (I Vespri Siciliani)			RIC

Miscellaneous Dramatic Songs

Bass

Cui	Hunger song	LM	E-F	DIT
Gretchaninoff	Over the steppe	LM	C-G	GSC
-----	Wounded birch	HL	B-EF	†
Grieg	A swan			†
-----	Autumnal gale	HL	A-F	CFI
-----	Jeg lever et liv i laengsel	L	BF-E	HAN
Koeneman	When the King went forth to war	ML	A-E	CHE
Korbay	Shepherd, see thy horse's foaming mane	L	B-DS	SC
Malashkin	O could I but express in song	LH		CHE
Mussorgsky	After the battle			GSC
-----	Siege of Kazan (Boris Godunoff)	L	F-E	GSC
-----	The song of the flea	L	AS-G	GSC
Rachmaninoff	Christ is risen	LM	D-F	GAL
-----	Floods of spring	HL		DIT
-----	O thou billowy harvest field	HL	CS-E	GSC
Sibelius	Black roses	M	A-ES	AMP
Tchaikovsky	Pilgrim's song	HLM	B-E	GSC

American Humorous Songs

Bass

Carpenter	Don't ceare	M	C-D	GSC
Diack	Little Jack Horner			CFI
Dougherty	Declaration of independence	L	C-C	GSC
Guion	What shall we do with a drunken sailor	HML	C-D	GSC
Malotte	Blow me eyes	MH	C-G	GSC
Mana-Zucca	The big brown bear	HML	C-F	GSC
Mason	A grain of salt	L	A-D	GSC
-----	I ain't afeared o' the Admiral	L	A-E	GSC
-----	Nautical lays of a landsman	L	A-E	GSC
Romberg	The fireman's bride (Up in Central Park)	M	D-EF	WIL
Schuman	Holiday song	M	C-F	GSC
Taylor	Captain Stratton's fancy	L	CS-F	JFI

British Humorous Songs

Bass

Arne, T.	Why so pale and wan?			GSC
Berners	Dialogue between Tom Filuter and his man	M	D-F	CHE
Boyce	The song of Momus to Mars	M	BF-EF	CFI
Charles, W.	The green eyed dragon	M	BF-E	BOH
Gibbs	Five eyes	HL	D-D	BOS
Head	Money Oh!			
-----	When I think upon the maidens	LM	D-G	BOO
Hely-Hutchinson	Old mother Hubbard	HL	B-E	CFI
Hughes	A Ballynure ballad	L	BF-D	BOH
Johnston	Because I were shy	L	B-E	CRA
Jones	Love is a babble			STB
Lawes	I am confirmed			BOO
Liddle	The garden where the praties grow	LMH	E-FS	STB
Lohr	The little Irish girl	HLM	C-E	CHA
Sanderson	Captain Mac	ML	G-E	BOO
Torrence	Smilin' Kitty O'Day	ML	CS-D	BOO

German Humorous Songs

Bass

Beethoven	Aus Goethes Faust			
-----	Ker Kuss			†
Brahms	Vergebliches Staendchen	LHM	E-FS	†
Mendelssohn	Ich bin ein vielgereister Mann (Heimkehr aus der Fremde)	ML		DIT
Mozart	Solche hergelaufne Laffen (Abduction from Seraglio)			†
-----	Warnung	HM	C-D	
Schubert	Heidenroeslein			
Wolf	Abschied			†
-----	Der Musikant	HL	CS-D	†
-----	Der Soldat 1	LH	E-FS	†
-----	Der Tambour	HL		†

Italian Humorous Songs

Bass

Mozart	La vendetta (Le Nozze di Figaro)			†
-----	Madamina (Don Giovanni)	L	A-E	†
-----	Non più andrai (Le Nozze di Figaro)	L	C-E	†
Pergolesi	Son imbrogliato io già (La Serva Padrona)	L		RIC
Rossini	La calunnia (Il Barbiere di Siviglia)			†
Scarlatti, A.	Chi vuole innamorarsi	HL	D-EF	DIT

Miscellaneous Humorous Songs

Bass

Bizet	Quand la flamme de l'amour (Le Jolie Fille de Perth)			CHO
Gounod	Sérénade de Mephistopheles (Faust)	L	G-G	CHO
Mussorgsky	The seminarian			GSC
-----	The song of the flea	L	AS-G	GSC
Poulenc	Chanson à boire	L	B-E	HEU
-----	La belle jeunesse	L	D-F	HEU

American Folk Songs (Arr.)

Bass

Bacon	Adam and Eve	M	B-D	CFI
-----	The Erie Canal	L	D-C	CFI
Brockway	Barbara Allen			GRA
-----	Sourwood mountain			GRA
Copland	I bought me a cat			
-----	Old American songs			
Davis	He's gone away	M	C-E	GAL
Dougherty	Across the western ocean	M	D-D	GSC
-----	Five sea chanties	L	A-EF	GSC
-----	Mobile bay	M	BF-EF	GSC
-----	Rio Grande	M	EF-EF	GSC
-----	Shenandoah	L	A-D	GSC
Guion	Home on the range	HLM	C-F	GSC

(Guion)	What shall we do with a drunken sailor	HML	C-D	GSC
Niles	Black is the color of my true love's hair			
-----	Down in the valley			GSC
-----	I wonder as I wander	HL	BF-D	GSC
-----	Jesus, Jesus rest your head	HL	A-D	GSC
-----	Oh who's goin' to shoe your pretty little foot			GSC
-----	The rovin' gambler	HL	BF-EF	GSC
Robinson	Water boy	M	B-E	BOS
Siegmeister	Bury me not on the lone prairie			
Wellesley	Sing me a chanty	HLM	B-E	FOX

British Folk Songs (Arr.)

Bass

Bantock	There was a jolly miller			
Britten	The ash grove			BOH
Broadwood	Some rival has stolen my true love	LM	D-E	BOO
Grainger	Shallow Brown	M	F-F	GSC
Harty	The game played in Erin-Go-Bragh			CFI
Hatton	The minstrel boy			BOO
Hopekirk	Annie Laurie			DIT
-----	Loch Lomond			DIT
-----	Ye banks and braes	LM	D-C	DIT
Hughes	A Ballynure ballad	L	BF-D	BOH
-----	Down by the Sally gardens			BOO
-----	The lark in clear air	ML	BF-D	BOO
Johnston	Because I were shy	L	B-E	CRA
Kennedy-Fraser	An Eriskay love lilt			BOO
Lawson	Turn ye to me	M	B-E	GSC
Liddle	The garden where the praties grow	LMH	E-FS	STB
Moss	The floral dance	HML	A-D	CHA
Page	The harp that once through Tara's halls			DIT
Quilter	Over the mountains			BOS
-----	Three poor mariners			BOO
Reid	Turn ye to me			BOO
Taylor	May day carol			JFI
Templeton	Wi' a hundred pipers	L	BF-EF	GSC

Vaughan				
Williams	King William	L	D-D	OXF
-----	Lullaby of the Madonna	L	BF-D	GRA
-----	Rollin in the dew			OXF
Warlock	Yarmouth Fair	HL	B-E	CFI
Welsh	All through the night			
Wilson	Come let's be merry			BOO
-----	When dull care			BOO

Miscellaneous Folk Songs (Arr.)

Bass

Brahms	Da unten in Thale			†
-----	Erlaube mir, fein's Maedchen			†
-----	Feinsliebchen, du sollst nicht barfuss geh'n			†
-----	In stiller Nacht			†
-----	Mein Maedel hat einen Rosenmund	M	F-F	†
Koeneman	The song of the Volga boatmen	L		CHE
Korbay	Marishka, Marishka			SC
-----	Shepherd, see thy horse's foaming mane		B-DS	SC
Liddle	An old French carol	LM	F-F	BOO
Obradors	Con amores a mi madre			RIC
Sinigaglia	Il cacciatore del bosco			
-----	Il maritino			
-----	Novara la bella			
Tiersot	L'amours de moi	M	EF-F	HEU
Weckerlin	Aminte	M	C-D	†
-----	Chanson normande			
-----	L'etoile du matin			
-----	O ma tendre musette	LM	A-E	GSC
-----	Pêche des moules			
-----	Trop aimable Sylvia	M	D-E	GSC

Negro Spirituals

Bass

Boatner	On mah journey	LH	EF-EF	RIC
-----	Trampin' (Tryin' to make Heaven my home)	L	D-F	ELK
Brown	Every time I feel de spirit	L		AMP
-----	Hammer song	L	A-C	AMP

162

Burleigh	Balm in Gilead	HL		RIC
-----	By and by	HL		RIC
-----	De gospel train	HL		RIC
-----	Deep river	HML		RIC
-----	Go down, Moses	HL		RIC
-----	Hard trials	M		RIC
-----	I stood on de ribber ob Jerdon	HL		RIC
-----	Nobody knows de trouble I've seen	HL		RIC
-----	Oh, Peter, go ring-a-dem bells			RIC
-----	Scandalize my name	M		RIC
-----	Weepin' Mary	HL		RIC
-----	Were you there?	HML		RIC
Collins	Safe by de Lawd			
Dett	Sit down servant			GSC
Johnson	At the feet of Jesus	L		
-----	City called Heaven			ROB
-----	Dere's no hidin' place down dere			
-----	Fix me Jesus	L	BF-DF	GSC
-----	Hold on			ROB
-----	John Henry			CFI
-----	Take my mother home	M	BF-EF	CFI
Kerby-Forrest	He's got the whole world in His hands	M	G-E	MLS
Mac Gimsey	Land uv degradashun	M	BF-F	CFI
Payne	Crucifixion	L	C-C	GSC
Ryder	Let us break bread together	LH	D-G	JFI
Saunders	The Lord's prayer	L	BF-C	BOH
Singer	Go down Moses	M	E-E	CFI

British Songs and Arias Employing Agility

Bass

Aiken	Sigh no more	HML		STB
Arne, T.	Now Phoebus sinketh in the west			GSC
-----	Preach not me your musty rules (Comus)	HML		ROW
German	Rolling down to Rio	ML	G-D	NOV
Handel	Arm, arm ye brave (Judas Maccabaeus)	L	B-E	†
-----	But who may abide (The Messiah)	L	G-E	†

163

(Handel)	His scepter is the rod of righteousness (Occasional Oratorio)	L	G-E	GSC
-----	Honour and arms (Samson)	L	G-EF	†
-----	How willing my paternal love (Samson)	L	B-E	DIT
-----	O ruddier than the cherry (Acis and Galatea)	L	G-F	DIT
-----	Revenge, Timotheus cries (Alexander's Feast)	L	G-D	†
-----	The trumpet shall sound (The Messiah)	L		†
-----	Thy glorious deeds (Samson)	M	C-F	†
-----	Wher'er you walk (Semele)	HML	C-D	†
---=-	Why do the nations (The Messiah)	L	B-E	†
Hely-Hutchinson	Old mother Hubbard	HL	B-E	CFI
Purcell	Arise, ye subterranean winds			GSC
-----	If music be the food of love	M	D-G	BOO
-----	I'll sail upon the dog star	HL	A-E	†
-----	Music for a while (Oedipus)	LH		SC
Wilson	Come let's be merry			BOO

French Songs and Arias
Employing Agility

Bass

Berlioz	Sérénade de Mephisto (La Damnation de Faust)			DIT
Chausson	Le colibri	M	F-GF	BOS
Gounod	Au bruit des lourds marteaux (Philémon et Baucis)	L	AF-EF	†
-----	Au rossignol	LMH	D-G	CHO
-----	Sous les pieds d'une femme (La Reine de Saba)			GSC
Meyerbeer	Piff, paff! (Les Huguenots)			BRH
Thomas	Le tambour major (Le Caid)			HEU

German Songs and Arias
Employing Agility

Bass

Bach, J.S.	Aechzen und erbaermlich Weinen (Cantata 13) Violin or flute	L	G-EF	PET
-----	Come blessed cross (St. Matthew Passion) Cello			†
-----	Doch weichet, ihr tollen vergeblichen (Cantata 8) Flute			NOV
-----	Endlich, endlich wird mein Joch (Cantata 56) Oboe			RIC
-----	Give, O give me back my Lord (St. Matthew Passion)			†
-----	Gladly will I all resigning (St. Matthew Passion)			†
-----	Gute Nacht, du Weltgetuemmel (Cantata 27) 2 Violins, viola and continuo			
-----	Hier in meines Vaters Staette (Cantata 32) Violin			AUG
-----	Make thee clean my heart from sin (St. Matthew Passion)			†
Brahms	Botschaft	HL	D-F	†
-----	O liebliche Wangen	MLH	E-G	GSC
Handel	Zweier Augen Majestaet (Almira)			MUP
Haydn	Now Heav'n in fullest glory shone (The Creation)	L		†
-----	Rolling in foaming billows (The Creation)	L	C-F	†
-----	With joy th' impatient husbandman (The Seasons)	L	B-E	†
Mendelssohn	Is not His word like a fire (Elijah)	M	B-F	†
Mozart	Solche hergelaufne Laffen (Abduction from Seraglio)			†
Schubert	Fruehlingsglaube	M	EF-F	†
-----	Mein!	HL		†
-----	Ungeduld	HML		†
Strauss	Staendchen	HM	A-FS	†
Weber	Hier im Ird'schen Jammertal (Der Freischuetz)			†

Bass

Bellini	Vi ravviso, o luoghi ameni (La Sonnambula)			DIT
Bononcini	L'esperto nocchiero (Astarte)	HL	B-E	†
Caldara	Alma del core			GSC
-----	Selve amiche, ombrose piante	HM	E-E	†
Carissimi	Filli, non t'amo più	HL	B-D	†
-----	Vittoria, mio core	HLM	B-E	†
Cavalli	Beato chi può (Serse)			HEU
Donizetti	Vieni la mia vendetta (Lucrezia Borgia)			BRO
Durante	Danza, danza fanciulla gentile	HM	BF-F	†
Handel	Confusa si miri (Rodelinda)	L	B-D	CFI
-----	Del minnacciar del vento (Ottone)	L		†
-----	Si, tra i ceppi (Berenice)	L	B-D	†
-----	Sei mia gioia (Parthenope)	HL	C-F	CFI
Mozart	Aprite un po quegl' occhi (Le Nozze di Figaro)			†
Pergolesi	Bella mia (Il Maestro di Musica)			GSC
Rossini	A un dottore (Il Barbiere di Siviglia)			GSC
Scarlatti, A.	Già il sole dal Gange	LH	EF-F	GSC
-----	La fortuna			BOS
-----	Rugiadose odorose (Il Pirro e Demetrio)	HL	D-E	DIT
Scarlatti, D.	Consolati e spara amante	L	BF-E	GSC
Verdi	Infelice è tu credevi (Ernani)	L	GF-EF	GSC
-----	O tu Palermo (I Vespri Siciliani)			RIC

American Songs Employing
Crescendo and Diminuendo

Bass

Bacon	A clear midnight			NEM
Barber	Rain has fallen	HM	D-E	GSC

Campbell-				
Tipton	The crying of water	LH	FS-GS	GSC
Carpenter	Go, lovely rose	M	DF-EF	GSC
-----	Looking glass river	M	B-D	GSC
-----	The day is no more	M	GS-DS	GSC
Duke	Loveliest of trees	L	C-D	GSC
Niles	I wonder as I wander	HL	BF-D	GSC
-----	Jesus, Jesus rest your head	HL	A-D	GSC
Rogers	At parting	LH	CS-FS	GSC
Thompson	Velvet shoes	M	C-E	ECS

German Songs Employing
Crescendo and Diminuendo

Bass

Brahms	Maienkaetzchen	L	D-E	†
-----	Sandmaennchen	LH	F-G	†
-----	Sonntag	H	D-G	†
-----	Wie Melodien zieht es	HL	A-E	†
Schubert	Der Juengling an der Quelle	LH	E-A	†
-----	Der Juengling auf dem Huegel	L	G-F	†
-----	Der Wanderer	HML	FS-D	†
-----	Lachen und Weinen	HL	C-EF	†
Schumann	Romanze	HL	C-E	†
Strauss	Die Nacht	HL		†
Wolf	Der Gaertner	HL		†
-----	Nun lass uns Frieden schliessen	HL		†
-----	Nun wandre, Maria	HL	EF-D	†
-----	Wenn du zu den Blumen gehst	HL	B-EF	†

Italian Songs Employing
Crescendo and Diminuendo

Bass

Caldara	Alma del core			GSC
-----	Sebben crudele	HML	E-DS	†
-----	Selve amiche, ombrose piante	HM	E-E	†
Carissimi	No, no, non si speri	HL	C-EF	†

Cesti	Intorno all'idol mio (Orontea)	MH	D-F	†
Falconieri	O bellissimi capelli	HL	B-D	†
-----	Vezzosette e care	M	CS-E	GSC
Frescobaldi	Se l'aura spira	HL	C-EF	DIT
Handel	Ombra mai fu (Serse)	HM	BF-EF	†
Marcello	Non m'è grave morir per amore	L	C-E	GSC
Monteverdi	Lasciatemi morire (Arianna)	ML	D-D	†
Mozart	Se vuol ballare (Le Nozze di Figaro)	L		†
Rontani	Se bel rio	ML	D-C	†
Scarlatti, A.	La fortuna			BOS

Miscellaneous Songs Employing
Crescendo and Diminuendo

Bass

Duparc	Chanson triste	MH	FS-AF	†
-----	L'invitation au voyage	HM	E-F	†
-----	Phidylé	MH	EF-AF	BOS
Goosens	Melancholy	M		CHE
Gretchaninoff	My native land	L	C-EF	GSC
Head	The ships of Arcady	ML	BF-EF	BOH
Martini	Plaisir d'amour	M	BF-EF	GSC
Mussorgsky	The banks of the Don			GSC
Nin	Minué cantado			ESC
Quilter	Now sleeps the crimson petal	LMH	EF-GF	BOO
Shaw	Song of the Palanquin bearers	LH	E-F	CUR

American Songs Employing
Piano Singing

Bass

Bacon	A clear midnight			NEM
Barber	Rain has fallen	HM	D-E	GSC
-----	With rue my heart is laden	HL	CS-D	GSC
Burleigh	Jean	HML		PRE
Campbell-Tipton	The crying of water	LH	FS-GS	GSC
Carpenter	Go, lovely rose	M	DF-EF	GSC

(Carpenter)	Looking glass river	M	B-D	GSC
-----	The cock shall crow	M	B-E	GSC
-----	The day is no more	M	GS-DS	GSC
-----	The green river	M	B-E	GSC
Charles	When I have sung my songs	HM	BF-EF	GSC
Farwell	These saw visions			GAL
Kramer	Minnelied	M	C-E	JFI
Manning	In the Luxembourg gardens	HML	BF-D	GSC
Niles	I wonder as I wander	HL	BF-D	GSC
-----	Jesus, Jesus rest your head	HL	A-D	GSC
Thompson	Velvet shoes	M	C-E	ECS

British Songs Employing
Piano Singing

Bass

Coleridge-Taylor	She rested by the broken brook	HL		DIT
Dunhill	The cloths of Heaven	LM	EF-G	STB
Forsyth	The bell man			DIT
Handel	Silent worship (Tolomeo)	LM	D-E	CUR
Head	The ships of Arcady	ML	BF-EF	BOH
Liddle	The garden where the praties grow	LMH	E-FS	STB
Quilter	Now sleeps the crimson petal	LMH	EF-GF	BOO
-----	O mistress mine	HML		BOO
Sanderson	Quiet	ML	AF-EF	BOH

French Songs and Arias Employing
Piano Singing

Bass

Debussy	La mer est plus belle	HL		†
Delibes	Lakmé ton doux regards (Lakmé)			HEU
Fauré	Après un rêve	HM	C-F	†
-----	Dans les ruines d'une abbaye	M	E-FS	†
Ferrari	Le miroir	M	E-F	GSC
Gounod	Au rossignol	LMH	D-G	CHO
Hahn	D'une prison	L	BF-EF	HEU
-----	L'heure exquise	M	DF-F	†

169

(Hahn)	Offrande	M	D-D	†
-----	Paysage	MH	EF-G	HEU
Lully	Bois épais (Amadis)	ML	C-EF	†
Pessard	L'adieu du matin	ML	BF-D	GSC
Poulenc	Invocation aux Parques			HEU
Ravel	Don Quichotte à Dulcinée	HM	A-F	DUR
Thomas	De son coeur j'ai calmé la fièvre (Mignon)	L	A-D	HEU
Weckerlin	Aminte	M	C-D	†
-----	O ma tendre musette	LM	A-E	GSC
-----	Trop aimable Sylvia	M	D-E	GSC
Widor	Je ne veux pas autre chose	HL	C-EF	HAM

German Songs and Arias Employing Piano Singing

Bass

Beethoven	Ich liebe dich	HL	BF-DF	†
Brahms	Botschaft	HL	D-F	†
-----	Der Gang zur Liebsten	HL		†
-----	In Waldeseinsamkeit	H	ES-G	†
-----	Sandmaennchen	LH	F-G	†
-----	Sapphische Ode	HML		†
-----	Staendchen	HL	BF-E	†
-----	Steig' auf, geliebter Schatten	HL	BF-EF	†
-----	Vergebliches Staendchen	LHM	E-FS	†
Mendelssohn	It is enough (Elijah)	L	A-E	†
-----	Lord God of Abraham (Elijah)	L	B-E	†
Mozart	An Chloe	LH	EF-AF	
Schubert	Ave Maria	LMH	F-F	†
-----	Du bist die Ruh	LMH	EF-AF	†
-----	Im Abendrot	HL	C-D	†
-----	Lachen und Weinen	HL	C-EF	†
-----	Totengraebers Heimweh	HL	G-EF	†
-----	Wohin?	HL	B-E	†
Schumann	Im Walde	HL	A-D	†
Strauss	Die Nacht	HL		†
-----	Freundliche Vision	HL	C-F	BOO
-----	Nachtgang			†
-----	Traum durch die Daemmerung	HML	BF-EF	†
Wolf	An die Geliebte			†
-----	Der Gaertner	HL		†
-----	Verborgenheit	HL	B-E	†

Italian Songs and Arias Employing
Piano Singing

Bass

Bononcini	Deh, più a me non v'ascondete	LH	EF-F	†
Castelnuovo-Tedesco	Ninna Nanna			
Cimara	Fiocca la neve	H	G-G	GSC
Durante	Vergin, tutta amor			
Frescobaldi	Se l'aura spira	HL	C-EF	DIT
Gagliano	Dormi, amore (La Flora)	HL	CS-E	DIT
Monteverdi	Lasciatemi morire (Arianna)	ML	D-D	†
Mozart	Deh vieni alla finestra (Don Giovanni)	L	D-E	†
Rontani	Se bel rio	ML	D-C	†
Secchi	Lungi dal caro bene	HL		DIT

Miscellaneous Songs Employing
Piano Singing

Bass

Cui	Dusk fallen	LH	E-GS	DIT
-----	The statue at Czarskoe-Selo	HM		†
Dvořák	God is my shepherd			AMP
-----	Goin' home			DIT
-----	I will life mine eyes			AMP
-----	Songs my mother taught me	HM	E-E	†
Grieg	A swan			†
-----	In the boat	LM	D-ES	†
-----	Snegl, Snegl	M	B-F	HAN
Mednikoff	The hills of Gruzia	H	DS-A	LAC

American Songs Employing
Rapid Enunciation

Bass

Boatner	Oh! what a beautiful city!	HL	D-E	GSC
Carpenter	Don't ceare	M	C-D	GSC
-----	The cock shall crow	M	B-E	GSC
Dichmont	Ma little banjo	ML	E-CS	GSC

171

British Songs Employing
Rapid Enunciation

Bass

Berners	Dialogue between Tom Filuter and his man	M	D-F	CHE
Charles, W.	The green eyed dragon	M	BF-E	BOH
Cowen	Border ballad	LM	D-E	BOO
Dowland	Shall I sue?			STB
Fisher	At Tankerton Inn	LM	B-G	BOO
German	Rolling down to Rio	ML	G-D	NOV
Gibbs	Five eyes	HL	D-D	BOS
Head	When I think upon the maidens	LM	D-G	BOO
Lehmann	Myself when young	LL	A-E	GSC
Leveridge	The beggar's song	L	G-D	BOO
Liddle	The garden where the praties grow	LMH	E-FS	STB
Moss	The floral dance	HML	A-D	CHA
Shaw	Song of the Palanquin bearers	LH	E-F	CUR
Sullivan	Ho, Jolly Jenkin (Ivanhoe)	LM	C-F	CHA
Templeton	Wi' a hundred pipers	L	BF-EF	GSC
Vaughan Williams	The water mill	L	C-D	OXF
Warlock	Good ale			AUG

French Songs and Arias Employing
Rapid Enunciation

Bass

Chausson	Le colibri	M	F-GF	BOS
Debussy	Le temps a laissié son manteau			DUR
Fauré	Dans les ruines d'une abbaye	M	E-FS	†
Meyerbeer	Piff, paff. (Les Huguenots)			BRH
Pessard	L'adieu du matin	ML	BF-D	GSC
Poulenc	La belle jeunesse	L	D-F	HEU
Saint-Saëns	Danse macabre	L	BF-EF	AXE
Thomas	Le tambour major (Le Caid)			HEU
Weckerlin	Aminte	M	C-D	†
-----	Trop aimable Sylvia	M	D-E	GSC

German Songs and Arias Employing
Rapid Enunciation

Bass

Beethoven	Hat man nicht auch Gold beineben (Fidelio)			†
Brahms	Meine liebe ist Gruen	MLH	ES-A	†
-----	O liebliche Wangen	MLH	E-G	†
-----	Staendchen	HL	BF-E	†
-----	Tambourliedchen			†
-----	Vergebliches Staendchen	LHM	E-FS	†
Mendelssohn	Ich bin ein vielgereister Mann (Heimkehr aus der Fremde)	ML		DIT
-----	O God, have mercy (Saint Paul)	L	B-D	†
Mozart	Solche hergelaufne Laffen (Abduction from Seraglio)			†
-----	Warnung	HM	C-D	
Schubert	Der Schiffer	LH	BF-A	†
-----	Der zuernende Barde			PET
-----	Die Forelle	MLH	EF-GF	†
-----	Die Post	HML	BF-EF	†
-----	Fischerweise	L	C-D	†
-----	Mein!	HL		†
-----	Ungeduld	HML		†
-----	Wohin?	HL	B-E	†
Strauss	Staendchen	HM	A-FS	†

Italian Songs and Arias Employing
Rapid Enunciation

Bass

Boito	Son lo spirito (Mefistofele)	L	G-E	RIC
Carissimi	Vittoria, mio core	HLM	B-E	†
Cavalli	Donzelle fuggite	HL	C-EF	†
Donizetti	Ah, un foco insolito (Don Pasquale)			RIC
-----	Udite, udite o rustici (L'Elisir d'Amore)			BRO
Durante	Danza, danza fanciulla gentile	HM	BF-F	†
Legrenzi	Che fiero costume	HML	C-D	†
Mozart	Aprite un po quegl' occhi (Le Nozze di Figaro)			†

173

(Mozart)	Finch' han dal vino (Don Giovanni)	L	D-EF	†
-----	Ho capito, Signor (Don Giovanni)			
-----	La vendetta (Le Nozze di Figaro)			†
-----	Madamina (Don Giovanni)	L	A-E	†
-----	Non più andrai (Le Nozze di Figaro)	L	C-E	†
-----	Se vuol ballare (Le Nozze di Figaro)	L		†
Pergolesi	Son imbrogliato io già (La Serva Padrona)	L		RIC
Rossini	A un dottore (Il Barbiere di Siviglia)			GSC
-----	La calunnia (Il Barbiere di Siviglia)			†
Scarlatti, A.	Chi vuole innamorarsi	HL	D-EF	DIT

Miscellaneous Songs Employing Rapid Enunciation

Bass

Grieg	In the boat	LM	D-ES	†
-----	Nu er aftenen lys og lang	L	C-E	HAN
-----	The way of the world			DIT
Korbay	Shepherd see thy horse's foaming mane			
Mussorgsky	The siege of Kazan (Boris Godunor)			
-----	The seminarian			GSC

American Songs Employing Sustained Singing

Bass

Andrews	Sea fever	L	A-D	GSC
Bacon	A clear midnight			NEM
Barber	Rain has fallen	HM	D-E	GSC
-----	With rue my heart is laden	HL	CS-D	GSC
Burleigh	Deep river	HML		RIC
-----	Jean	HML		PRE
-----	Sometimes I feel like a motherless child	HML		RIC

174

(Burleigh)	Were you there?	HML		RIC
Campbell-Tipton	The crying of water	LH	FS-GS	GSC
Carpenter	Go, lovely rose	M	DF-EF	GSC
-----	Looking glass river	M	B-D	GSC
-----	The day is no more	M	GS-DS	GSC
-----	The green river	M	B-E	GSC
-----	To one unknown	M	A-DS	GSC
Charles	When I have sung my songs	HM	BF-EF	GSC
Coombs	Her rose	ML	D-C	GSC
Edwards	By the bend of the river	HML	C-E	GSC
-----	Into the night	HML	C-DF	GSC
Farwell	These saw visions			GAL
Foote	I'm wearing awa'	HL		ASC
Guion	Home on the range	HLM	C-F	GSC
Hawley	Ah, 'tis a dream	L	G-C	JCH
Kramer	Minnelied	M	C-E	JFI
Levitzki	Do you remember?	HML	BF-EF	GSC
Manning	In the Luxembourg gardens	HML	BF-D	GSC
Metcalf	At nightfall	HML	C-DF	ASC
Naginski	The ship starting	M	BF-B	GSC
Robinson	Water boy	M	B-E	BOS
Rogers	At parting	LH	CS-FS	GSC
Skiles	You will know my love			CFI
Speaks	Sylvia	HML	AF-DF	GSC
Tyson	Noon and night	LH	F-AF	GSC

British Songs and Arias Employing
Sustained Singing

Bass

Bantock	Silent strings	MH	F-G	BOO
Campion	Follow thy fair			STB
-----	There is a garden in her face			DIT
Clarke	The blind ploughman	HML	C-D	CHA
Coleridge-Taylor	She rested by the broken brook	HL		DIT
Del Riego	Homing	HML	BF-E	CHA
Dunhill	The cloths of Heaven	LM	EF-G	STB
Ford	Since first I saw your face			DIT
Forsyth	The bell man			DIT
Goossens	Melancholy	M		CHE
Handel	But who may abide (The Messiah)	L	G-E	†

(Handel)	Hear me, ye winds and waves (Scipione)	ML	G-EF	BOO
-----	How willing my paternal love (Samson)	L	B-E	DIT
-----	Leave me, loathsome light (Semele)	L		DIT
-----	Shall I in Mamre's fertile plain (Joshua)	L	G-EF	DIT
-----	Silent worship (Tolomeo)	LM	D-E	CUR
-----	Thy glorious deeds (Samson)	M	C-F	NOV
-----	Vouchsafe, O Lord (Dettingen Te Deum)	HM		ELV
-----	Wher'er you walk (Semele)	HML	C-D	†
Head	The ships of Arcady	ML	BF-EF	BOH
Holst	The heart worships	ML	BF-D	STB
Keel	Trade winds	HL	BF-EF	BOH
Mc Gill	Duna	HML	BF-D	BOO
Milford	So sweet love seemed Cello	HL	D-D	GRA
Purcell	If music be the food of love	M	D-G	BOO
-----	Music for a while (Oedipus)	LH		SC
-----	Next winter comes slowly (The Faery Queen)			GSC
Quilter	Now sleeps the crimson petal	LMH	EF-GF	BOO
Sanderson	Quiet	ML	AF-EF	BOH
Stephenson	Love is a sickness	HML	C-D	BOO
Sullivan	The lost chord	HL	C-F	GSC
Vaughan Williams	Four nights	L	AF-EF	OXF
-----	The roadside fire	HML	BF-EF	BOO
Wood	I look into your garden	LMH	F-AF	CHA

French Songs and Arias Employing Sustained Singing

Bass

Berlioz	O misère des rois (L'Enfance du Christ)			CST
Chausson	Le colibri Violin or cello	M	F-GF	BOS
-----	Le temps des lilas	MH	D-GS	†
Debussy	Beau soir	LH	C-FS	†
-----	Colloque sentimental			DUR

Delibes	Lakmé ton doux regards (Lakmé)			HEU
Duparc	Chanson triste	MH	FS-AF	†
-----	Lamento	ML	EF-EF	†
-----	L'invitation au voyage	HM	E-F	†
-----	Phidylé	MH	EF-AF	BOS
Fauré	Après un rêve	HM	C-F	†
-----	Automne	MH	D-FS	GSC
-----	Le parfum impérissable	LH	GF-GF	
-----	Les berceaux	LMH	BF-G	†
-----	Nocturne	H	F-A	MAR
-----	Prison	LH		†
-----	Rencontre	H	EF-AF	†
Ferrari	Le miroir	M	E-F	GSC
Gounod	Au rossignol	LMH	D-G	CHO
-----	Que les songes heureux			GSC
-----	Sous les pieds d'une femme (La Reine de Saba)			GSC
Hahn	D'une prison	L	BF-EF	HEU
-----	L'heure exquise	M	DF-F	†
-----	Paysage	MH	EF-G	HEU
Halévy	Si la rigeur (La Juive)			†
-----	Vous qui du Dieu vivant (La Juive)			
Honegger	Chanson (Ronsard) Flute and string quartet			SEN
Hue	J'ai pleuré en rêve	HL	D-E	BOS
Indy	Madrigal			DIT
Lenormand	Quelle souffrance	HM	AF-F	HAM
Lully	Bois épais (Amadis)	ML	C-EF	†
Martini	Plaisir d'amour	M	BF-EF	GSC
Massenet	Elégie	LM	C-GF	GSC
-----	Les grands mots (Manon)			GSC
Poulenc	Chanson à boire	L	B-E	HEU
Ravel	Ronsard à son âme	L	CS-E	DUR
Severac	Les hiboux			ROU
Thomas	De son coeur j'ai calmé la fièvre (Mignon)	L	A-D	HEU
Tiersot	L'amours de moi	M	EF-F	HEU
Weckerlin	O ma tendre musette	LM	A-E	GSC
Widor	Je ne veux pas autre chose	HL	C-EF	HAM

Bass

Bach, J.S.	Aechzen und erbaermlich Weinen (Cantata 13) Violin or flute	L	C	
-----	Consider, O my soul (St. John Passion)			†
-----	Come blessed cross (St. Matthew Passion) Cello			†
-----	Gute Nacht, du Weltgetuemmel (Cantata 27) 2 Violins, viola and continuo			
-----	Hier in meines Vaters Staette (Cantata 32) Violin			AUG
-----	Ich will den Kreuzstab (Cantata 56)			BRO
-----	Make thee clear my heart from sin (St. Matthew Passion)			†
Beethoven	Adelaide	HML	BF-E	†
-----	An die ferne Geliebte	HL	C-E	†
-----	Die Ehre Gottes	HL	AF-EF	†
-----	Ich liebe dich	HL	BF-DF	†
-----	In questa tomba	ML	A-CS	†
-----	Vom Tode	L	A-EF	GSC
-----	Wonne der Wehmut			†
Brahms	An die Nachtigall	H	DS-G	†
-----	Auf dem Kirchhofe	HL	BF-EF	CFI
-----	Dein blaues Auge	MH	BF-G	†
-----	Der Ueberlaeufer			†
-----	Die Mainacht	HL	BF-FF	†
-----	Erinnerung	H	E-G	†
-----	Feldeinsamkeit	HL	C-EF	†
-----	In Waldeseinsamkeit	H	ES-G	†
-----	Minnelied	MHL	C-EF	†
-----	Mit vierzig Jahren	HL	FS-D	†
-----	Nachtigall	MHL	BF-FS	†
-----	O kuehler Wald	MH	A-F	†
-----	O wuesst' ich doch den Weg zurueck	H	E-FS	†
-----	Ruhe, Suessliebchen	HL	BS-E	†
-----	Sapphische Ode	HML		†
-----	Steig' auf, geliebter Schatten	HL	BF-EF	†
-----	Treue Liebe	LMH	DS-E	†
-----	Wie bist du meine Koenigin	HL	C-E	†

(Brahms)	Wie Melodien zieht es	HL	A-E	†
-----	Wir wandelten	LH	EF-GF	†
Franz	Dedication	HML	BF-C	†
-----	Es ragt ins Meer der Runenstein	HL	G-F	†
-----	For music	ML	C-D	†
-----	Im Herbst	HM	A-F	†
-----	Mutter, o sing mich zur Ruh	HL	E-G	GSC
Haydn	Now Heav'n in fullest glory shone (The Creation)	L		†
Loewe	Der heilige Franziskus	L	A-E	SC
Mendelssohn	It is enough (Elijah)	L	A-E	†
-----	Lord God of Abraham (Elijah)	L	B-E	†
-----	O God, have mercy (Saint Paul)	L	B-D	†
Mozart	In diesen heiligen Hallen (Die Zauberfloete)	L	FS-C	†
-----	O Isis und Osiris (Die Zauberfloete)			†
-----	Wer ein Liebchen hat gefunden (Abduction from Seraglio)			†
Schubert	Am Bach im Fruehling			PET
-----	Am Meer	HML	B-D	†
-----	An die Leier	LM	BF-F	†
-----	Ave Maria	LMH	F-F	†
-----	Das Wirtshaus	HL	C-D	†
-----	Der Doppelgaenger	HL	G-D	†
-----	Der Juengling an der Quelle	LH	E-A	†
-----	Der Juengling auf dem Huegel	L	G-F	†
-----	Der Leiermann	ML	C-D	†
-----	Der Lindenbaum	HL	A-D	†
-----	Der Wanderer	HML	FS-D	†
-----	Der Wegweiser	L	D-EF	†
-----	Die Allmacht	HML	G-E	GSC
-----	Die Kraehe	HL	A-E	†
-----	Die Stadt	HL	A-E	†
-----	Du bist die Ruh	LMH	EF-AF	†
-----	Fruehlingsglaube	M	EF-F	†
-----	Gute Nacht	LH	C-FS	†
-----	Im Abendrot	HL	C-D	†
-----	Sei mir gegruesst	LH	G-G	†
-----	Staendchen	MH	B-E	†
Schuetz	Aus dem 119th Psalm			
Schumann	An den Sonnenschein	HL	A-D	†
-----	Die Lotusblume	HLM	BF-F	†

(Schumann)	Du bist wie eine Blume	HM	F-EF	†
-----	Ich grolle nich	HL	BF-D	†
-----	Im Rhein, im heiligen Strome	HM	D-F	
-----	Romanze	HL	C-E	†
-----	Wenn ich in deine Augen seh'	HL	EF-FF	†
-----	Wer nie sein Brot			†
Strauss	Breit ueber mein Haupt	LH	GF-AF	HSC
-----	Der Einsame			†
-----	Die Nacht	HL		†
-----	Freundliche Vision	HL	C-F	†
-----	Heimliche Aufforderung	HL	B-E	†
-----	Im Spaetboot			
-----	Madrigal	LH	EF-GF	
-----	Mit deinen blauen Augen	LH	C-GS	DIT
-----	Morgen	HML	E-F	†
-----	Nachtgang			†
-----	Ruhe meine Seele			†
-----	Traum durch die Daemmerung	HML	BF-EF	†
Wagner	Auf wolkigen Hoeh'n (Siegfried)			†
-----	Gebet des Amfortas (Parsifal)			GSC
-----	Koenigs Gebet (Lohengrin)	M	F-EF	GSC
-----	Leb' wohl du kuehnes, herrliches Kind (Die Walkuere)	L	B-E	†
-----	Moegst du, mein Kind (Der Fliegende Hollaender)			†
-----	Pogners Anrede (Die Meistersinger)	L	A-F	†
Wolf	Alles endet, was entstehet	HL	F-C	†
-----	Anakreons Grab	HL	D-D	†
-----	An die Geliebte			†
-----	Biterolf	HL	D-F	†
-----	Fuehlt meine Seele	L	A-D	†
-----	Gebet	HL		†
-----	Gesang Weylas	HL	DF-F	†
-----	Gesegnet sei, durch den die Welt	HL		†
-----	Heb' auf dein blondes Haupt	HL	G-DF	†
-----	Herr, was traegt der Boden	HL	B-DS	INT
-----	In der Fruehe	HL	C-C	†
-----	Michelangelo Lieder			†
-----	Nun lass uns Frieden schliessen	HL		†

(Wolf)	Nun wandre, Maria	HL	EF-D	†
-----	Um Mitternacht	HL	G-EF	†
-----	Verborgenheit	HL	B-E	†
-----	Wenn du zu den Blumen gehst	HL	B-EF	†
-----	Wohl denk' ich oft	M	C-EF	†
Wolff	Ewig			

Italian Songs and Arias Employing Sustained Singing

Bass

Bellini	Vi ravviso, o luoghi ameni (La Sonnambula)			DIT
Caccini	Amarilli, mia bella	ML	C-D	†
Caldara	Alma del core			GSC
-----	Come raggio di sol	HL	D-F	†
Carissimi	No, no, non si speri!	HL	C-EF	†
Castelnuovo-Tedesco	Ninna Nanna			
Cavalli	Beato chi può (Serse)			HEU
Cesti	Che angoscia, che affanno (Il Pomo d'Oro)	HL	C-DF	DIT
-----	Intorno all'idol mio (Orontea)	MH	D-F	†
Cimara	Fiocca la neve	H	G-G	GSC
Diaz	O splendore infinito (Benvenuto)	L	A-F	GRU
Donizetti	Udite, udite o rustici (L'Elisir d'Amore)			BRO
-----	Vieni la mia vendetta (Lucrezia Borgia)			BRO
Durante	Vergin, tutta amor	LM	C-EF	†
Gagliano	Dormi, amore (La Flora)	HL	CS-E	DIT
Handel	Ombra mai fu (Serse)	HM	BF-EF	†
Mattei	Non è ver	HML		DIT
Monteverdi	Ahi, troppo è duro (Il Balletto delle Ingrate)	HL	C-EF	DIT
-----	Lasciatemi morire (Arianna)	ML	D-D	†
Mozart	Deh vieni alla finestra (Don Giovanni)	L	D-E	†
Paisiello	Nel cor più non mi sento	HL	C-EF	†
Pergolesi	Bella mia (Il Maestro di Musica)			GSC
-----	Nina	HL	CS-D	DIT
Peri	Invocazione di Orfeo (Euridice)	HL	E-CS	DIT

Ponchielli	Si, morir ella de' (La Gioconda)			RIC
Respighi	Nebbie			†
Rosa	Star vicino	HL	D-E	†
Stradella	Per pietà (Il Floridoro)	HM	D-F	DIT
-----	Pietà, Signore	HM	C-F	GSC
Torelli	Tu lo sai	HL	BF-F	†
Tosti	The last song	HL		RIC
Verdi	Ella giammai m'amò (Don Carlos)	L	A-E	RIC
-----	Il lacerato spirito (Simon Boccanegra)	L	FS-D	GSC
-----	Infelice è tu credevi (Ernani)	L	GF-EF	GSC
-----	O tu Palermo (I Vespri Siciliani)			RIC
-----	Tu sul labbro de' veggenti (Nabucco)			RIC

Miscellaneous Songs Employing Sustained Singing

Bass

Dvořák	God is my shepherd			AMP
-----	Hear my prayer, O Lord			AMP
-----	I will life mine eyes			AMP
-----	Lord thou art my refuge and shield			AMP
-----	Songs my mother taught me	HM	E-E	†
-----	Turn Thee to me			AMP
Gretchaninoff	Over the steppe	LM	C-G	GSC
-----	Wounded birch	HL	B-EF	†
Grieg	A swan			†
-----	I love thee	HML	E-F	†
-----	The old mother	ML	D-D	DIT
-----	Two brown eyes	LM	EF-F	GSC
Malashkin	O could I but express in song	LH		CHE
Mussorgsky	Sphinx			BRH
-----	The grave			BRH
Rachmaninoff	Christ is risen	LM	D-F	GAL
-----	O thou billowy harvest field	HL	CS-E	GSC
Sibelius	Black roses	M	A-ES	AMP
Tchaikovsky	Don Juan's serenade	HLM	B-E	GSC
-----	Pilgrim's song	HLM	B-E	GSC

American Songs Employing
Spirited Singing

Bass

Bacon	The Erie canal	L	D-C	CFI
Barber	I hear an army	LH	D-AF	GSC
Boyd	Cape Horn gospel	L	BF-D	GAL
Carpenter	Dansons la gigue	M	B-E	GSC
-----	Don't ceare	M	C-D	GSC
-----	The cock shall crow	M	B-E	GSC
Damrosch	Danny Deever	L	A-F	PRE
Griffes	An old song resung	LM	EF-F	GSC
Guion	What shall we do with a drunken sailor	HML	C-D	GSC
Huhn	Cato's advice	L	G-C	GSC
Kountz	The sleigh	HL	D-FS	GSC
Mana-Zucca	I love life	LM	F-F	PRE
Margetson	Tommy, lad	HML	A-D	BOH
Mason	A sea dirge			WIT
Niles	The rovin' gambler	HL	BF-EF	GSC
Rogers	The last song	MLH	E-AF	GSC
Schuman	Holiday song	M	C-F	GSC
Speaks	On the road to Mandalay	HL	BF-F	PRE
-----	Shepherd, see thy horse's foaming mane			FLA
Taylor	Captain Stratton's fancy	L	CS-F	JFI
Wolfe	Short'nin' bread	LHM	D-D	FLA

British Songs and Arias Employing
Spirited Singing

Bass

Arne, T.	By the gaily circling glass	L		DIT
-----	Now Phoebus sinketh in the west			GSC
-----	Preach not me your musty rules (Comus)	HML		ROW
-----	Why so pale and wan?			GSC
Charles, W.	The green eyed dragon	M	BF-E	BOH
Cowen	Border ballad	LM	D-E	BOO
Dowland	Shall I sue			STB
German	My song is of the sturdy north	ML		CHA
-----	Rolling down to Rio	ML	G-D	NOV
Gibbs	Five eyes	HL	D-D	BOS

183

Handel	Arm, arm ye brave (Judas Maccabaeus)	L	B-E	†
-----	His scepter is the rod of righteousness (Occasional Oratorio)	L	G-E	GSC
-----	Honour and arms (Samson)	L	G-EF	†
-----	O ruddier than the cherry (Acis and Galatea)	L	G-F	DIT
-----	Revenge, Timotheus (Alexander's Feast)	L	G-D	†
-----	Thy glorious deeds (Samson)	M	C-F	†
Harrison	I hear an army			CRA
Head	When I think upon the maidens	LM	D-G	BOO
Holst	The sergeant's song			ASH
Hopekirk	Ye banks and braes	LM	D-C	DIT
Johnston	Because I were shy	L	B-E	CRA
Jones	Love is a babble			STB
Keel	Trade winds	HL	BF-EF	BOH
Lawes	I am confirmed			BOO
Leveridge	The beggar's song	L	G-D	BOO
Liddle	The garden where the praties grow	LMH	E-FS	STB
Martin	Come to the fair	HML	D-D	BOO
Moss	The floral dance	HML	A-D	CHA
Purcell	Arise, ye subterranean winds			GSC
-----	I'll sail upon the dog star	HL	A-E	†
Quilter	It was a lover and his lass	HL	CS-E	BOO
-----	O mistress mine	HML		BOO
Sanderson	Captain Mac	ML	G-E	BOO
Shaw	Song of the Palanquin bearers	LH	E-F	CUR
Sullivan	Ho, Jolly Jenkin (Ivanhoe)	LM	C-F	CHA
Toye	The inn	L	C-E	CUR
Vaughan Williams	The roadside fire	HML	BF-EF	BOO
Warlock	Good ale			AUG

French Songs and Arias Employing
Spirited Singing

Bass

Berlioz	Chanson de la puce (La Damnation de Faust)		CST
-----	Sérénade de Mephisto (La Damnation de Faust)		DIT

Bruneau	L'heureux vagabond	LH	EF-G	GSC
Debussy	La mer est plus belle	HL		†
-----	Le faune			DUR
-----	Le temps a laissié son manteau			DUR
Duparc	Le manoir de Rosamunde	HL	B-F	BOS
Fauré	Fleur jetée	HM	BF-FS	†
Gluck	C'est en vain que l'enfer compte (Alceste)			†
Gounod	Au bruit des lourds marteaux (Philémon et Baucis)	L	AF-EF	†
-----	Au printemps	LMH	DF-AF	GSC
-----	Le veau d'or (Faust)	L	C-EF	†
Hahn	The gay vagabond			
Lully	Il faut passer (Alceste)			LEM
Massenet	Chanson de la Touraine (Panurge)	M	EF-EF	HEU
Meyerbeer	Piff, paff! (Les Huguenots)			BRH
Poulenc	La belle jeunesse	L	D-F	HEU
Saint-Saëns	Danse macabre	L	BF-EF	AXE
-----	Les pas d'armes du roi Jean	HML	A-F	RIC
Thomas	Le tambour major (Le Caid)			HEU

German Songs and Arias Employing Spirited Singing

Bass

Bach, J.S.	Doch weichet, ihr tollen vergeblichen (Cantata 8) Flute			NOV
-----	Endlich, endlich wird mein Joch (Cantata 56) Oboe			RIC
Beethoven	An die Geliebte	M	E-E	†
-----	Aus Goethes Faust			
-----	Der Kuss			†
-----	Ha! welch ein Augenblick (Fidelio)			†
-----	Hat man nicht auch Gold beineben (Fidelio)			†
Brahms	Botschaft	HL	D-F	†
-----	Der Gang zur Liebsten	HL		†
-----	Meine Liebe ist gruen	MLH	ES-A	†
-----	O liebliche Wangen	MLH	E-G	†
-----	Tambourliedchen			†
-----	Vergebliches Staendchen	LHM	E-FS	†
Haydn	Rolling in foaming billows (The Creation)	L	C-F	†

(Haydn)	With joy th' impatient husbandman (The Seasons)	L	B-E	†
Mendelssohn	Ich bin ein vielgereister Mann (Heimkehr aus der Fremde)	ML		DIT
-----	Is not His word like a fire? (Elijah)	M	B-F	GSC
Mozart	An Chloe	LH	EF-AF	
-----	Solche hergelaufne Laffen (Abduction from Seraglio)			†
Nicolai	Als Bueblein klein (Die Lustigen Weiber)			GSC
Schubert	Aufenthalt	HLM	A-F	†
-----	Der Schiffer	LH	BF-A	†
-----	Der zuernende Barde			PET
-----	Die Forelle	MLH	EF-GF	†
-----	Die Post	HML	BF-EF	†
-----	Fischerweise	L	C-D	†
-----	Heidenroeslein			
-----	Lachen und Weinen	HL	C-EF	†
-----	Mein!	HL		†
-----	Mut	HL		†
-----	Rastlose Liebe	M	B-F	†
-----	Wohin?	HL	B-E	†
Schumann	Im Walde	HL	A-D	†
-----	Wanderlied	HL	A-E	†
-----	Widmung	HL	BF-F	†
Strauss	Caecilie	MH	E-B	†
-----	Heimliche Aufforderung	HL	B-E	†
-----	Staendchen	HM	A-FS	†
-----	Wie sollten wir geheim sie halten	LH	D-A	
-----	Zueignung	HL	CS-FS	†
Wagner	Jerum! jerum! (Die Meistersinger)			GSC
-----	Moegst du, mein Kind (Der Fliegende Hollaender)			†
Weber	Hier im Ird' shen Jammertal (Der Freischuetz)			†
Wolf	Auf einer Wanderung	HL		†
-----	Der Rattenfaenger	HL		†
-----	Der Soldat 1	LH	E-FS	†
-----	Er ist's	H	D-G	†
-----	Fussreise	HL	D-E	†
-----	Seemanns Abschiedslied	H	C-A	†
-----	Trunken muessen wir alle sein	M	ES-FS	†

Italian Songs and Arias Employing
Spirited Singing

Bass

Bononcini	L'esperto nocchiero (Astarte)	HL	B-E	†
Caldara	Sebben crudele	HML	E-DS	†
Carissimi	Filli, non t'amo più	HL	B-D	†
-----	Vittoria, mio core!	HLM	B-E	†
Cavalli	Donzelle fuggite	HL	C-EF	†
Donizetti	Ah, un foco insolito (Don Pasquale)			RIC
-----	Udite, udite o rustici (L'Elisir d'Amore)			BRO
-----	Vieni la mia vendetta (Lucrezia Borgia)			BRO
Durante	Danza, danza fanciulla gentile	HM	BF-F	†
Falconieri	Vezzosette e care	M	CS-E	GSC
Handel	Confusa si miri (Rodelinda)	L	B-D	CFI
-----	Del minnacciar del vento (Ottone)	L		†
-----	Si, tra i ceppi (Berenice)	L	B-D	†
Legrenzi	Che fiero costume	HML	C-D	†
Mozart	Aprite un po quegl' occhi (Le Nozze di Figaro)			†
-----	Finch' han dal vino (Don Giovanni)	L	D-EF	†
-----	La Vendetta (Le Nozze di Figaro)			†
-----	Madamina (Don Giovanni)	L	A-E	GSC
-----	Non più andrai (Le Nozze di Figaro)	L	C-E	†
-----	Se vuol ballare (Le Nozze di Figaro)	L		†
Pergolesi	Son imbrogliato io già (La Serva Padrona)	L		RIC
Ponchielli	Si, morir ella de' (La Gioconda)			RIC
Rossini	A un dottore (Il Barbiere di Siviglia)			GSC
Scarlatti, A.	Chi vuole innamorarsi	HL	D-EF	DIT
-----	Già il sole dal Gange	LH	EF-F	GSC
Scarlatti, D.	Consolati e spara amante	L	BF-E	GSC
Tosti	The last song	HL		RIC

Miscellaneous Songs Employing
Spirited Singing

Bass

Alnaes	Nu brister i all de klofter	L	A-F	HAN
Dvořák	I will sing new songs of gladness	HL		†
-----	Sing ye a joyful song			AMP
Grieg	Hunter's song	L	DS-E	GSC
-----	Jeg lever et liv i laengsel	L	BF-E	HAN
Koeneman	When the King went forth to war	ML	A-E	CHE
Mussorgsky	Siege of Kazan (Boris Godunoff)	L	F-E	GSC
Rachmaninoff	Floods of spring	HL		DIT
Tchaikovsky	At the ball	MH		GSC
-----	Don Juan's serenade	HLM	B-E	GSC

American and British Songs
of Popular Appeal

Bass

Andrews	Sea fever	L	A-D	GSC
Arden and Wille	Roses in your hair	ML	C-EF	ROW
Brown	Your song from paradise	LMH	D-G	BOO
Burleigh	Jean	HML		PRE
Cadman	The builder	HML	B-D	FLA
Charles, E.	When I have sung my songs	HM	BF-EF	GSC
Charles, W.	The green eyed dragon	M	BF-E	BOH
Clarke	The blind ploughman	HML	C-D	CHA
Cowen	Border ballad	LM	D-E	BOO
Damrosch	Danny Deever	L	A-F	PRE
Del Riego	Homing	HML	BF-E	CHA
D'Hardelot	Because	MH	E-G	CHA
Diack	Little Jack Horner			CFI
Dichmont	Ma little banjo	ML	E-CS	GSC
Dix	The trumpeter	HML	A-C	BOH
Dougherty	Everyone sang			
Edwards	By the bend of the river	HML	C-E	GSC
-----	Into the night	HML	C-DF	GSC
Elvey	Great and fair is she			
Fisher	At Tankerton Inn	LM	B-G	BOO

188

(Fisher)	Tavern song			BOO
Forsyth	The bell man			DIT
Foster	My journey's end	HLM	DF-G	GSC
Fox	The hills of home	HML	BF-DF	CFI
German	Rolling down to Rio	ML	G-D	NOV
Guion	Home on the range	HLM	C-F	GSC
-----	What shall we do with a drunken sailor	HML	C-D	GSC
Head	When I think upon the maidens	LM	D-G	BOO
Hely-Hutchinson	Old mother Hubbard	HL	B-E	CFI
Huhn	Invictus	ML	BF-DF	ASC
Ireland	Sea fever	HLM	D-F	AUG
Johnston	Because I were shy	L	B-E	CRA
Kountz	Prayer of the Norwegian child	ML	C-C	GSC
-----	The sleigh	HL	D-FS	GSC
La Forge	To a messenger	HLM	CF-G	GSC
Lehmann	Myself when young	LL	A-E	GSC
Levitzki	Do you remember?	HML	BF-EF	GSC
Lohr	The little Irish girl	HLM	C-E	CHA
Mac Gimsey	Down to de river	M	B-G	CFI
-----	Jeri Jericho	M	C-G	CFI
-----	Land uv degradashun	M	BF-F	CFI
-----	Thunderin' wonderin'	L	C-D	CFI
-----	To my mother	HML	C-C	CFI
-----	Trouble	ML	C-D	CFI
-----	Twilight meditation			MCG
Malotte	Blow me eyes	MH	C-G	GSC
-----	For my mother	HLM	BF-EF	GSC
-----	Song of the open road			ABC
Mana-Zucca	I love life	LM	F-F	PRE
-----	The big brown bear	HML	C-F	GSC
Manning	In the Luxembourg gardens	HML	BF-D	GSC
Margetson	Tommy, lad	HML	A-D	BOH
Martin	Come to the fair	HML	D-D	BOO
Mason	A grain of salt	L	A-D	GSC
-----	I ain't a'feared o' the Admiral	L	A-E	GSC
Mc Gill	Duna	HML	BF-D	BOO
Rogers	At parting	LH	CS-FS	GSC
Sanderson	Captain Mac	ML	G-E	BOO
-----	Shipmates of mine	LL	G-D	BOO
-----	Until	LMH	E-A	BOO
Schuman	Holiday song	M	C-F	GSC
Shields	The friar of orders gray			
Skiles	You will know my love			CFI

Speaks	Fuzzy wuzzy			JCH
-----	On the road to Mandalay	HL	BF-F	PRE
-----	Sylvia	HML	AF-DF	GSC
Spross	Gunga Din			JCH
Squire	Three for Jack			CHA
Stickles	The open road			DIT
Stothart	The song of the shirt	L	A-E	ROB
Strelezki	Dreams	LMH	B-A	GSC
Sullivan	The lost chord	HL	C-F	GSC
Tours	Mother o' mine	HML	C-D	CHA
Tyson	Moon and night	LH	F-AF	GSC
Wellesley	Sing me a chanty	HLM	B-E	FOX
Wolfe	Who's gonna mourn for me	LMH	D-A	ROB
Wood	I look into your garden	LMH	F-AF	CHA

(See also Humorous Songs, Negro Spirituals,
Folk Songs, Operetta Songs and Opera Arias.)

Miscellaneous Songs of Popular Appeal

Bass

Cavalli	Donzelle, fuggite	HL	C-EF	†
D' Esposito	Anima e core			
Dvořák	Songs my mother taught me	HM	E-E	†
Flégier	Le cor	ML	D-D	GSC
Franz	Dedication	HML	BF-C	†
Gounod	Au printemps	LMH	DF-AF	GSC
Grieg	I love thee	HML	E-F	†
Lara	Granada			
Massenet	Elégie	LM	C-GF	GSC
Mattei	Non è ver	HML		DIT
Saint-Saëns	Danse macabre	L	BF-EF	AXE
Schubert	Ave Maria	LMH	F-F	†
-----	Staendchen			
Schumann	Widmung	HL	BF-F	†
Sibella	La Girometta	HML	D-E	GSC
Strauss	Staendchen	HM	A-FS	†
-----	Zueignung	HL	CS-FS	†
Tagliaferri	Nun me sceta			
Tchaikovsky	Pilgrim's song	HLM	B-E	GSC
Tosti	The last song	HL		RIC

Arias From British Operas

Bass

Arne, T.	Preach not me your musty rules (Comus)	HML		ROW
Handel	Hear me, ye winds and waves (Scipione)	ML	G-EF	BOO
-----	Leave me, loathsome light (Semele)	L		DIT
-----	Silent worship (Tolomeo)	LM	D-E	CUR
Purcell	Music for a while (Oedipus)	LH		SC
-----	Next winter comes slowly (The Faery Queen)			GSC
-----	Ye twice hundred deities			
Sullivan	Ho, Jolly Jenkin (Ivanhoe)	LM	C-F	CHA

Arias From French Operas

Bass

Berlioz	Chanson de la puce (La Damnation de Faust)			CST
-----	Sérénade de Mephisto (La Damnation de Faust)			DIT
Debussy	Récit d'Arkel (Pelléas et Melisande)			DUR
Delibes	Lakmé, ton doux regards (Lakmé)			HEU
Gluck	C'est en vain que l'enfer compte (Alceste)			†
Gounod	Au bruit des lourds marteaux (Philémon et Baucis)	L	AF-EF	†
-----	Le veau d'or (Faust)	L	C-EF	†
-----	Que l'hymne nuptial (Roméo et Juliette)			CHO
-----	Sérénade de Mephistopheles (Faust)	L	G-G	CHO
-----	Sous les pieds d'une femme (La Reine de Saba)			GSC
Halévy	Si la rigeur (La Juive)			†
-----	Vous qui du Dieu vivant (La Juive)			
Lully	Bois épais (Amadis)	ML	C-EF	†
-----	Il faut passer (Alceste)			LEM
Massenet	Chanson de la Touraine (Panurge)	M	EF-EF	HEU
-----	Les grands mots (Manon)			GSC

Meyerbeer	Nonnes qui reposez			GSC
	(Robert le Diable)			
-----	O jours heureux			BRO
	(L'Etoile du Nord)			
-----	Piff! paff! (Les Huguenots)			BRH
Offenbach	J'ai des yeux			GSC
	(Tales of Hoffman)			
Paladihle	Pauvre martyr obscur (Patrie)			
Rameau	Invocation et hymne au soleil			LEM
	(Les Indes Galantes)			
Thomas	De son coeur j'ai calmé	L	A-D	HEU
	la fièvre (Mignon)			
-----	Fugitif et tremblant			HEU
	(Mignon)			
-----	Le tambour major (Le Caid)			HEU

Arias From German Operas

Bass

Beethoven	Ha! welch ein Augenblick			†
	(Fidelio)			
-----	Hat man nicht auch Gold			†
	beineben (Fidelio)			
Handel	Zweier Augen Majestaet			MUP
	(Almira)			
Lortzing	Auch ich war ein Juengling L		A-D	CFI
	(Der Waffenschmied)			
Mendelssohn	Ich bin ein vielgereister ML			DIT
	Mann (Heimkehr aus der Fremde)			
Mozart	In diesen heiligen Hallen	L	FS-C	†
	(Die Zauberfloete)			
-----	O Isis und Osiris			†
	(Die Zauberfloete)			
-----	Solche hergelaufne Laffen			†
	(Abduction from Seraglio)			
-----	Wer ein Liebchen hat gefunden			†
	(Abduction from Seraglio)			
Nicolai	Als Bueblein klein			GSC
	(Die lustigen Weiber)			
Strauss	Waltz scene (Der Rosenkavalier)			BOO
Wagner	Auf wolkigen Hoeh'n (Siegfried)			†
-----	Gebet des Amfortas			GSC
	(Parsifal)			
-----	Jerum! Jerum!			†
	(Die Meistersinger)			
-----	Koenigs Gebet	M	F-EF	GSC
	(Lohengrin)			

(Wagner)	Leb' wohl, du kuehnes herrliches Kind (Die Walkuere)	L	B-E	†
-----	Moegst du, mein Kind (Der Fliegende Hollaender)			†
-----	Pogners Anrede (Die Meistersinger)	L	A-F	†
-----	Wahn! wahn! ueberall wahn! (Die Meistersinger)	L	A-E	†
-----	Was duftet doch der Flieder (Die Meistersinger)			
Weber	Hier im Ird'schen Jammertal (Der Freischuetz)			†

Arias From Italian Operas

Bass

Bellini	Tu non sai (La Sonnambula)			RIC
-----	Vi ravviso, o luoghi ameni (La Sonnambula)			DIT
Boito	Prologue (Ave Signor) (Mefistofele)			RIC
-----	Son lo spirito (Mefistofele)	L	G-E	RIC
Diaz	O splendore infinito (Benvenuto)	L	A-F	GRU
Donizetti	Ah, un foco insolito (Don Pasquale)			RIC
-----	Udite, udite o rustici (L'Elisir d'Amore)			BRO
-----	Vieni la mia vendetta (Lucrezia Borgia)			BRO
Monteverdi	Ahi, troppo è duro (Il Balletto delle Ingrate)	HL	C-EF	DIT
-----	Lasciatemi morire (Arianna)	ML	D-D	†
-----	Oblivian soave (L'Incoronazione di Poppea)			HEU
Mozart	Aprite un po quegl' occhi (Le Nozze di Figaro)			†
-----	Deh vieni alla finestra (Don Giovanni)	L	D-E	†
-----	Finch' han dal vino (Don Giovanni)	L	D-EF	†
-----	Ho capito, Signor (Don Giovanni)			
-----	La vendetta (Le Nozze di Figaro)			†
-----	Madamina (Don Giovanni)	L	A-E	†

(Mozart)	Non più andrai (Le Nozze di Figaro)	L	C-E	†
-----	Se vuol ballare (Le Nozze di Figaro)	L		†
Pergolesi	Son imbrogliato io già (La Serva Padrona)	L		RIC
Ponchielli	Si, morir ella de' (La Gioconda)			RIC
Porrino	Io per l'antico diritto (Gli Orazi)			
Puccini	Colline's song (La Boheme)			RIC
Rossini	A un dottore (Il Barbiere di Siviglia)			GSC
-----	Eterno! immenso! (Mose in Egitto)			
-----	La calunnia (Il Barbiere di Siviglia)			†
Verdi	Ella giammai m'amò (Don Carlos)	L	A-E	RIC
-----	Il lacerato spirito (Simon Boccanegra)	L	FS-D	GSC
-----	Infelice è tu credevi (Ernani)	L	GF-EF	GSC
-----	O tu Palermo (I Vespri Siciliani)			RIC
-----	Tu sul labbro de' veggenti (Nabucco)			RIC

Miscellaneous Opera Arias

Bass

Borodin	I hate a dreary life (Prince Igor)			BOO
-----	Konchak's aria (Prince Igor)			
Dvořák	Alas, alas (Air of the water fay) (Rusalka)			
-----	Burgrave's aria (The Jacobin)			
Gershwin	I got plenty o' nuttin' (Porgy and Bess)	L	B-D	CHA
-----	It ain't necessarily so (Porgy and Bess)			CHA
Glinka	Prayer of Susanin (A Life for the Czar)			
Mussorgsky	Clock scene (Ah give me air, this suffocates my soul) (Boris Godunoff)			BES
-----	Death scene (Boris Godunoff)			BES

(Mussorgsky)	Monologue and hallucination scene (Boris Godunoff)			BES
-----	Pimen's monologue (Boris Godunoff)			BES
-----	Siege of Kazan (Boris Godunoff)	L	F-E	GSC
Rachmaninoff	Aleko's aria (Aleko)			
Rimsky-Korsakov	Song of the Viking guest (Sadko)		A-EF	BRO
Rubinstein	The demon's song (The Demon)			
Smetana	Everything is ready (The Bartered Bride)			BOO
Tchaikovsky	Prince Gremin's aria (Eugene Onegin)			GSC

Arias From Oratorios and Latin Works

Bass

Bach, J.S.	At evening hour of calm and peace (St. Matthew Passion)			†
-----	Consider o, my soul (St. John Passion)			†
-----	Come blessed cross (St. Matthew Passion) Cello			†
-----	Give, o give me back my Lord (St. Matthew Passion)			†
-----	Gladly will I all resigning (St. Matthew Passion)			†
-----	Make Thee clean my heart from sin (St. Matthew Passion)			
-----	Mighty Lord (Christmas Oratorio)			
-----	My darkened heart (Christmas Oratorio)			
Berlioz	O misère des rois (L'Enfance du Christ)			CST
Dvořák	Give ear, ye people (St. Ludmilla)			
-----	I was not deceived (St. Ludmilla)			
Handel	Arm, arm ye brave (Judas Maccabaeus)	L	B-E	†
-----	But who may abide (The Messiah)	L	G-E	†
-----	His scepter is the rod of righteousness (Occasional Oratorio)	L	G-E	GSC

195

(Handel)	Honour and arms (Samson)	L	G-EF	†
-----	How willing my paternal love (Samson)	L	B-E	DIT
-----	O ruddier than the cherry (Acis and Galatea)	L	G-F	DIT
-----	Revenge, Timotheus cries (Alexander's Feast)	L	G-D	†
-----	Shall I in Mamre's fertile plain (Joshua)	L	G-EF	DIT
-----	The Lord worketh wonders (Judas Maccabaeus)			
-----	The people that walked in darkness (The Messiah)			†
-----	The trumpet shall sound (The Messiah) Trumpet	L		†
-----	Thy glorious deeds (Samson)	M	C-F	†
-----	Turn not, O Queen, thy face away (Esther)			DIT
-----	What though I trace each herb and flower (Solomon)		CS-E	†
-----	Wher'er you walk (Semele)	HML	C-D	†
-----	Why do the nations (The Messiah)	L	B-E	†
-----	With pious hearts (Judas Maccabaeus)	L	G-E	†
Haydn	Behold along the dewy grass (The Seasons)			
-----	Now heav'n in fullest glory shone (The Creation)	L		†
-----	Rolling in foaming billows (The Creation)	L	C-F	†
-----	With joy th' impatient husbandman (The Seasons)	L	B-E	GSC
Mendelssohn	But the mountains shall depart (Elijah)			
-----	Consume them all (Saint Paul)			
-----	For know ye not (Saint Paul)			
-----	Is not His word like a fire (Elijah)	M	B-F	†
-----	It is enough (Elijah)	L	A-E	†
-----	Lord God of Abraham (Elijah)	L	B-E	†
-----	O God, have mercy (Saint Paul)	L	B-D	†
Rossini	Pro peccatis (Stabat Mater)			DIT

Sullivan	Honor the Lord with thy substance (Prodigal Son)			
Verdi	Confutatis maledictis (The Requiem)			GSC

Cantata Arias

Bass

Bach, J.S.	Aechzen und erbaermlich Weinen (Cantata 13) Violin or flute	L	G-EF	PET
-----	Die Welt mit allen Koenigreichen (Cantata 59) Violin		A-D	
-----	Doch weichet, ihr tollen vergeblichen (Cantata 8) Flute			NOV
-----	Endlich, endlich wird mein Joch (Cantata 56) Oboe			
-----	Es ist vollbracht (Cantata 159) Oboe			AUG
-----	Gleich wie die Wilden Meereswellen (Cantata 178) Violin			
-----	Greifet zu, fasst das Heil (Cantata 174) Violin or viola			
-----	Gute Nacht, du weltgetuemmel (Cantata 27) 2 Violins, viola and continuo			
-----	Herr, nun laessest du 'deinen Diener (Cantata 83) Violin or viola			
-----	Lass, o Welt, mich aus Verachtung (Cantata 123) Flute			PET
-----	Wenn Trost und Huelf' (Cantata 117) Violin			
Blow	Music's the cordial of a troubled breast (Begin the Song)	L	D-E	PET
Buck	The virgin's lullaby (The Coming of the King)	HL	B-CS	GSC
Elgar	Oh, my warriors (Caractacus)			NOV
Handel	Vouchsafe, O Lord (Dettingen Te Deum)	HM		ELV
Righini	Al nome tuo temuto (La Selva Incantata)			CFI

Operetta Musical Comedy
or Show Songs

Bass

Berlin	A pretty girl is like a melody (Ziegfeld Follies 1919)			BER
-----	The girl that I marry (Annie Get Your Gun)			BER
-----	White Christmas (Holiday Inn)			BER
De Koven	Armorer's song (Robin Hood)	L		GSC
-----	Brown October ale (Robin Hood)	L	E-E	GSC
Herbert	Every day is ladies' day with me (The Red Mill)			WIT
-----	Gypsy love song (The Fortune Teller)	LHM	C-E	WIT
-----	Thine alone (Eileen)			WIT
Kern	Ah still suits me (Show Boat)			BRO
-----	Ol' man river (Show Boat)	LM	BF-G	HAR
-----	The song is you (Music in the Air)	M	C-F	HAR
-----	The way you look tonight (Swing Time)			CHA
-----	Yesterdays (Roberta)			CHA
Loewe	I still love Elisa (Paint Your Wagon)			
-----	I talk to the trees (Paint Your Wagon)			
Milloecker	Dunkelrote Rosen bring'ich (Mme. Dubarry)			CHA
Porter	So in love (Kiss Me Kate)			CHA
Rodgers	If I loved you (Carousel)			WIL
-----	Oh, what a beautiful morning (Oklahoma)			WIL
-----	Some enchanted evening (South Pacific)	M	C-E	CHA
-----	This nearly was mine (South Pacific)			WIL
Romberg	Stouthearted men (New Moon)	L	C-F	HAR
-----	The fireman's bride (Up in Central Park)	M	D-EF	WIL
Strauss, J.	Ja, mein idealer Lebenszweck (The Gypsy Baron)			CRZ
Weill	September song (Knickerbocker Holiday)			CHA

Song Cycles (Or Groups of Songs)

Bass

Babin	Beloved stranger	L		AUG
Beethoven	An die ferne Geliebte	HL	C-E	†
Brahms	Vier ernste Gesaenge			†
Copland	Old American songs			
Cornelius	Six Christmas songs	HL		BOS
Dougherty	Five sea chanties	L	A-EF	GSC
Dvořák	Biblical songs	HL		AMP
Mahler	Kindertotenlieder	L	G-GF	INT
Mason	Nautical lays of a landsman	L	A-E	GSC
Poulenc	Chansons gaillardes	L		HEU
Ravel	Don Quichotte à Dulcinée	HM	A-F	DUR
Schubert	Die Winterreise			†
-----	Gesaenge des Harfners, 1, 2 and 3			PET
-----	Three Italian songs			
Schumann	Dichterliebe			†
-----	Vier Husarenlieder	L	D-EF	BRH
Wolf	Harfenspieler Lieder (1, 2 and 3 Goethe)			
-----	Michelangelo Lieder			

Solo Cantatas

Bass

Bach, J.S.	Ich habe genug (Cantata 82) Oboe, strings and continuo		RIC
-----	Ich will den Kreuzstab (Cantata 56)		BRO

(See Solo Cantatas of Pergolesi, Handel and Scarlatti, Kirchenkantaten of Buxtehude and Symphoniae Sacrae of Schuetz.)

Concert Arias

Bass

Mozart	Alcandro, lo confesso		INT
-----	Così dunque tradisci		INT
-----	Io ti lascio, o cara addio		
-----	Mentre ti lascio	L	BOO

(Mozart)	Per questa bella mano			INT
-----	Rivolgete a lui lo sguardo			INT
-----	Un bacio di mano			INT

Christmas Songs

Bass

Andrews	I heard the bells on Christmas day	L	A-E	GAL
Bach, J.S.	Mighty Lord (Christmas Oratorio)			
-----	My darkened heart (Christmas Oratorio)			
-----	So appears thy natal day	L		GAL
Berlin	White Christmas (Holiday Inn)			BER
Berlioz	O misère des rois (L'Enfance du Christ)			CST
Branscombe	Hail ye time of holidays			
Buck	The Virgin's lullaby (The Coming of the King)	HL	B-CS	GSC
Coerne	A rhyme for Christmas-tide	L	CS-CS	DIT
Coombs	Bethlehem	HM	D-F	GSC
De Koven	The white Christ	L	C-D	GSC
Elmore and Reed	Come all ye who weary	L	C-C	JFI
Evans	The Virgin had a baby	L	C-EF	BOH
Harker	A Child is born in Bethlehem	LH	D-G	GSC
-----	There's a song in the air	HL	BF-D	GSC
Jewell	The vision of the shepherds	HL	A-D	ASC
Liddle	An old French carol	LM	F-F	BOO
Lynn	Gently little Jesus	L	BF-BF	DIT
-----	The magic night of Christmas	M	D-D	DIT
Neidlinger	The manger cradle	L	EF-F	GSC
Niles	The cherry tree			GSC
Prokoff	Christmas cradle song	LM	D-E	CHA
Rodney	A dream of Bethlehem	MML	G-DF	ENO
Taylor	Christmas folk song	L	BF-EF	GRA
Thiman	In the bleak midwinter	L	A-E	NOV

Bass

Cadman	Hail joyous morn	HL	BF-DF	WIL
Duke	Calvary	L	G-F	CFI
Granier	Hosanna	HH	F-BF	DIT
Handel	The trumpet shall sound (The Messiah) Trumpet	L		†
Harker	As it began to dawn	ML	G-DF	GSC
La Forge	Before the crucifix	HML	BF-EF	GSC
Mac Farlane	On wings of living light	MH	D-G	GSC
O' Hara	There is no death	LMH	EF-AF	CHA
Parker	Come see the place	HL		GSC
Rachmaninoff	Christ is risen	LM	D-F	GAL
Turner	Hail your risen Lord	HL	C-D	GSC
Wolf	Herr, was traegt der Boden	HL	B-DS	†

Patriotic Songs

Bass

Bone and Fenton	Prayer for a waiting world	L		CFI
Candlyn	O God of armies	L	DF-DF	GRA
Chadwick	He maketh wars to cease	ML		ASC
De Koven	Recessional			
Dix	The trumpeter	HML	A-C	BOH
Dungan	Eternal life	HL		PRE
Handel	Arm, arm ye brave (Judas Maccabaeus)	L	B-E	†
Lester	Greater love hath no man	LH	B-E	CFI
O' Hara	Guns	M	C-F	DBH
-----	There is no death	LMH	EF-AF	CHA
Steffe	Battle hymn of the Republic			

Sacred Songs

Bass

Beethoven	The worship of God in nature			
Bone and Fenton	First Psalm	LM	DF-F	CFI
-----	Thy word is a lamp	LH	C-F	ROW
Brown	The twenty-third Psalm	LH	E-G	GRA

(Brown)	What are these which are arrayed	HLM	C-F	ASC
Buck	Blessed are they which love Thee	L	BF-D	GSC
-----	Fear not ye, O Israel	HLM		GSC
-----	Judge me, O God	L	GS-D	GSC
-----	O ye that hear and understand	L	A-D	GSC
Campbell-Tipton	I will give thanks unto the Lord	LMH	DF-AF	GSC
Candlyn	O God of armies	L	DF-DF	GRA
Chadwick	A ballad of trees and the Master	HML	A-F	DIT
-----	He maketh wars to cease	ML		ASC
Charles	Incline Thine ear	HL	BF-D	GSC
Clokey	God is in everything	LH	D-G	JFI
Davis	Be ye kind, one to another	L		GAL
Dungan	Eternal life	HL		PRE
Dvořák	God is my shepherd			AMP
-----	Hear my prayer, O Lord			AMP
-----	I will lift mine eyes			AMP
-----	Turn Thee to me			AMP
Edmunds	Praise we the Lord	HL	D-D	ROW
Eville	Psalm 130 (Out of the Deep)	HML		BOO
Faure, J.	The palms	HM	C-EF	DIT
Franck	O Lord most Holy	LM	A-FS	BOS
Godard	Lead kindly light			
Guion	The cross bearer	HM	B-DS	GSC
Handel	Thanks be to Thee	M	CS-E	†
Holst	The heart worships	ML	BF-D	STB
Kountz	What shall I ask	L		GAL
La Forge	They that trust in the Lord	HL	BF-EF	GAL
-----	What shall I render unto the Lord	HL	C-D	GSC
Lederer	Psalm 104	L	A-E	CFI
Liddle	How lovely are Thy dwellings?	HML		BOS
Mac Dermid	In my Fathers house are many mansions	HML		FRS
Mac Dermid	Ninety-first Psalm	HLM		FRS
Mac Gimsey	Think on these things	LM	BF-EF	CFI
Malotte	The Lord's Prayer			
-----	The twenty-third Psalm	HLM	C-F	GSC
Mc Gill	Thine eternal peace	HL	A-CS	GSC
Mendelssohn	But the mountains shall depart (Elijah)			

(Mendelssohn)	For know ye not (Saint Paul)			
-----	Lord God of Abraham (Elijah)	L	B-E	†
-----	O God, have mercy (Saint Paul)	L	B-D	†
Milligan	Hear my cry	HM	C-EF	GSC
O'Connor-Morris	Fill Thou my life, O Lord	L	BF-EF	CFI
O'Hara	Art Thou the Christ	HML	A-D	GSC
-----	Let God rule the world			
Rogers	Great peace have they which love Thy law	HML	B-CS	GSC
Sanderson	Green pastures	HL	BF-EF	BOO
Schubert	The Omnipotent			
-----	To the Infinite			
Scott	Repent ye	HML	A-D	GSC
Sowerby	The Lord is my shepherd			GRA
Speaks	Thou wilt keep him in perfect peace	HML		GSC
Stickles	Saith the Lord	LH	D-F	CHA
Sullivan	Honor the Lord with thy substance (The Prodigal Son)			
Tchaikovsky	Pilgrim's song	HLM	B-E	GSC
Van de Water	The publican	HL	C-E	DIT
Weaver	Build thee more stately mansions	M	C-E	GAL
Wolf	Give praise to Him through whom the world arose			
-----	Prayer (Gebet)			

Wedding Songs

Bass

Beethoven	Ich liebe dich	HL	BF-DF	†
De Koven	Oh promise me (Robin Hood)	HML	C-D	†
D'Hardelot	Because	MH	E-G	CHA
Grieg	I love thee	HML	E-F	†
Lippe	How do I love Thee?			BOS
Schubert	Du bist die Ruh	LMH	EF-AF	†
-----	Ungeduld	HML		†
Schumann	Widmung	HL	BF-F	†
Sharp	Possession	MH	D-A	DIT
Thiman	The God of love my Shepherd is	ML	A-D	NOV
Youmans	Through the years (Through the Years)	HML	A-F	MLR

203

Songs and Arias With Added
Accompanying Instrument

Bass

Bach, J.S.	Aechzen und erbaermlich Weinen (Cantata 13) Violin or flute	L	G-EF	PET
-----	Come blessed cross (St. Matthew Passion) Cello			†
-----	Die Welt mit allen Koenigreichen (Cantata 59) Violin		A-D	
-----	Endlich, endlich wird mein Joch (Cantata 56) Oboe			RIC
-----	Es ist vollbracht (Cantata 159) Oboe			AUG
-----	Gleich wie die wilden Meereswellen (Cantata 178) Violin			
-----	Greifet zu, fasst das Heil (Cantata 174) Violin or viola			
-----	Herr, nun laessest du deinen Diener (Cantata 83) Violin or viola			
-----	Hier in meines Vaters Staette (Cantata 32) Violin			AUG
-----	Ich habe genug (Cantata 82) Oboe, strings and continuo			RIC
-----	Lass, o Welt, mich aus Verachtung (Cantata 123) Flute			PET
-----	Wenn Trost und Huelf' (Cantata 117) Violin			
Buxtehude	Mache dich, mein Herz, bereit Trumpet and strings			
Chausson	Le colibri Violin or cello	M	F-GF	BOS
Handel	The trumpet shall sound (The Messiah) Trumpet	L		†
Honegger	Chanson (Ronsard) Flute and string quartet			SEN
Milford	So sweet love seemed Cello	HL	D-D	GRA
Mozart	Per questa bella mano Cello			INT

American and British Songs of Limited Range

Baritone or Bass

Athay	City streets	M	E-EF	CFI
Bacon	The Erie Canal	L	D-C	CFI
Barber	Rain has fallen	HM	D-E	GSC
-----	With rue my heart is laden	HL	CS-D	GSC
Bartholomew	Pretty Saro	M	D-D	GSC
Bellini	Ninna nanna a liana	LH	G-G	GSC
Boatner	Oh what a beautiful city	HL	D-E	GSC
-----	On mah journey	LH	EF-EF	RIC
Bowles	Cabin	ML	CS-CS	GSC
-----	David	M	E-D	AMP
-----	Lonesome man	M	DF-EF	GSC
Bridge	Een as a lovely flower	HM	FS-E	BOH
Broadwood	Some rival has stolen my true love	LM	D-E	BOO
Burleigh	Joshua fit de battle ob Jericho	LH	DS-E	RIC
Carpenter	Don't ceare	M	C-D	GSC
Carter	Dust of snow	M	D-E	AMP
Clarke	The blind ploughman	HML	C-D	CHA
Cowen	Border ballad	LM	D-E	BOO
De Koven	Brown October ale (Robin Hood)	L	E-E	GSC
-----	Oh promise me (Robin Hood)	HML	C-D	GSC
Dello Joio	Mill doors	M	D-E	CFI
Dichmont	Ma little banjo	ML	E-CS	GSC
Dougherty	Across the western ocean	M	D-D	GSC
-----	Blow ye winds	L	C-D	GSC
-----	Declaration of independence	L	C-C	GSC
-----	Rio Grande	M	EF-EF	GSC
Dowland	Awake sweet love	M	E-F	STB
-----	Come again, sweet love	M	D-E	STB
-----	Fine knacks for ladies	M	E-F	STB
-----	Flow, my tears	M	D-E	STB
-----	I saw my lady weep	M	E-E	STB
-----	Now, O now, I needs must part	M	D-D	DIT
-----	Sorrow, sorrow stay	M	D-D	BOS
-----	What if I never speede	M	D-D	BOS
Duke	Loveliest of trees	L	C-D	GSC
Elgar	My old tunes	M	D-EF	ELK
Ford	There is a lady sweet and kind	M	D-E	STB
Gibbs	Five eyes	HL	D-D	BOS

Griffes	An old song resung	LM	EF-F	GSC
Guion	All day on the prarie	M	EF-F	GSC
-----	Mam'selle Marie	M	D-E	GSC
-----	What shall we do with a drunken sailor	HML	C-D	GSC
Handel	Love's a dear deceitful jewel	LH	F-F	RBR
-----	Wher'er you walk (Semele)	HML	C-D	GSC
Harris	Agatha Morley	M	C-D	CFI
Hindemith	The whistling thief	M	E-F	AMP
Holst	The heart worships			
Hook	Bright Phoebus	M	EF-F	GSC
Hughes	The stuttering lovers	M	E-FS	CHA
Johnson	Roll Jerd'n roll	M	EF-F	GSC
Johnston	Ould John Braddleum	L	A-B	CRA
-----	Roger's courtship	M	C-D	CRA
Liddle	The garden where the praties grow	LMH	E-FS	STB
Mac Dowell	The Sea	HL	D-D	BRH
Mac Gimsey	Sweet little Jesus Boy	ML	D-D	CFI
-----	To my mother	HML	C-C	CFI
-----	Trouble	ML	C-D	CFI
Mana Zucca	I love life	LM	F-F	PRE
-----	Nichavo	HML	F-G	JCH
Manning	Shoes	M	EF-F	GSC
Martin	Come to the fair	HML	D-D	BOO
Metcalf	At nightfall	HML	C-DF	ASC
Naginski	Night song at Amalfi	M	D-EF	GSC
-----	The ship starting	M	BF-B	GSC
Oberbrunner	Giuseppe, da barber	HML	E-E	GSC
Payne	Crucifixion	L	C-C	GSC
Peterkin	The garden of bamboos	M	EF-F	OXF
Pinsuit	Bedouin love song	HL	FS-DS	GSC
Porter, Q.	Music when soft voices die	HM	D-C	MUP
Quilter	Barbara Allen	M	D-D	BOO
-----	Believe me if all those endearing young charms	M	EF-EF	BOO
-----	Drink to me only	LMH	GF-GF	BOH
-----	The Ash Grove			
-----	Ye banks and braes	M	DF-EF	BOO
Rodgers	Oh what a beautiful morning (Oklahoma)	L		WIL
Romberg	The fireman's bride (Up in Central Park)	M	D-EF	WIL
Rosseter	When Laura smiles	LM	D-E	STB
Russell	Children of men	HL	EF-F	FLA
Sacco	Mexican serenade	HL	D-EF	BOS
-----	Revelation	HL	DF-EF	BOS
Sanderson	Susan is her name	LM	D-E	BOH

Scott	Lord Randal	L	E-F	GAL
-----	Think on me	HML	D-EF	GAL
-----	Wailie wailie	M	D-E	DIT
Shaw	Song of the palanquin bearers	LH	E-F	CUR
Speaks	In May time	HL	D-E	JCH
Stanford	A soft day	ML	DF-DF	STB
Stephenson	Love is a sickness	HML	C-D	BOO
-----	Ships that pass in the night	HML	DF-DF	BOO
Torrence	Smilin' Kitty O'Day	ML	CS-D	BOO
Tours	Mother o' Mine	HML	C-D	CHA
Vaughan Williams	King William	L	D-D	OXF
-----	Linden Lea	HML	C-D	BOS
-----	The water mill	L	C-D	OXF
-----	The woodcutter's song	M	D-E	OXF
Warlock	Fair and true	M	EF-EF	CFI
-----	Sigh no more	M	EF-F	CFI
-----	The night	M	D-E	OXF
Warren	If you have forgotten	LH	GF-GF	GSC
-----	White horses of the sea	LH	F-G	GSC
Watts	Blue are her eyes	H	FS-FS	DIT

French Songs of Limited Range

Baritone or Bass

Chausson	Apaisement	MH	EF-G	HAM
-----	Chanson de clown	M	D-EF	ROU
Duparc	Lamento	M	EF-EF	BOS
-----	L'invitation au voyage	HM	E-F	O
Fauré	Adieu	MH	F-F	MAR
-----	Arpege	MH	E-FS	HAM
-----	Chant d'automne	LH	G-G	HAM
-----	Dans les ruines d'une abbaye	M	E-FS	GSC
-----	Le parfum imperissable	LH	GF-GF	
-----	Madrigal	MH	F-F	HAM
-----	Mandoline	HL	F-E	GSC
-----	Serenade Toscane	MH	G-AF	HAM
-----	Spleen	H	E-FS	MAR
Franck	Le mariage des roses	M	E-FS	BOS
-----	Lied	LH	FS-FS	
Hue	J'ai pleuré en rêve	HL	D-E	BOS
Massenet	Crepuscule	M	D-E	GSC
Pierné	En barque	L	D-DF	GSC
Poulenc	Reine des mouettes	M	EF-F	SAL
Quilter	My lady's garden	M	D-EF	DIT

Saint Saens	Mai	H	G-FS	DUR
Tiersot	L'amours de moi	M	EF-F	HEU
Weckerlin	Aminte	M	C-D	GSC
-----	Bergère légère	M	D-E	BOS

German Songs of Limited Range

Baritone or Bass

Ahle	Bruenstiges Verlangen	M	E-E	GSC
Beethoven	An die Geliebte	M	E-E	AUG
Brahms	Bei dir sind meine Gedanken	MH	E-FS	GSC
-----	Der Schmied	HL	EF-EF	GSC
-----	Kein Haus, keine Heimat	HL	D-D	CFI
-----	Klage	LH	FS-FS	CFI
-----	Maienkaetzchen	L	D-E	CFI
-----	Mein Maedel hat einen Rosenmund	M	F-F	GSC
-----	Mit vierzig Jahren	HL	FS-D	CFI
-----	Muss es eine Trennung geben	LH	FS-FS	CFI
-----	O wuesst ich doch dem Weg zurueck	H	E-FS	CFI
-----	Treue Liebe	LMH	DS-E	GSC
-----	Verrat	HL	FS-EF	GSC
Franz	For Music	ML	C-D	DIT
-----	Sterne mit den gold'nen Fuesschen	HL	DS-E	DIT
-----	Stille Sicherheit	M	E-F	GSC
Haydn	She never told her love	M	D-EF	
Liszt	Die Lorelei	LH	DF-BF	CFI
Loewe	Edward	HL	F-E	GSC
Mendelssohn	An die Entfernte	M	F-F	
-----	Pagenlied	M	E-E	
-----	Schilflied	M	F-FS	
-----	Venetianisches Sondellied	LM	E-FS	AUG
Mozart	Abendempfindung	M	E-F	
-----	Der Vogelfaenger bin ich (Die Zauberfloete)	L	D-E	PET
-----	Warnung	HM	C-D	
Schubert	An den Mond	HL	F-GF	GSC
-----	Auf dem Flusse	HL	F-E	GSC
-----	Danksagung an den Bach	HL	E-F	GSC
-----	Das Wandern	HLM	E-E	GSC
-----	Das Wirtshaus	HL	C-D	GSC
-----	Der Blumenbrief	L	F-EF	GSC
-----	Der Leiermann	ML	C-D	GSC

(Schubert)	Der Musensohn	LH	FS-G	DIT
-----	Der Wegweiser	L	D-EF	DIT
-----	Der Zwerg	M	A-GF	PET
-----	Die Hoffnung	HM	E-E	
-----	Die Rose	M	G-FS	PET
-----	Die Taubenpost	HL	D-EF	GSC
-----	Du liebst mich nicht	LH	E-FS	GSC
-----	Fruehlingsglaube Sehnsucht	M	EF-F	GSC
-----	Im Abendrot	HL	C-D	GSC
-----	Lob der Traenen	LM	F-F	GSC
-----	Nacht und Traeume	HL	C-DF	CFI
-----	Sei mir gegruesst	LH	G-G	GSC
-----	Seufzer	M	CS-D	BIR
-----	Wanderers Nachtlied, 2	LH	F-F	GSC
Schumann	Alte Laute	HL	DF-DF	DIT
-----	Du bist wie eine Blume	HM	F-EF	GSC
-----	Mondnacht	M	E-FS	GSC
-----	Vier Husarenlieder	L	D-EF	BRH
Wolf	Morgenthau	M	C-C	PRE

Italian Songs of Limited Range

Baritone or Bass

Bassani	Dormi, bella dormi tu	L	EF-F	GSC
Bononcini	Deh piu a me non v'ascondete	LH	EF-F	GSC
Caccini	Amarilli, mia bella	ML	C-D	GSC
Caldara	Sebben crudele	HML	E-DS	GSC
-----	Selve amiche, ombrose piante	HM	E-F	GSC
Carissimi	A morire	ML	C-D	
Cesti	Ah! quanto à vero (Il Pomo d'Oro)	HL	F-F	DIT
-----	Che angoscia che affanno (Il Pomo d'Oro)	HL	C-DF	DIT
Cimara	Fiocca la neve	LMH	G-G	GSC
Donaudy	O del mio amato ben	M	EF-F	RIC
Falconieri	Non più d'amore	HL	C-D	DIT
-----	Nuio arcisro	HL	AF-AF	DIT
Gasparini	Caro laccio, dolce nodo	M	EF-EF	GSC
Handel	Cara sposa (Rinaldo)	M	CS-D	
-----	Rendi'l sereno al ciglio (Sosarme)	LH	EF-F	GSC
Legrenzi	Che fiero costume	HML	C-D	GSC
Lotti	Pur dicesti, o bocca bella	LMH	E-FS	GSC

Other Songs of Limited Range

Baritone or Bass

Monteverdi	Lasciatemi morire	ML	D-D	DIT
Mozart	Deh vieni alla finestra (Don Giovanni)	L	D-E	GSC
Paradies	M'ha preso alla sua ragna	M	EF-F	GSC
Pergolesi	Nina	HL	CS-D	DIT
Rontani	Se bel rio	ML	D-C	GSC
Rosa	Star vicinio	M	D-E	RIC
Scarlatti, A.	Chi vuole innamorarsi	HL	D-EF	DIT
-----	O cessate di piagarmi	HL	DS-E	GSC
-----	Son tutta duolo	M	D-EF	GSC
Stradella	Col mio sangue comprenderei (Il Floridoro)	HL	E-F	DIT
Tosti	La Serenata	HLM	D-EF	GSC

Other Songs of Limited Range

Candlyn	O God of armies	L	DF-DF	GRA
Dvořák	Songs my mother taught me	HM	E-E	GSC
Edmunds	Praise we the Lord	HL	D-D	ROW
Cui	The Statue at Czarskoe-Selo	HM	DF-EF	DIT
Elmore-Reed	Come all ye who weary	L	C-C	JFI
Franck	O Lord most Holy	LM	A-FS	BOS
Goodhall	The mountain	M	D-E	GAL
Gounod	There is a green hill far away	LMH	E-F	GSC
Grandi-Clokey	O fair art thou	ML	BF-C	JFI
Grieg	Hunter's song	L	DS-E	GSC
-----	I love thee	HML	E-F	GSC
-----	In the boat	LM	D-ES	DIT
-----	The old mother	ML	D-D	DIT
-----	Two brown eyes	LM	EF-F	GSC
Hinchliffe	Tranquillity	M	E-F	CFI
Lynn	Gently little Jesus	L	BF-BF	DIT
-----	The magic night of Christmas	M	D-D	DIT
Martin	The Holy Child	HML	G-G	ENO
Prokoff	Christmas cradle	LM	D-E	CHA
Rachmaninoff	To the children	MH	F-G	DIT
Rogers	Great peace have they which love Thy law	HML	B-CS	GSC
Schubert	They sang that night in Bethlehem	LMH	EF-EF	GSC

Scott	The first Easter morn	LH	F-G	GSC
Tchaikovsky	A legend	M	D-E	GSC
Turner	Hail your risen Lord	HL	C-D	GSC
Tuthill	Prayer for those at home	HL	C-D	BOH
Vaughn Williams	And all in the morning	L	D-E	GAL

Operatic Duets

Baritone or Bass

Balfe	This is they deed (Bohemian Girl)	A&Bs	
Bellini	Oh ciel che tento (La Sonnambula)	S&Bs	RIC
-----	Suoni la tromba (I Puritani)	Br&Bs	RIC
Berlioz	Par Bacchus ils sont fous (Les Troyens)	T&Br	CHO
Bizet	Au fond du temple (Les Pêcheurs de Perles)	T&Br	CHO
-----	Je suis Escamillo (Carmen)	T&Br	†
Boito	Se tu mi doni un'ora di riposo (Mefistofele)	T&Bs	†
Borodin	Duet of Jaroslavna and Galitsky (Prince Igor)	S&Bs	†
-----	Duet of Jaroslavna and Igor (Prince Igor)	S&Br	BOO
Charpentier	L'enfant serait sage (Louise)	S&Br	HEU
Debussy	Ah! ah! tout va bien (Pelleas et Melisande)	S&Br	DUR
-----	Duo de la lettre (Pelleas et Melisande)	A&Br or S&Br	DUR
-----	Prenez garde (Pelleas et Melisande)	T&Br	
-----	Prenez garde (Pelleas et Melisande)	Br&Br	DUR
Donizetti	Cheti, cheti immantinente (Don Pasquale)	Br&Bs	BRO
-----	Non sai tu (La Favorita)	T&Bs	
-----	Prender moglie (Don Pasquale)	T&Bs	
-----	Quando le soglie paterne (La Favorita)	A&Bs	BRO
-----	Tu che a Dio spiegasti (Lucia di Lammermoor)	T&Bs	BRO

(Donizetti)	Un buon servo del visconte (Linda di Chamounix)	T&Br	RIC
-----	Venti scudi! (L'Elisir d'Amore)	T&Br	BRO
-----	Voglio dire (L'Elisir d'Amore)	T&Br	
Dvořák	Julie and Bohuse (The Jacobin)	S&Bs	
Flotow	Solo, profugo, rejetto (Martha)	T&Br	BRO
Gershwin	Bess you is my woman now (Porgy and Bess)	S&Br	CHA
Halévy	Ta fille en ce moment (La Juive)	T&Bs	
Leoncavallo	A kiss (Zaza)	S&Br	SON
-----	Sei là? credea che te non fossi (I Pagliacci)	S&Br	GSC
-----	Silvio! a quest'ora (I Pagliacci)	S&Br	GSC
Lortzing	Im Wein ist Wahrheit (Undine)	T&Bs	
Massenet	Death of Don Quichotte (Don Quichotte)	S&Bs	HEU
-----	Duo de l'oasis (Thais)	S&Br	HEU
-----	Pardon! mais j'étais là (Manon)	S&Bs	GSC
-----	Quand apparaissent les étoiles (Don Quichotte)	S&Br	HEU
-----	Te souvient-il du lumineux voyage (Thais)	S&Br	HEU
Meyerbeer	Dans la nuit (Les Huguenots)	S&Bs	
Mozart	Bei Maennern, welche Liebe (Die Zauberfloete)	S&Bs	GSC
-----	Cinque, dieci (Le Nozze di Figaro)	S&Br	RIC
-----	Crudel! perchè finora (Le Nozze di Figaro)	S&Br	DIT
-----	Giovanette, chè fate all'amore (Don Giovanni)	S&Br	GSC
-----	Ich gehe, doch rate ich dir (Abduction from Seraglio)	S&Br	
-----	Il core vi dono (Così fan tutte)	S&Br	INT
-----	Là ci darem la mano (Don Giovanni)	S&Bs or S&Br	GSC
-----	Pa, Pa, Pa, Pa, Papagena (Die Zauberfloete)	S&Br	GSC

(Mozart)	Se a caso Madama (Le Nozze di Figaro)	S&Bs or S&Br	RIC
-----	Vivat Bacchus! (Abduction from Seraglio)	T&Bs	
Mussourgsky	Duet Boris and Prince Shuisky (Boris Godunoff)	T&Bs	BES
Pergolesi	Lo conosco, a quegli occhietti (La Serva Padrona)	S&Bs	RIC
-----	Per te ho io nel core (La Serva Padrona)	S&Bs S&Bs	RIC RIC
Ponchielli	Enzo Grimaldo principe di Santafior (La Gioconda)	T&Br	RIC
Puccini	Addio, fiorito asil (Madama Butterfly)	T&Br	
-----	Dovunque al mondo (Madama Butterfly)	T&Br	RIC
-----	Già! Mi dicon venal (Tosca)	S&Br	RIC
-----	O Mimi tu più non torni (La Bohême)	T&B RIC	
Rossini	Ah! Mathilde idole de mon âme (Guillaume Tell)	T&Br	RIC
-----	All'idea di quel metallo (Il Barbiere di Siviglia)	T&Br	GSC
-----	Bell image (Semiramide)	A&Bs	
-----	Oh! che muso (L'Italiana in Algeri)	S&Bs	
-----	Pace e gioia (Il Barbiere di Siviglia)	T&Bs	GSC
Saint-Saens	Il faut pour assouvir ma haine (Samson et Dalila)	S&Br	DUR
Smetana	Everyone praises his own girl (The Bartered Bride)	T&Bs	
Strauss, R.	Herr Cavalier (Der Rosenkavalier)	A&Bs	BOO
-----	Love Duet, Act 2 (Arabella)	S&Br	BOH
Thomas	As tu souffert (Mignon)	A&Bs	HEU
-----	Doute de la lumiere (Hamlet)	S&Br	HEU
-----	Legeres hirondelles (Mignon)	A&Bs	GSC
-----	O ma gaselle (Le Caid)	S&Bs	HEU
Verdi	Amici in vita e in morta (La Forza del Destino)	T&Br	
-----	Ciel mio padre (Aida)	S&Br	RIC
-----	Dio, che nell'alma infondere (Don Carlos)	T&Br	RIC

(Verdi)	Dite alla giovine (La Traviata)	S&Br	GSC
-----	Figlia a tal nome io palpito (Simon Boccanegra)	S&Br	RIC
-----	Figlia! Mio padre! (Rigoletto)	S&Br	GSC
-----	La Vergine degli angeli (La Forza del Destino)	S&Bs	RIC
-----	Lo vedremo, o vogli audace (Ernani)	Br&Bs	RIC
-----	Mira, di acerbe lagrime (Il Trovatore)	S&Br	DIT
-----	Prima di tutto (Falstaff)	Br&Br	RIC
-----	Pura siccome un angelo (La Traviata)	S&Br	RIC
-----	Quando al mio ben per te parlava (I Vespri Siciliani)	T&Br	RIC
-----	Si, pel ciel marmoreo giuro! (Otello)	T&Br	RIC
-----	Sleale! Il segretto fu dunque violato? (La Forza del Destino)	T&Br	RIC
-----	Solenne in quest'ora (La Forza del Destino)	T&Br	CFI
-----	Tardo per gli anni (Attila)	Br&Bs	
-----	Tutte le feste al tempie (Rigoletto)	S&Br	RIC
-----	Veglia o donna (Rigoletto)	S&Br	GSC
-----	V'ho ingannato (Rigoletto)	S&Br	GSC
Wagner	Wirst du des Vaters Wahl nicht schelten? (Der Fliegende Hollaender)	S&Br	GSC

Operetta Duets

Baritone or Bass

Berlin	It's a lovely day today (Call Me Madam)	A&Br	BER
-----	Let's take an old fashioned walk (Miss Liberty)	S&Br	BER
-----	They say it's wonderful (Annie Get Your Gun)	S&Br	BER
-----	White Christmas (Holiday Inn)	S&Br	BER
-----	You're just in love (Call Me Madam)	A&Br	BER

Caryll	Wait till the cows come home (Jack o Lantern)	A&Br	CHA
Coward	I'll see you again (Bitter Sweet)	S&Br	HAR
Donaldson	You (The Great Ziegfeld)	S&Br	FEI
-----	You never looked so beautiful (The Great Ziegfeld)	S&Br	FEI
Forrest-Grieg	Strange music (Song of Norway)	S&Br	CHA
Friml	Charms are fairest when they're hidden (Katinka)	S&Br	GSC
-----	Indian love call (Rose Marie)	S&Br	HAR
-----	Love me tonight (The Vagabond King)	S&Bs or S&Bs	FAM
-----	Only a rose (The Vagabond King)	S&Br	FAM
-----	Rose Marie (Rose Marie)	S&Br	HAR
-----	Sympathy (The Firefly)	S&Br	GSC
Gershwin	Embraceable you (Girl Crazy)	S&Br	NEM
-----	Of thee I sing (Of Thee I Sing)	S&Br	BRO
Hahn	Chanson de route (Ciboulette)	S&Br	SAL
-----	Duo de la lettre (Ciboulette)	T&Br	SAL
Herbert	A kiss in the dark (Orange Blossoms)	A&Bs or A&Br	WIT
-----	Ah sweet mystery of life (Naughty Marietta)	S&Br	HAR
-----	All for you (Princess Pat)	S&Br	WIT
-----	Because you're you (The Red Mill)	A&Br or S&Br	WIT
-----	Gypsy love song (The Fortune Teller)	A&Bs or S&Br	WIT
-----	I'm falling in love with someone (Naughty Marietta)	S&Br	WIT
-----	In old New York (The Red Mill)	S&Br	GSC
-----	In the isle of our dreams (The Red Mill)	A&Br	WIT
-----	Kiss me again (Mlle. Modiste)	S&Br	WIT
-----	Moonbeams (The Red Mill)	S&Br	WIT
-----	Rose of the world (The Rose of Algeria)	S&Br	WIT
-----	Sweethearts (Sweethearts)	S&Br	GSC
-----	Thine alone (Eileen)	S&Br	WIT

(Herbert)	To the land of my own romance (Enchantress)	S&Br	WIT
-----	When you're away (The Only Girl)	S&Br	
Heuberger	Im chambre separée (Der Opernball)	A&Bs	
Hirsch	Kiss me (Going Up)	S&Br	WIT
Jacobi	I'll be true to you (Apple Blossoms)	S&Br	HAR
-----.-	On the banks of the Bronx (Apple Blossoms)	S&Br	HAR
-----	You are free (Apple Blossoms)	S&Br	HAR
Johnstone	Can it be love at last (Fiddler's Three)	S&Br	WIT
Kalman	In the garden of romance (Miss Springtime)	S&Br	HAR
-----	Love's own sweet song (Sari)	S&Br	MAR
Kern	D'ya love me (Sunny)	S&Br	HAR
-----	Look for the silver lining (Sally)	S&Br	HAR
-----	Make believe (Show Boat)	S&Br	CHA
-----	Why do I love you (Show Boat)	S&Br	HAR
Koschna	Every little movement (Madame Sherry)	S&Br	WIT
Lehar	Are you going to dance (The Count of Luxembourg)	S&Br	CHA
-----	My little nest of heavenly blue (Frasquita)	A&Br	MAR
-----	You're in love (Gypsy Love)	S&Br	CHA
Luders	Heidelberg stein song (The Prince of Pilsen)	T&Br	WIT
Messager	The Swing Song (Veronique)	S&Br	CHA
-----	Trot Here and There (Veronique)	S&Br	CHA
Porter	In the Still of the Night (Rosalie)	A&B	CHA
-----	Night and Day (Gay Divorcee)	S&Br	HAR
-----	Wunderbar (Kiss Me Kate)	S&Br	CHA
Reinhardt	Day Dreams (The Spring Maid)	S&Br	MAR
-----	Two Little Love Bees (The Spring Maid)	S&Br	MAR
Rodgers	A Fellow needs a Girl (Allegro)	S&Br	CHA

(Rodgers)	Here in my arms (Dearest Enemy)	S&Br	HAR
-----	If I Loved You (Carousel)	S&Br	WMS
-----	My Heart Stood Still (Connecticut Yankee)	S&Br	HAR
-----	People will say we're in love (Oklahoma)	S&Br	WIL
-----	So Far (Allegro)	S&Br	CHA
-----	This nearly was mine (South Pacific)	S&Br	WIL
-----	We Kiss in a Shadow (The King and I)	S&Br	BRO
-----	With a Song in my Heart (Spring is Here)	S&Br	HAR
-----	You'll never walk alone (Carousel)	A&Br	CHA
Romberg	Auf Wiedersehn (The Blue Paradise)	S&Br	GSC
-----	Deep in my heart dear (The Student Prince)	S&Br	HAR
-----	Just we two (The Student Prince)	S&Br	HAR
-----	Once upon a time	S&Br	WIT
-----	One Kiss (New Moon)	S&Br	HAR
-----	Serenade (The Student Prince)	S&Br	HAR
-----	Silver moon (My Maryland)	S&Br	HAR
-----	Song of love (Blossom Time)	S&Br	FEI
-----	Will you remember (Maytime)	S&Br	GSC
Schwartz	Dancing in the dark (The Band Wagon)	S&Br	HAR
Straus, O.	A waltz dream (A Waltz Dream)	S&Br	BRO
Strauss, J.	Komm mit mir zum Souper (Die Fledermaus)	T&Br	BOO
Sullivan	None shall part us (Iolanthe)	S&Br	
Tierney	Castle of dreams (Irene)	S&Br	FEI
-----	If you're in love you'll waltz (Rio Rita)	S&Br	FEI
-----	Rio Rita (Rio Rita)	S&Br	FEI
-----	You're always in my arms (Rio Rita)	S&Br	FEI
Youmans	Sometimes I'm happy (Hit the Deck)	S&Br	HAR
-----	Tea for two (No, No, Nanette)	S&Br	HAR

Oratorio, Mass or Cantata Duets

Baritone or Bass

Bach, J. S.	Der Herr segne Euch (Wedding Cantata)	Br&Bs	
-----	Peasant Cantata	S&Bs	
Berlioz	L'arrivée à sais (L'Enfance du Christ)	S&Br	CST
-----	L'etable de Bethleem (L'Enfance du Christ)	S&Br	NOV
Elgar	Doubt not Thy Father's care (The Light of Life)	S&Br	NOV
Handel	Apollo and Daphne (Cantata)	S&Br	
-----	Go, baffled coward (Samson)	T&Br	NOV
-----	The Lord is a man of war (Israel in Egypt)	Bs&Bs	NOV
Haydn	Graceful consort (The Creation)	S&Bs	NOV
Mendelssohn	Help me, oh man of God (Elijah)	S&Br	GSC

British Song Duets

Baritone or Bass

Britten	Underneath the abject willow	S&Br	BOH
Henschel	Gondoliera	S&Br	DEI
Hughes	When thro' life unblest we rove	S&Br	BOO
Huhn	Be Thou exalted	A&Br	GSC
-----	The Hunt	S&Br	GSC
Lawes	The angler's song	S&Br	ECS
Purcell	Let us wander	S&Br	AUG
-----	Lost is my quiet	S&Br	AUG
-----	My dearest, my fairest	S&Br	AUG
-----	Shepherd leave decoying	S&Br	AUG
-----	Sound the trumpet	S&Br	AUG
Ronald	Down in the forest	A&Br	BOH
-----	O lovely night	A&Br	ENO
Somervell	Under the greenwood tree	S&Br	BOO

French Song Duets

Baritone or Bass

Berlioz	Chanson à boire	T&Bs	LAC
-----	Chant guerier	T&Bs	LAC
Chaminade	Angelus	S&Br	GSC
Charpentier	La chanson de chemin	T&Br	
Faure, G.	Pleurs d'or	S&Br	
Faure, J.	Crucifix	T&Br	HEU
Franck	O Lord most Holy	S&Br	BOS
Milhaud	Prends cette rose	S&Br	
Rameau	Les amants trahis – cello	S&Br	DUR

German Song Duets

Baritone or Bass

Brahms	Der Jaeger und sein Lieb-chen	A&Br	PET
-----	Die Nonne und der Ritter	A&Br	PET
-----	Es rauschet das Wasser	A&Br	
-----	Four Duets for alto and baritone with piano, Op. 28	A&Br	PET
-----	Nun lass uns wandern	S&Br	DIT
-----	Vor der Tuer	A&Br	
Buxtehude	O wie selig – 2 violins, cello and harpsichord	T&Bs	
Cornelius	Ein wort der liebe	S&Br	PET
Goetze	Calm as the night	S&Br	GSC
Hildach	Now thou art mine	S&Br	GSC
-----	Passage birds farewell	S&Br	GSC
Hindemith	Acht kanons	S&Br	
Mendelssohn	Gruess	S&Bs or S&Br	WOO
-----	My bark is bound to the gale	S&Br	
Schuetz	Die furcht des Herren	T&Br	BAR
Schumann	Blaue Augen	T&Bs	PET
-----	Ich bin dein Baum	A&Bs	PET
-----	Intermezzo	T&Bs	PET

Italian Song Duets

Baritone or Bass

Carissimi	Vaghirai pupille ardente	S&Br	
Clari	Cantando un di	S&Br	ECS

Floridia	A lover's duet	S&Br	DIT
Handel	Caro autor	S&Br	
-----	Rimanti in pace omai	S&Br	
Legrenzi	Fierezza si vaga	Br&Br	

Other Song Duets

Baritone or Bass

Dargomijshky	Vanka tanka	S&Bs	
Hoffman	I feel thy angel spirit	S&Br	GSC
Mendelssohn	They have taken away my Lord	S&Br	ECS
Pergolesi	Salve Regina, 2	S&Br	ROM
Rachmaninoff	Two partings	S&Br	BOO

Trios

Baritone or Bass

Debussy	L'enfant Prodigue (Cantata)	S&T&Br	DUR
Gounod	Anges purs anges radieux (Faust)	S&T&Bs	
------	Il m'amie, Act 2 (Faust)	S&T&Bs	
Handel	Disdainful of danger (Judas Maccabaeus)	T&A&Bs	NOV
-----	The flocks shall leave (Acis and Galatea)	S&T&Br	NOV
-----	Thou sittest (Dettingen Te Deum)	S&T&B	NOV
Haydn	Most beautiful appear (The Creation)	S&T&Bs	NOV
------	On Thee each living soul (The Creation)	S&T&Bs	NOV
Herbert	When you're wearing the ball and chain (The Only Girl)	T&B&Bs	WIT
Menotti	Trio (The Consul)	S&A&Br	GSC
Mozart	Ah taci ingiusto core (Don Giovanni)	S&Br&Bs	
-----	Due pupille amabili	S&S&Br	
-----	Ecco quel fiero istante	S&S&Br	
-----	Grazie agl inganni tuoi	S&T&Br	
-----	Liebes mandel wo is s bandel	S&T&Br	
-----	Luci care luci belle	S&B&B	
-----	Mandina amabile	S&T&Br	

(Mozart)	Mi lagnero tacendo	S&S&Br	
-----	Se lontan ben mio tu sei	S&Br&Bs	
Offenbach	Tu ne chanteras plus (Tales of Hoffman)	S&Ms&B	GSC
Puccini	Terzetto delle maschere (Turandot)	T&T&B	RIC
Purcell	Saul and the witch of Endor	S&T&Br	BOO
Saint-Saens	Je viens celebrer la victoire (Samson et Dalila)	A&T&Bs	DUR
Strauss, J.	Frank, you set my doubts at rest (Die Fledermaus)	S&T&Br	BOO
-----	To part is such sweet sorrow (Die Fledermaus)	S&T&Br	BOO
-----	When these lawyers don't believe (Die Fledermaus)	S&T&Br	BOO
Talbot	The joy of life (The Arcadians)	T&A&Br	CHA
Tchaikovsky	Trio and couplets (Eugene Onegin)	S&T&B	GSC
Verdi	Io muojo (La Forza del Destino)	S&T&Br	RIC
-----	Ma dimmi (Aida)	S&T&Br	GSC
-----	Qual volutta trascorrere (I Lombardi)	S&T&Br	RIC
-----	Te sol quest anima (Attila)	S&T&Bs	GSC
-----	Tu se Ernani (Ernani)	S&T&Br	
-----	Vieni l'sula e deserta (Otello)	T&T&Br	RIC

Contemporary Chamber Operas

Baritone or Bass

		(minutes)	
Allen	Mamselle Figaro	60 S, T, BS-BAR	WHB
Barab	Chanticleer	40 S, C, T, BR	BOO
-----	A Game of Chance	35 2S, M, BS-BR	BOO
-----	Reba	40 T, S, C, BAR	BOO
-----	The Rajah's Ruby	45 2S, T, BAR, BS, mute	BOO
Bartok	Bluebeard's castle	66 S, BS-BAR, speaker	BOO
Bucci	The Dress	30 2S, BAR	CHA
Collins	Catherine Parr	20 M, BAR, BS	LEE
Davis	The Sailing of the Nancy Belle	30 S, T, BS & cho.	BOO
Delaney	A Very Special Date	20 BR, S, small boy	

diGiovanni	Medea	60 S, C, T, BAR & cho.	SPA
Elkus	Tom Sawyer	60 S, C, BS	NOV
Engel	The Malady of Love	30 S, BAR, 2 mutes	Manu-script
Floyd	Slow Dusk	38 S, M, T, BAR	BOO
Gillis	The Libretto	30 2 singers	MLS
Holst	Savitri	40 S, T, BS & wom. cho.	GCS
Johnson	A Letter to Emily	SOP., MEZZO, BAR, BAS-BAR	MER
Kastle	The Swing	13 S, BAR & speaker	TEM
Kupferman	In a Garden	20 S, T, BS	MER
Lochrem	A Letter to Emily	40 S, M, BAR, BS-BR	MER
Low	Rapunzel	40 S, C, BAR	SOU
Martin	The Marriage	90 S, M, T, BAR	BOO
Mennini	The Rope	48 C, T, BAR, BS	BOO
Menotti	The Old Maid and the Thief	55 2S, M, BAR	RIC
-----	The Telephone	25 SOP, BAR	GSC
Milhaud	Le Pauvre Matelot	60 S, T, BAR, BS	MER
Moore	Gallantry	35 BR, S, M, T (dancers opt.)	GSC
Patacchi	The Secret	65 3S, BS-BAR	ASB
Perry	The Cask of Amontillado	30 M, T, BAR	SOU
Petit	The Game of Love and Chance	25 S, M, BAR	MER
Phillips	Don't We All	30 four	
Ratner	The Necklace	40 S, M, BAR	MER
Rorem	The Robbers	20 BS, BR, T, LYR BAR	BOO
Rosenthal	The Weeping Willow	45 S, T, BAR, cho & speaker	MER
Siegmeister	Miranda and the Dark Young Man	60 S, M, BAR, BS-BAR	TEM
Stravinsky	Les Noces	25 4 & cho.	GSC
Townsend	Lima Beans	25 S, T, BAR	MER
Weisgall	The Stronger	25 COL-SOP, BAR & mate	

Standard Chamber Operas

Baritone or Bass

Bach, J.S.	The Coffee Cantata	35 S, T, BAR & quartet	GSC

(Bach, J. S.)	The Peasant Cantata	40	2S, BAR, BS	CFI
Bizet	Djamileh	60	M, T, BAR speaker & cho.	PET
Byrd	The Music Master		S, T, BAR	AMI
Cadman	The Willow Tree	55	S, C, T, BAR	MER
Chabrier	The Incomplete Education	45	S, T, BAR	
Debussy	The Prodigal Son	50	S, T, BAR	MER
Delibes	The Omlet	4	2sp	HEU
Donizetti	Il Campanello	50	S, T, BAR	RIC
Massenet	Portrait of Canon	45	S, M, T, BAR, cho.	MER
Monteverdi	Orfeo	60	S, C, T, BS, Sp	AMP
Mozart	Bastien and Bastienne	35		MAR
-----	The Impressario	60	2S, T, BS	GSC
Offenbach	Forty Winks	20	S, T, BS	
-----	Lady to Raffle	45	three	MER
Pergolesi	Jealous husband	100	S, M, T, BS	MER
-----	La Serva Padrona	42	S&BS, & mute	
Purcell	Saul and the witch of Endor	30	3 and cho.	BOO
Rimsky-Korsakov	Mozart and Salieri	43	T, BAR	BOO
Wolf-Ferrari	The Secret of Suzanne	45	S&BR & speaker	GSC